Brendan Behan
Interviews and Recollections

Volume 1

Also by E. H. Mikhail

The Social and Cultural Setting of the 1890s
John Galsworthy the Dramatist
Comedy and Tragedy
Sean O'Casey: A Bibliography of Criticism
A Bibliography of Modern Irish Drama 1899–1970
Dissertations on Anglo-Irish Drama
The Sting and the Twinkle: Conversations with
Sean O'Casey (*co-editor with John O'Riordan*)
J. M. Synge: A Bibliography of Criticism
Contemporary British Drama 1950–1976
J. M. Synge: Interviews and Recollections (*editor*)
W. B. Yeats: Interviews and Recollections (two volumes) (*editor*)
English Drama 1900–1950
Lady Gregory: Interviews and Recollections (*editor*)
Oscar Wilde: An Annotated Bibliography of Criticism
Oscar Wilde: Interviews and Recollections (two volumes) (*editor*)
A Research Guide to Modern Irish Dramatists
The Art of Brendan Behan
Brendan Behan: An Annotated Bibliography of Criticism
An Annotated Bibliography of Modern Anglo-Irish Drama
Lady Gregory: An Annotated Bibliography of Criticism

BRENDAN BEHAN

Interviews and Recollections

Volume 1

Edited by

E. H. Mikhail

BARNES & NOBLE BOOKS
TOTOWA, NEW JERSEY

Selection and editorial matter © E. H. Mikhail 1982

All rights reserved. No part of this publication may be reproduced or transmitted, in any form or by any means, without permission

First published in the USA 1982 by
BARNES & NOBLE BOOKS
81, Adams Drive
Totowa, New Jersey 07512

ISBN 0-389-20221-5

Printed in Hong Kong

Library of Congress Cataloging in Publication Data

Main entry under title:
Brendan Behan, interviews and recollections.

   Bibliography: p.
   Includes index.
   1. Behan, Brendan—Interviews. 2. Authors, Irish—20th century—Biography—Addresses, essays, lectures.
I. Behan, Brendan. II. Mikhail, E. H.
PR6003. E417Z63   1981   822'.914 [B] 81-8042
ISBN 0-389-20221-5   AACR2

Contents

Acknowledgements	vii
Introduction	ix
A Note on the Text	xii
Chronological Table	xiii

INTERVIEWS AND RECOLLECTIONS

The Golden Boy *Stephen Behan*	1
Schooldays	2
Moving Out *Dominic Behan*	2
A Bloody Joke *Dominic Behan*	7
Dublin Boy Goes to Borstal	9
The Behan I Knew Was So Gentle *C. A. Joyce*	10
In Prison *Sean Kavanagh*	13
In Jail with Brendan Behan *Sean O'Briain*	16
I Knew the Real Brendan Behan *Seamus G. O'Kelly*	20
The Catacombs *Anthony Cronin*	23
To France with Brendan Behan *Anthony Cronin*	30
Brendan Behan in Paris *Sindbad Vail*	38
Brendan *Joseph Cole*	39
Night Out in Dublin *Joseph Cole*	44
At Kelly's Pawn Office *Dominic Behan*	52
'Get the Rozzers' *Anthony Cronin*	55
The First Play *Mary Lodge*	58
Making up my Mind *Beatrice Behan*	65
A Memorable Occasion *Seamus de Burca*	68
A Terrible Man *Seamus de Burca*	69
Borstal Boy *John Murdoch*	70
Ex-IRA Man Returns as Poet *Edward Goring*	73
The Years of Fame Had Begun *Anthony Cronin*	74
A Celebrated Interview *Beatrice Behan*	76
Drunk? Sure, I'd Had a Bottle *Vincent Mulchrone*	80
Brendan Behan at Lime Grove *Malcolm Muggeridge*	82
Behanism *Myles Na Gopaleen [Brian O'Nolan]*	83
Fourteen-Pint Behan Switches to Milk	85

CONTENTS

The Woman on the Corner of the Next Block to Us *Brendan Behan*	86
My First Meeting with Brendan Behan *Iain Hamilton*	88
His New Play Is Loaded *Kenneth Allsop*	90
Half Angel, Half Beast *John Montague*	92
Brendan Behan Fought for Franco! *Beatrice Behan*	93
Brendan Behan *Roderick W. Childers*	96
Encounter with an Irish Genius *Olof Lagerlöf*	103
My First Visit to Dublin *Rae Jeffs*	108
Book and Author *Michael Campbell*	109
Behan: the Last Laugh *Alan Simpson*	111
Talk with the Author *Frank Melville*	119
My Husband Brendan Behan *Beatrice Behan*	120
Brendan Behan Insists on Use of Irish in Bray Court	122
'The Only Thing I Blame Paris For' *Brendan Behan*	125
A Cry *Georges Wilson*	127
'Success Is Damn Near Killing Me' *Rae Jeffs*	130
The Doctors Warn Behan	132
I Swear I'll Beat It Yet *Brendan Behan*	133
His London Appearances *Donal Foley*	136
His Tremendous Humanity *David Astor*	142
Meet the Quare Fella	142
But Not in the Pejorative Sense *W. J. Weatherby*	149
Meet the New Brendan Behan *Alan Bestic*	152

Acknowledgements

I wish to express my gratitude to Dr Brian Tyson and Dr Colbert Kearney, who read this work in typescript and made many valuable suggestions. At various stages I also received useful comments, information, support or assistance from Mrs Beatrice Behan; Mrs Kathleen Behan; Mr Rory Furlong; Mrs Paula Furlong; Mr Seamus de Burca; Ms Marianne Levander; Dr Olof Lagerlöf; Mr Louis Burke; Mr Desmond Mac Namara; Mr Paddy O'Brien; Mrs Teresa Monaghan; Mr Brian McCoy; the Canadian Broadcasting Corporation; Mr Manus Canning; Mr Tony Aspler; Mr John O'Riordan; Mr Cathal Goulding; Mr Michael Cormican; Miss Alice E. Einhorn of Doubleday Publishers; Miss Kate Mackay of Eyre Methuen Ltd; Research Assistance Routledge Associates, London; Microfilming Executors and Methods Organisation Ltd, Dublin; and Radio Telefís Éireann.

I am grateful to Miss Bea Ramtej for her usual skill in preparing the final typescript.

Thanks are due to the University of Lethbridge for granting me a sabbatical leave, during which this work was completed.

It is also a pleasant duty to record my appreciation to the staff of the University of Lethbridge Library; the British Library, London; the Newspaper Library, Colindale; the National Library of Ireland, Dublin; Trinity College Library, Dublin; the Bibliothèque Nationale, Paris; and the New York Public Library.

The editor and publishers wish to thank the following, who have kindly given permission for the use of copyright material:

Granada Publishing Ltd, for the extracts from *Brendan Behan* by Ulick O'Connor.
The *Daily News*, for 'Behan Back on Booze Binge'; © 1960 New York News Inc.; reprinted by permission.
Mr Iain Hamilton, for 'Among the Irish' in *Encounter*.
Gill and Macmillan Ltd, for the extracts from *Remembering How We Stood* by John Ryan.
The *North American Review*, for 'Brendan Behan: Vital Human Being'; reprinted with permission; © 1964 by the University of Northern Iowa.
Mr Seamus de Burca, for the extracts from his book *Brendan Behan: A Memoir*.

ACKNOWLEDGEMENTS

The *Irish Press*, for 'In Jail with Brendan Behan' by Sean O'Briain; and 'Brendan Behan' by Francis MacManus.

The *Sunday Press*, for 'The Behan I Knew Was So Gentle' by C. A. Joyce; and 'Rich in Talent and a Great Personality' by Benedict Kiely.

The *Evening Press*, for 'The Man Brendan Behan' by Tim Pat Coogan; 'He Ran Too Quickly' by Sean O'Casey; 'Great Man' by Sean Kenny; and 'Behan's Mother Wasn't There' by Clare Boylan.

The *Manchester Evening News*, for 'Behan Takes Swallow' by John Alldridge.

The *Observer*, for 'Deckhand on Collier' by Maurice Richardson; and the untitled obituary of Brendan Behan by Joan Littlewood.

The New English Library, for the extracts from *The World of Brendan Behan*, edited by Sean McCann.

Mr Brian Behan, for the extracts from his book *With Breast Expanded*.

Mrs Peter A. Sebley, for the extracts from her book *Brendan Behan: Man and Showman*; for her Preface to *Confessions of an Irish Rebel*; and for her Afterword to *The Scarperer*.

The *Daily Telegraph*, for 'Brendan Behan: Uproarious Tragedy' by Alan Brien.

A. D. Peters and Co. Ltd, for 'Behan: a Giant of a Man, Yet Gentle' by Kenneth Allsop in the *Daily Mail*.

Mrs Beatrice Behan, for the extracts from her book *My Life with Brendan*; for 'The Only Thing I Blamed Paris for' by Brendan Behan in *L'Express*; and for 'The Woman on the Corner of the Next Block to Us' by Brendan Behan in *Vogue*.

The *Guardian*, for 'But Not in the Pejorative Sense' by W. J. Weatherby.

The *Irish Times*, for 'Dublin Boy Goes to Borstal'; 'Behanism'; 'Book and Author'; 'Brendan Behan Insists on Use of Irish in Bray Court'; 'Brendan Behan Fined £30 on Assault Charges'; 'Talking to Mrs Stephen Behan' by Marion Fitzgerald; and 'Tribute'.

The *New Statesman*, for 'Brendan Behan at Lime Grove' by Malcolm Muggeridge.

The *Sunday Independent*, for 'Was Poet, Comedian, Rebel and Lover of People' by Proinsias MacAonghusa; and 'He Was So Much Larger Than Life' by Frank O'Connor.

The *Washington Post*, for 'The Behan' by Walter Hackett.

The editor has made every effort to trace all the copyright-holders, but if he has inadvertently overlooked any he will be pleased to make the necessary arrangements at the first opportunity.

Introduction

Although it would not be fair to either writer to compare Brendan Behan and Oscar Wilde, it might be instructive to examine some intriguing similarities. Behan found himself cast in the role of the precursor of the permissive generation as Wilde epitomised the aesthetic revolution. Both Behan and Wilde were versatile writers who eventually achieved fame as successful dramatists. Unlike Sean O'Casey, W. B. Yeats and James Joyce – who gave the totality of their life to their art and created illustrious literary works – both Wilde and Behan were too busy living to write. They sometimes even needed to be pushed into the job of producing a masterpiece. George Alexander, the actor–manager of the St James's Theatre, once commissioned Wilde to write a social comedy and offered him an advance of £100 on royalties. This Oscar readily accepted. It was soon spent; still no play. Alexander then tried to badger Wilde with letters; but whenever they met Wilde said 'I am in what I call the invention period', and would not make any promises. Likewise, Iain Hamilton of Hutchinson once interrupted Behan at a party to ask how much more work he had to do on *Borstal Boy*, and at once there was a note of irritation in Behan's reply as he dismissed the subject. 'It's all lies', he said. When Wilde and Behan submitted *Lady Windermere's Fan* and *The Quare Fellow* respectively to George Alexander and Joan Littlewood, both directors badly needed a money-maker, as their theatres were in financial straits.

Both Wilde and Behan died when they were still in their early forties and after suffering the agony of not being able to write any more. The full span of their respective careers bridged only a few years. Both appeared at Bow Street Police Court in London – Wilde on charges of homosexuality and Behan on assault charges. Neither of them had any sense of money or practical affairs. The two dramatists delighted in shocking other people and did not mind making enemies. Both of them joined the journalist profession at an earlier period in their lives, and later suffered at the hands of journalists. Paris attracted both writers, who were cosmopolitan in their outlook. When they achieved success, the limelight attracted – and then eventually destroyed – them. In both cases Constance Wilde and Beatrice Behan were not particularly interested in the social glamour that went with fame. Critical evaluations of the achievement of both men vitiate themselves in accepting biased popular judgements of the writers' personalities, which pervaded all they wrote. Wilde once told Lillie

Langtry that he was going to Australia. She asked why. 'Well, do you know,' he replied, 'when I look at the map and see what an awfully ugly-looking country Australia is, I feel that I want to go there and see if it cannot be changed into a more beautiful form.' And, when Australia banned *Borstal Boy*, Behan refused to meet members of the Australian press in London to give his views on the banning, and his only comment, 'Oh! God, Oh! Canberra. Where's Australia?', was considered best left unrecorded.

André Gide reported Wilde as saying 'Would you like to know the great drama of my life? It is that I have put my genius into my life – but only my talent into my works.' Brian Behan tells us in his autobiography that his brother Brendan 'was too much a person. He expressed himself in what he did and said, much more than in what he wrote.' Brendan Behan wrote brilliantly as a young man, but as he grew older he truly believed that a bawdy song and a jig on a tabletop were ultimately more essential to life than literary output; and so he gave his art to his life.

Both Wilde and Behan were brilliant conversationalists and both had a great sense of humour. Behan's aphorisms recall those of Wilde: 'The first duty of a writer is to let his country down'; 'An honest God is the noblest work of man.' Both Wilde's and Behan's ability as conversationalists was certainly inherited from their parents. Seldom can there have been such an ill-assorted couple as Sir William and Lady Wilde: the husband debauched and almost deformed, the wife idealistic and statuesque. But, whatever the future difficulties of their marriage, because of their shared curiosity in people and books and their love of conversation it can be said that their marriage was a success and that they were never bored in each other's company. Up to a year before Stephen Behan died, he was getting up at 6.30 every morning to go to his work. 'On the way home he used to go in for a pint and a chat. Kathleen often met him, and they'd go into a pub together. He was a brilliant conversationalist and could talk on any subject. He could adjust himself to any company', recalls Seamus de Burca.

Brendan first appeared publicly as a brilliant raconteur, singer and mime at McDaid's pub in Harry Street. Often it took time for him to grip his audience. But after a while he would get on the beam and keep them entertained for hours. Although his abilities were often spoiled by drinking, there are many witnesses to his being a very good conversationalist, the possessor of a rich and beautiful voice and a sparkling wit. Alan Simpson says that he 'was not a compulsive writer; he was a compulsive thinker and talker'. Thomas Quinn Curtiss writes that 'His scenes in public . . . have attracted a wider audience than the excellent scenes in his plays.' The extraordinary thing was that he could embark on these long hours of performance with the remains of a stutter still in his speech. The slight stoppage which he retained from his childhood was much more noticeable on tapes and records: it is probable that his magnetic personality and the mobility of his face diminished the deficiency once he was face to face with his listeners. Rae Jeffs remembers that 'His huge, red face expressed everything from the angelic to the diabolical as he told one uproarious anecdote after another.'

With worldwide acclaim for *The Hostage*, which had been produced in the week preceding the publication of *Borstal Boy*, Behan began to devote less of his time to writing. More and more did he parade the public figure of the irrepressible drunken Irishman, and the newspapers helped enthusiastically. He has to his credit few plays and autobiographical books; and an incredible number of anecdotes and legends surrounding his personal life. He is still highly thought of in Dublin, and the play about him based on *Borstal Boy* was a hit of the 1967 Dublin Theatre Festival and of the 1970 theatrical season in New York. It has the attraction of *Dylan*, based on the life of Dylan Thomas. Behan's writing is quite clearly autobiographical. But, while it is certainly true to say that he left for posterity a part of himself somewhere in his writing and in every place he visited, his works have been collected and published while his personal impressions have not.

It is the intention of this book to fill this gap. Shortly after Behan's death, Rae Jeffs said that it was 'too soon for the compilation of these impressions, and the memory of him is too close for unprejudiced appraisal. A man would emerge possessing every virtue and fault alike, for Brendan inspired love or hatred but never indifference.' Another difficulty was suggested by Beatrice Behan: 'Behan lived life so fully that it would be difficult for any one person, even I who was closest to him, to recall many of its moments without reminders from others who knew him well.' In tracing those 'who knew him well', however, a third difficulty arose. As Beatrice herself remarked, 'I resented after his death the writings of persons who professed they had known him, often persons who had denigrated him during his lifetime, and some of them then tried to ingratiate themselves with me. A few tried to smear his reputation, but those who had been close to him preferred to ignore this denigration.' A great many accounts of Behan are grossly inaccurate or merely superficial. Not nearly enough personal research went into many interviews; they were often the result of very short meetings with him. 'They've got a job to do. I can't refuse them an interview', Behan used to say about journalists. As an international celebrity, therefore, Behan was the easiest in the world to interview. John Murdoch quotes him as always saying, 'Write what you like about me. You can quote me for anything.' And many people did! He helped a lot, of course, with his own inimitable wit and original phrases. But there is probably nobody who could have taken more libel actions against newspapers and magazines than Behan. No such action ever occurred to him and he never complained. Or maybe he believed in Wilde's axiom, 'There is only one thing worse than being talked about; that is, not being talked about!'

E. H. MIKHAIL

A Note on the Text

In the extracts given, spelling errors in the originals have been silently corrected, American spellings have been anglicised and the spelling of names has been rendered consistent throughout.

Chronological Table

1923 (9 Feb) Brendan Behan born in Dublin, the first child of Stephen and Kathleen (Kearney) Behan. Mrs Behan had been married before to Jack Furlong, who left her a young widow with two sons, Rory and Sean.

1928–34 Attends School of the French Sisters of Charity of St Vincent de Paul, North William Street, Dublin.

1931 Joins Fianna Eireann (the Republican scout organisation founded by Countess Markievicz).

1934–7 Attends Irish Christian Brothers' School at St Canice's, Brunswick Street, Dublin.

1937 Attends Day Apprentice School to learn the trade of house-painting. Dublin Corporation relocates the Behans in a housing estate in Crumlin.
Joins the Irish Republican Army (IRA), transferring from Fianna Eireann.

1939 (Nov) Arrested in Liverpool for illegal IRA activity and held in Walton Jail.

1940 (Feb) Tried and sentenced to three years' Borstal (i.e. reform) treatment in Hollesley Bay Borstal Institution, Suffolk, England.

1941 (Nov) Released and deported to Ireland under an Expulsion Order.

1942 (Apr) Shooting incident at Glasnevin Cemetery, Dublin, on the day of the annual Easter Sunday commemoration of the Rising of 1916; sentenced to fourteen years for shooting at a policeman; begins sentence in Mountjoy Prison, Dublin.
(June) 'I Become a Borstal Boy', his first story, published in *The Bell*.

1943 (July) Transferred to Arbour Hill Military Prison, Dublin.

1944 (June) Transferred to the Curragh Internment Camp, County Kildare.

1946 (Nov) Released from prison in the General Amnesty.

1946–51 House-painter, seaman and smuggler.

1947 (Jan) Goes to the Blasket Islands, County Kerry.
(Mar) Arrested in Manchester for attempting to free an IRA prisoner from an English jail.
(July) Released from Strangeways Jail.

1948 (May) Sentenced to one month with hard labour in Mountjoy Prison for assaulting a policeman.
(Aug) Goes to live in Paris.

1951–6 Freelance journalist.

1952 (Oct) Arrested at Newhaven for breaking deportation order.
(Nov) Released from Lewes Prison, Sussex; visits Samuel Beckett in Paris.
1953 (Oct–Nov) *The Scarperer*, by 'Emmet Street', published serially in the *Irish Times*.
1954 (Apr) Begins weekly column in the *Irish Press*.
(Nov) *The Quare Fellow*, directed by Alan Simpson, opens at the Pike Theatre, Dublin.
1955 (Feb) Marries Beatrice ffrench-Salkeld, daughter of the Irish artist Cecil Salkeld, at the Sacred Heart Church, Donnybrook.
1956 (May) *The Quare Fellow*, directed by Joan Littlewood, opens at the Theatre Royal, Stratford, East London.
(Sep–Oct) *Borstal Boy* published serially in the Irish edition of the *Sunday Dispatch*.
(Nov) *The Quare Fellow* published.
1957 (Jan) Draft of *Borstal Boy* accepted for publication by Hutchinson.
(Mar) Begins *An Giall* (*The Hostage*) in Irish.
1958 (Jan) Goes to Ibiza, Spain.
(Apr) Goes to Paris to discuss the production of *The Quare Fellow*.
(June) *An Giall* opens at Damer Hall, Dublin.
(Aug) Goes to Sweden. Starts translation of *An Giall*.
(Oct) *The Hostage*, directed by Joan Littlewood, opens at the Theatre Royal, Stratford, East London. *Borstal Boy* published.
(Nov) *The Quare Fellow*, directed by José Quintero, opens off-Broadway, New York.
(Dec) *The Hostage* published.
1959 (Mar) Goes to Berlin for the opening of *The Quare Fellow*.
(Apr) Goes to Paris. *The Hostage* selected to represent Great Britain at the Théâtre des Nations Festival.
(July) *The Hostage* moves to Wyndham's Theatre in the West End of London.
First serious breakdown.
1960 (Jan) Tapes *Brendan Behan's Island* in Dublin.
(Mar) Begins *Richard's Cork Leg*.
Goes to London. Second breakdown.
(Sep) Goes to New York for the opening of *The Hostage* at the Cort Theatre.
(Dec) Returns to Dublin.
1961 (Jan) Translates *Richard's Cork Leg* into Irish.
Failure of *A Fine Day in the Graveyard*.
(Mar) Travels 11,000 miles across the United States and Canada. Two periods in hospital.
(July) Returns to Dublin.
(Sep–Oct) 'The Big House' published in *Evergreen Review*.
(Oct) Film version of *The Quare Fellow* opens in London.

1962 (Feb) Returns to New York for the off-Broadway production of *The Hostage*.
(Mar) Returns to Dublin.
(July) *The Hostage* selected in France as the best play of the season.
(Sep) Goes to London. Enters home for alcoholics.
(Oct) *Brendan Behan's Island* published.
(Nov) Goes to France to recuperate.
Returns to Dublin after failure of cure.
1963 (Feb) Final trip to America.
(Apr) Tapes *Confessions of an Irish Rebel* in New York.
(July) Returns to Dublin and to hospital.
(Sep) *Hold Your Hour and Have Another* published.
(Nov) Tapes *Brendan Behan's New York* in Dublin.
Blanaid Behan born.
(Dec) Enters hospital.
1964 (Jan) In and out of hospital.
(20 Mar) Dies in Meath Hospital, Dublin.
(June) *The Scarperer* published.
(Sep) *Brendan Behan's New York* published.
1965 (Sep) *Confessions of an Irish Rebel* published.
1967 'Moving Out' and 'A Garden Party', ed. Robert Hogan, published.
1972 (Mar) *Richard's Cork Leg*, directed by Alan Simpson, opens at the Abbey Theatre, Dublin.
1973 *Richard's Cork Leg* published.

The Golden Boy*

STEPHEN BEHAN

Brendan was a very good-looking child and was usually very even tempered. But he had another side. Because he was the golden boy, he always wanted his own way. There was a vicious streak in him side by side with the personality of a sensitive little boy. I remember finding him one day with a little boy half his size up against the railings and the child nearly throttled. We pulled him off, but Brendan still wanted a go at the child who had angered him. Another time I discovered that he had tortured a dog which had bitten him a few minutes before. He played a dastardly trick on one of our neighbours in Russell Street.[1] He put sacks over the windows of her room so that when she woke up she thought she was blind. She didn't know whether it was night or day until someone opened the door three days later and let the light in. Brendan was also very jealous of any of the other children who managed to attract his granny's[2] attention. He didn't want his position to be usurped. Once he discovered that Seamus (his younger brother)[3] had scrounged a penny from the granny. Brendan rushed up the stairs, grabbed Seamus and threw him down shouting, 'She is my granny, not yours'.

NOTES

Stephen Behan (1891–1967), Brendan's father. A house-painter, he married Kathleen Furlong in 1922. See 'Mr Stephen Behan: a Dublin Character', *The Times*, 15 July 1967, p. 12.

1. The Behans lived at that time in 14 Russell Street, off North Circular Road. Russell Street was on the perimeter of the Georgian slum area in Dublin. 'Our street was a tough street, and the last outpost of toughness you'd meet as you left North Dublin for the red brick respectability of Jones's Road, Fitzroy Avenue, Clonliffe Road, and Drumcondra generally' – Brendan Behan, *Hold Your Hour and Have Another* (London: Hutchinson, 1963) p. 149. (All subsequent page-references are to first editions of Behan's works.)

2. Granny English. When Stephen Behan's father died, his mother married another house-painter, Patrick English.

3. Brendan Behan had three brothers: Brian, Dominic, and Seamus; two stepbrothers: Rory and Sean; and one sister: Carmel.

* Ulick O'Connor, *Brendan Behan* (London: Hamish Hamilton, 1970) p. 20. Editor's title.

Schooldays*

The young Behan of schooldays[1] was recalled by two of his teachers, Bred Costello and Brother O'Donnell. Bred remembered his torrent of Gaelic ('he loved roaring out the Irish'). Another teacher had told her that he was 'brassy bold', and that she could not stop him talking in English and Irish. But he was full of personality.

Brother O'Donnell remembered him as a 'thin, spare, little boy' in 1934, but he was an avid reader of the Irish novelists when his schoolmates were reading books of their own age.
   He caught Brendan one day with Daniel Corkery's[2] *Hidden Ireland*, and found he understood it very well. 'He had matured thoughts, weaved his sentences very well, and, where other boys would write one page of an essay, Brendan would write six.'
   He said he thought that he was unmarked by Borstal and said, 'I don't think he had it in him to be bitter to anyone' and said that when he was there he read everything from the *Catholic Herald* to the *Daily Worker*.

* *Irish Times* (Dublin), 21 Mar 1964, p. 9. Editor's title.

NOTES

1. Behan attended the Irish Christian Brothers' School, Dublin, from 1934 to 1937.
2. Daniel Corkery (1878–1964), Irish writer, professor of English, and Senator.

Moving Out †

DOMINIC BEHAN

I first met him in 1937[1] when he was fourteen and I was nine. On the back of an ass and cart we were sitting, and it going to Kimmage. He had an answer for everything – or so I was led to believe. 'Why are we leaving

† *My Brother Brendan* (London: Leslie Frewin, 1965) pp. 9–16. Editor's title.

Russell Street?' I asked. Without looking at me he replied, 'Because me mother's country blood is getting unsettled and she wants to get back to the cows and cowshite.' His handsome face scowled anger and he placed his arm around my shoulder, 'Ah, it's not your fault, sondown.' When he was like this he would take time with us. He had great patience in affection. Most of the other kids in the street would get a dig from their elder brothers for nothing, and two for anything else. Brendan never touched me. Oh, he'd go for Seamus all right; but me? well, 'God help yeh', he'd say, 'but yer not the size of threepence in coppers.' At the top of North Great Georges Street he asked, 'Have yeh ever been here before?' I hadn't, but I felt such an eejit because the place was no more than a stone's throw from my granny's tenements. 'Oh yes', I lied, 'Charlie Mac and meself hunted a cow up here one time.' He looked seriously to the front of his twinkling eyes. 'Did yeh?' he asked. I felt uncomfortable and said, 'Isn't it great to drink the milk up at the market when it's hot from the cow?' 'Don't for the love of jazes mention anything even remotely connected with farming to me again this evening', in the middle of which I bowed my head because he had taken the Lord's name in vain. As yet I wasn't quite sure if it was the 'vein' or the 'vain', but in the religion of my mother's people yeh sort of caught on quick. Even the kids at St John of God's, who are as nutty as fruit-cakes, learn the way to detect such a sinner.

As the cart turned into Parnell Street towards the monument he pointed to a great big building behind Charles Stewart Parnell and said, 'That's where I was born.' 'Yes,' I replied, 'Ma showed it to me when we were shopping here one time. How did Da go down in the world?' For a moment he looked puzzled. 'Down where?' he asked. 'Well,' I said, 'from a nice big clean house like that one to the dirty oul place where we're livin' in now.' He jumped down off the back of Mrs Farrell's cart and ran the length of O'Connell Street with my hand in his. At the tram terminus he stopped to let other people go before us and asked, 'Do you know what that place is?' I wasn't quite sure because there was something going on in his head I didn't know about. 'Seamus says Da was born there and it was part of his grandfather's estate that was taken over from him by the British after Easter week.'[2] He looked at me in amused astonishment. 'Are you really as much of a gobshite as yeh seem? That is the Rotunda Maternity Hospital where women go to give birth to their children.' 'They buy them there?' He flew up the stairs of the tram with a backward glance. 'Oh, Mother of jazes! And you're nine years of age.' He stared, and after a moment, seeing the tears in my eyes, he said, 'Lord God Almighty, did nobody ever tell yeh anything? What do yeh talk about with yerself and Charlie Mac and all when yer by yerselves?' So gentle, so understanding. I looked at the fond face set in the jet-black hair over a smiling set of teeth in ivory and replied, 'About the time me ma's granny was burned on a rack by the English and the farm taken for Scots settlers and how someday we'll win the lot back.' His face contorted with rage and his cheeks bulged, ready for a torrent of abuse, but all that came out was, 'Oh, for jazes' sake!' And not another word did he speak until we were well on the south side of the Liffey.

As the tramcar rumbled along around Dame Street and by the headquarters of the Irish National Painters' and Decorators' Trades Union, my brother said, 'Did yeh ever hear Da talk about the "Hall"?[3] Well, that's it.' I leaned over his knees and peered down at the place. This was one very important building and I didn't want to miss it. I was disappointed. To me it had always been as great at least as the Bank of Ireland. My hearing of the place had built a more imposing image than the rather ordinary neo-Georgian house fronted by a gilt fascia. Da got money from this place when he was idle. Security cried out from its picture in my mind. Christmas and unemployment would never be the same again. And it seemed to me that the very next time Da went to sign on at this 'Hall' for his money that rock of sustenance, the secretary, would be gone, buried under a load of old rubbish no better than the place we were leaving and the Corporation was pulling down.

Now that Brendan had spoken first, it was safe for me to talk. 'Where's Kimmage?' I asked. 'Near the Hill of Midcain,' he replied, 'and I wouldn't be one bit surprised if we had to give three shouts when we get there.' 'Why should we have to do that, Brendan?' He smiled at my puzzled look and said, 'There were three sons of Turenn who had done a great wrong in killing an enemy, and for that they were punished by the son of him they killed. They were ordered to bring three apples from the Garden of Hesperides; the skin of the King of Greece's healing pig; the poisoned spear of Pisar; two horses and a chariot from the King of Sicily; the seven pigs of Asal; a puppy dog belonging to the King of Iruad; a cooking spit from the faery women of Finchory; and they were to give three shouts from the Hill of Midcain. All the tasks were far more dangerous than you could think.' 'Did they do them?' 'They did,' he replied, 'and got killed for their trouble.' 'Oh Lord!' I thought.

At the top of Clanbrassil Street, by the junction of the South Circular Road, I saw Rory, my eldest brother, sitting beside Seamus on the front of a horse-dawn cart. Ma's furniture was piled precariously on the float, pinnacled by the horse-hair sofa through which the strong stuffing protruded with cutting edge. Da had been going to mend it for as long as I could remember; he had thought about it a great deal. Just now, as it wagged from side to side, it seemed all Da's worries would soon be over. 'Brendan,' I said, 'there's Rory with the things for the new house. And if they don't stop and tie up the load that sofa will fall off.' He looked along the line of my pointing finger with little interest and said, 'It will that', and it seemed to me that he would have derived immense satisfaction from such an occurrence.

At the military barracks taken over from the British in 1922, and named after Arthur Griffiths [sic],[4] Brendan said, 'Did yeh ever hear Ma talkin' about the man who wrote *Twenty Men from Dublin Town*?' I did, but whenever Brendan began like that we knew that the question would be rhetorical, so I said nothing. 'Well, that place there is called after him.' 'Was he the one who was shot with Michael Collins?'⁵ I asked. 'How did yeh know about things like that? He was a close friend of Collins' but he wasn't shot. He died before Collins – overworked, Ma said. Though she also said that to her it was obvious Collins himself knew he wouldn't be long after Griffiths.' 'How could she know that?' I asked. 'She was behind him at Griffiths' funeral and all the time Collins kept looking over his shoulder.' 'What was he like, Brendan, Collins I mean?' 'I can't say personally, because I wasn't born at the time of his death, but, according to Father O'Flanagan, Collins was a good man, and that's alright by me.' 'Bernard Keegan's mother said Father O'Flanagan was in favour of those people in Spain. And would be unfrocked.' 'Well,' said Brendan, 'if he's unfrocked twenty times a day it won't be half as many times as Bernard Keegan's mother.'

Kids were playing under a street-lamp by the tram-stop at Sally's Bridge. 'P'liceman, p'liceman, don't take me. Take that boy behind the tree. He took silver, he took gold, p'liceman, p'liceman, please take hold.' Very grand songs. Very grand kids and not one of them but had trousers and coats to match. Indeed most of them had school caps. Where we lived in Russell Street it was, 'Limpy Dan, Limpy Dan, lift yer leg and yeh'll see a wee man.' This place appealed to me, for I'd always had a yearning for nice clothes and people who spoke well, who came home on trains at the end of mysterious times called 'terms'. The *Hotspur* comic was full of great things, like schools with places 'out of bounds' and 'tuck' shops. Maybe it was all true after all. 'Is the whole of Kimmage like this?' I asked. 'Kimmage!' said Brendan indignantly, 'Kimmage! Would yeh for God's sake look at the size of the houses. Shabby genteel maybe. But big. Closed Hall doors, but enough to keep a body warm for a few hours if chopped up nicely. Grass enough at the front but nothin' a few bags of sand and cement couldn't very quickly eradicate. Yer still in some sort of civilisation. Those kids singin' out there are the last yeh'll ever hear, because the chisellers in Kimmage don't have time to play games, they have to go huntin' with their fathers. Take it from me, sondown, we're on our way to the wild west.'

Brendan sat, staring, sightless, as the long circular snake slipped southwards. He sighed. My heart was filled with a sense of adventure, but all he had ever wanted was behind him: the smell of Mountjoy Brewery, the roar from Croke Park Stadium, the sound of 'city' cattle on their way to the docks down the North Circular Road. The view from Granny's grandstand window of a street teeming with life. Even the smell of Mrs Cullen's pigs in the lane.

It was dark and with the sky for a roof the top of the tram was very cold. 'Could we go downstairs, Brendan?' I asked. 'It's not worth it now, Dom', he said. 'We'll soon be in Dolphin's Barn.' 'Is that near Kimmage?' 'Well,' he thought for a moment, 'to be quite honest I don't know where it really is, though I passed it one time in a cab with me granny. They used to come out here durin' the summertime, me granny and her friends. Out to the Red Cow in Clondalkin, or maybe the Cuckoo's Nest near Tallaght or Lena Delaney's in Bohernbreena, Kennedy's of Old Bawn, or to the pub of many names in Rathcool. Then back into the cab stocious drunk while the driver unable to do anything about it would let the horse steam back to Dublin. Then she'd lift me out of the cab and explain to the neighbours how "we've just had a lovely day in the country, messrs, and of course the air is too strong for poor Bren". I've often inhaled more air in a picture house.' He laughed at what he had just said and then sat back, his head turned away from me. Granny was on his mind now. His granny and nobody else's. She had died some few months before and her act he construed as some sort of betrayal. He had lived by her and with her. He slept in our place but that was about all. A lot of his life died when she did, for his granny was everything in the world to him. 'Poor little Bren', she would say, 'loves his gran.' His granny had never much time for me, Rory and Sean were greeted civilly enough, Seamus she couldn't stand since he was named after her first husband, our grandfather. In later times I wrote about his granny in a somewhat critical way and Brendan never forgave me. But, then it was only after he had refused forgiveness for a million other real and imaginary wrongs perpetrated against him by a brother who was always 'a bit of a gobshite'.

We came to a junction of village size and the conductor cried, 'Dolphin's Barn! All off here!'

We gained the foot of the stairs in time to see the driver and conductor slip around the corner on the north side of Dolphin's Barn. Brendan swore and muttered, 'Jazes, I wanted to ask him about a bus goin' out to this kip. Ah, they won't be long anyway; probably just gone for a pint.' He looked down at me and with a smile said, 'Go across to that place with the light on and ask them where the sheriff is. We should report to him at once, I'm sure.' I was halfway across the road when he called, 'Will yeh come back out of that, yeh thick, before one of these country eejits captures yeh for a leprechaun!'[6] I didn't like people making fun of my height, so I crossed back to him and sat sullen with bowed head on the corner of the kerb. He put his arm around me and I shook it away. He asked me did I want to hear about Fiann Macool, and though I would have loved to have the story of Ireland's legendary hero related I just turned my head further away. 'Alright,' he said, 'keep yer anger in and me out. But yeh'll want me company when we have to leave here and walk into the night:'

Although 'Dolphin's Barn' was connected to the city by an unbroken stream of streets and houses it had lost none of its village characteristics. The tallest house in it would not have come up to the chest of one of our Georgian slums. There was no sound of singing children here, and people passing went by and spoke to each other with a touch of that 'God Bless all Here Irish', and the Catholic chapel surveyed the scene with evident satisfaction. It was then – and, I suppose, it still is – three and one half miles from Dublin. The driver and conductor came across the road and Brendan said, 'We're tryin' to get to Kimmage, please.' 'Out there over the bridge,' replied the driver. 'But we want to get a bus,' said Brendan, as the driver got on to his tram. He looked at Brendan and unlocked his lever and contemplated the glass in front. The conductor straightened his bag, pulled the bell strap, said, 'A bus! To Siberia!', and as the tram sped away, retracing its steps, the conductor's loud laughter could be heard singing in the distance.

NOTES

Dominic Behan (1928–), Brendan's younger brother; left Ireland for England in 1947; became involved in trade unionism; and has written ballads, television documentaries, a play, *Posterity Be Damned*, and an autobiography, *Teems of Times and Happy Returns*.
1. In 1937 the Behan family moved from 14 Russell Street to 70 Kildare Road, Crumlin (Kimmage).
2. The Easter Rising in 1916.
3. Liberty Hall, headquarters of the Irish Transport and General Workers Union.
4. Arthur Griffith (1872–1922), Irish political leader.
5. Michael Collins (1890–1922), Irish revolutionary leader and soldier.
6. In Irish folklore, a sprite or goblin resembling a little old man.

A Bloody Joke*

DOMINIC BEHAN

Da came home from work, left his bike at the corner of the house, and I scooted it round to the back. He looked at the weeds growing high in the garden and laughed. 'Yeh know,' he said, 'in the famine times people would have been delighted to take a bag of those and boil them.'
'I wonder how they tasted', I asked.
'Like weeds that have been boiled, I'd imagine.'
Brendan came whistling up the path and Da said, 'C'mere; I want just a word with you.'
'What's that, Da?' asked Brendan.
'What were you up to today?'

* *My Brother Brendan* (London: Leslie Frewin, 1965) pp. 29–31. Editor's title.

Brendan with a half-smile and blushing look said, 'Well I . . .'

'I know yeh weren't in Tech[1] because only tonight I met Charlie O'Byrne and he nearly died of shock on account you told him that yeh were takin' the day off because of my death.' I was shocked. Fancy anybody making up a thing like that about their father – or even their mother. Brendan was embarrassed. 'I didn't mean it, Da,' he began, 'it was a sort of a joke. A poor one, I admit, but at the time I didn't think of it in bad taste. I'm sorry.'

'It doesn't interest me, Brendan. It doesn't interest me one little bit even if yeh told your teacher I was bloody well cremated. What does worry me is why you did it.'

'I told yeh,' said Brendan irritably, 'it was a bloody joke. Now surely we can drop the whole bastardin' subject.' Da ignored Brendan's anger and said, 'Before we go inside to where yer mother is I want to know how you spent the time you took off.' He was getting into a temper now, the sort where he sat and boiled. He wouldn't beat us, for he didn't believe a child was a match for a man and that was an end to corporal punishment. 'What I do with my time is my own', replied Brendan.

'Not', said my father, 'if it concerns me.'

'What do you mean, concern you?' demanded Brendan. 'How could anything I do concern you?'

'I'll tell you,' said Da, 'if you were in Killiney Castle today where they're makin' the stuff for the English campaign[2] that concerns me.'

Brendan looked surprised. 'How d'ye know about Killiney?' he asked.

'That doesn't matter,' said Da, 'what matters is that I don't agree with this campaign in England.'

'So?' asked Brendan sullenly.

'So,' my father replied, 'under no circumstances are you to make 70 Kildare Road one of the jumpin'-off grounds for it.'

'Same as all the other Staters',[3] muttered Brendan, and Da heard him. He went white with temper and I could see the knuckles sticking through the taut skin on his hands.

'Don't you dare call me a Stater. I fought against the murder gang before yeh were born. I was in jail – their bloody jail – *when* yeh were born.[4] If you're ever *half* the Republican I was you'll be damned lucky.' And as if by some prearranged signal they both turned in their own circles and walked, Da into the house where Ma was waiting and Brendan down to the pub where somebody was waiting for him.

'Strange people,' I thought, 'let's hope to God they don't start arguing tonight during "Band Wagon".'[5]

They have a saying in Dublin, 'Yer better off idle than walkin' about.' So far as I can discover, Brendan got two things from attending Mr O'Byrne's painting class at Bolton Street Technical School: enough knowledge of signwriting to enable him to write a fascia for a Parisian restaurateur which read: 'There is but one Au Fait Café in Paris and this is fucking well it.' And it got him away from Kimmage and back to the land he was fighting for – North Dublin. He was as well off walking around Liverpool with a suitcase full of stuff as being idle on the ratepayers of Dublin at fifteen shillings a week which he never brought home anyway. Though I do remember how Ma used to commiserate with him every time he lost his wages – each week. 'Poor Brendan,' she'd say, 'still, yeh have your health. Thank God!'

NOTES

For a note on Dominic Behan see p. 7.
1. In 1937 Behan attended the Day Apprentice School to learn the trade of house-painting.
2. In 1939 there was a wave of IRA bombings in England.
3. When the Irish Free State was established in 1922 following the signing of the treaty between Britain and Southern Ireland, a civil war broke out between the Free-Staters, who were satisfied with the new state, and the Republicans, who wanted complete independence for Ireland, including Ulster.
4. When Brendan Behan was born in 1923, during the Irish Civil War, his father Stephen was confined as a Republican prisoner in Kilmainham Jail.
5. 'Band Wagon' was a BBC Radio comedy show starring Arthur Askey and Richard Murdoch.

Dublin Boy Goes to Borstal*

A sixteen years old boy, who was said by the police to have stated that he had been sent over by an illegal organisation to 'reorganise further operations in Liverpool', was sentenced at Liverpool Assizes today to three years' Borstal detention. He was Brendan Behan, a painter, of Kildare Road, Dublin, who smiled as he stood in the dock accused of being in possession of explosives, and declared that he had no interest in the proceedings of the court. His 'No Interest' remark was construed as a plea of not guilty.

While Detective-Sergeant Earps was giving evidence, the boy shouted, 'That's a lot of damned lies', and was warned by Mr Justice Hallett that if he did not remain quiet he would be removed from court and the case conducted in his absence.

The detective gave evidence that the boy made a statement in which he said, 'I have been sent over to take the places of Chris Kenneally, Nick

* *Irish Times* (Dublin), 8 Feb 1940, p. 6.

Lynch and the others who have been arrested. I was to reorganise further operations in Liverpool. I intended to put bombs in big stores – Lewis's and Hughes's I think they call it. I was making up some to put in letter-boxes tonight. I would have put one in Cammell Lairds if I had the chance. I am only sixteen and they can't do much with me.'

Behan interposed that he did not make such 'ridiculous assertions'. The Judge asked if there was any truth that Behan was only sixteen. The maximum penalty for an adult in his position would be fourteen years' penal servitude.

Behan – 'It is my proud privilege and honour to stand in an English court to testify to the unyielding determination of the Irish people to regain every inch of our national territory, and to give expression to the noble aspirations for which so much Irish blood has been shed and so many hearts have been broken, and for which so many friends and comrades are languishing in English jails.'

Sentencing Behan to three years' Borstal detention, the Judge said that Parliament in recent years had taken an extremely lenient view of what ought to be done with young persons found guilty of offences.

As Behan went below he shouted, 'God save Ireland.'

Mr Eric Errington, MP, prosecuting, said that the boy was found in a house in Aubrey Street, Liverpool, standing by an open suitcase, which contained a bottle of acid. He had a fountain-pen filler in his hand. In his possession were also found twenty ounces of potassium chlorate and sugar and sixteen rubber balloons. Later he made a statement to the effect that he was a member of an organisation, and that he would blow up places if he got the chance.

The Behan I Knew Was So Gentle*

C. A. JOYCE

'Brendan Behan came to me towards the end of 1939 to serve a three-year sentence', began Mr Joyce in slow matter-of-fact tones, 'I was impressed by him immediately. I did not, of course, treat him any differently from any

* *Sunday Press* (Dublin), 5 Apr 1964, p. 12.

other prisoner but he struck me as having a high sense of humour, an exceptional degree of honesty and quite unusual intelligence. His intelligence showed itself mainly by his approach to problems; his extraordinarily sharp and quick wit and the colourful choice of words in his ordinary speech. In ways he was so refreshing, so out of the ordinary.

'To start with the end of his sentence first. I recommended that he be released after eighteen months. He was duly allowed to go free to return to Ireland or to stay in England if he wished. But I recommended that he be released only after he had given me a definite promise that he would not attack my countrymen as the IRA had been doing in 1939 in England.[1] I said to Brendan, "You know we are already fighting one enemy. Do you understand?" The humour and wit of his character came out like a flash when he said, "Sure, I promise not to do anything until we have done with this bastard Hitler and after that I can always consider it again, can't I?"

'I told him that while he loved his country, I also loved mine and I had to play my part in its protection. He understood my point of view perfectly.

'Then I was amazed to read in the newspapers that Brendan, before the war was over, was sentenced[2] to fourteen years imprisonment in a Dublin court for attempting to shoot two detectives. I could not understand this because when he was released from Borstal I trusted him. Unexpectedly, I got a letter from him at a time when I thought he was still in prison. He wrote, "I didn't break my promise. I snatched the gun from a fellow who was going to use it on the detectives and when I was arrested it was, of course, found in my possession."

'Whether Brendan's statement to me in that letter was true or not I am not going to say, one way or the other,' added Mr Joyce, 'and I want to make it perfectly clear that I am not suggesting that the police framed him. I am merely giving the blunt bald statement as I got it.'

Mr Joyce saw much on the 'positive and creditable' side of the playwright's character.

'Most people will be surprised to know that Brendan Behan was an intensely religious young man. But he did not wear his religion on his cuff. It was deep down in his soul, fundamental and solid. He came to me as a member of the IRA and, as such, he was excommunicated. That worried him a great deal because he was not allowed to attend Mass. He came to me one day and said, "You must understand, sir, that the freedom of Ireland is to me a second religion. I was bred to believe in it and work for it." And very often he would come to me and say, "Governor, couldn't you persuade the Father to let me go to Mass for I feel all lost without its consolation." I knew that the priest was helpless in the matter. He was merely acting on the instructions of his Bishop. But to satisfy Brendan I did ask the priest and he explained. Brendan was very sad when I told him.

'Then I said to the boy, "Listen, son, I am not a Roman Catholic but I would like to go to Mass with you. We'll sit together. I can't receive it for one reason and you for another, but we will pray to the same God together, Brendan." And we did.

'Sometimes we would go into the chapel together when nobody was there. I would play the organ for him. We sang, "I'll Sing a Hymn to Mary" and "Sweet Sacrament Divine". I have no doubt at all that Brendan was a good boy at heart and he loved his religion.'

Mr Joyce continued, 'I was not interested in whether the boy was in the IRA or not, I saw there was much good in him if only he would give himself a chance. I was not interested in his past but in his future. As a governor, I was always more interested in rogues than in roguery. I regarded Brendan as I did the other prisoners – not just a number but a man with a soul, a living human being.'

Ex-Governor Joyce said that the Dublin playwright could not have used the bad language in Borstal that he claimed to have used in *Borstal Boy*.[3]

'This claim was just an aspect of Brendan's character. It was merely a pose, all part of the mask that he wore even in Borstal. He appeared to be a loudmouth aggressive type but at heart he was a kindly soul. In his book, he described incidents retrospectively and put in the lurid language as part of the colour to make, what he thought, was good reading. We were not unreasonable in regard to bad language in Borstal in my time. If somebody said, "bloody stupid", or something like that, nothing was done. But four-letter words were certainly forbidden. Brendan never used them. I remember on one occasion he apologised to me for using bad language. He said he was not aware that I was present. But I did not hear what he was supposed to have said.[4] I always found him kindly, charitable and generous. He loved his mother and his country.'

Mr Joyce said that Behan and he never lost touch with each other over the twenty-five year period until Behan's death. Frequently Brendan phoned him at one o'clock in the morning for a friendly chat from Dublin.

'The last time he phoned me at that hour my wife answered', said Mr Joyce. 'She said, "Brendan dear, will you go back to bed and phone about ten in the morning." And in his rich Irish voice he replied, "Shure that is drinking time in Ireland." Whenever he phoned at one in the morning he usually explained that, to use the jockey's language, he was "under pressure".'

Brendan Behan and his old Borstal boss corresponded a lot and Brendan's mother wrote a couple of letters to Mr Joyce thanking him for the kindness shown to her son while he was in Borstal. For many years after his release, Brendan sent Mr Joyce lovely Easter Cards expressing highly religious sentiments and scribbled inside 'with fond remembers to the "Old Man" and Mrs Joyce; see you in Church'.

At his home in Ryde, Mr Joyce was saddened by the death of the Irish playwright. 'He was one of the most lovable characters that ever passed through Borstal,' said Mr Joyce, 'no matter what he did you could not help liking the man.'

NOTES

In November 1939 Behan was arrested in Liverpool for illegal IRA activity and was sentenced to three years' Borstal (i.e. reform) treatment. C. A. Joyce was Governor of Hollesley Bay Borstal Institution, Suffolk, England, when Behan came under his care at the age of sixteen years. This interview with Joyce is edited by John Murdoch, a journalist and friend of Behan.

1. This promise was challenged by Behan's father. 'It is not a custom for Republican prisoners to compromise with their jailers, and Brendan's promise was somewhat contrary to the code' – Stephen Behan, 'Defence of His Son's Republicanism', *Evening Herald* (Dublin), 29 Nov 1965, p. 5. See reply by Anthony Butler, ibid., 1 Dec 1965, p. 6; and counter-reply by Seamus G. O'Kelly, ibid., 2 Dec 1965, p. 10.
2. In April 1942.
3. Brendan Behan, *Borstal Boy* (London: Hutchinson, 1958; New York: Alfred A. Knopf, 1959).
4. Cf. 'bad language, of which I am extremely fond. In my very early childhood I never used bad language because I didn't hear it in my home, except when my father had a few oils on him, and that was only at weekends' – Brendan Behan, *Confessions of an Irish Rebel* (London: Hutchinson, 1965) pp. 120–1.

In Prison*

SEAN KAVANAGH

The Brendan Behan who arrived in Mountjoy Prison in April 1942 was a slim, good-looking youth of nineteen, five feet eight and 130 pounds. He had been released from Borstal in England only a very short time before so he was in very good physical condition.

His arrival in Mountjoy was awaited with no a little interest owing to the circumstances of his arrest. He was captured in De Courcy Square near Glasnevin after a gun battle with Special Branch detectives (in which nobody was hurt) following the discharge of a volley of revolver shots by himself and a couple of other IRA men at a commemoration ceremony in the cemetery. However, meeting this mild-mannered boy gave one a feeling of anti-climax; surely this was no desperado, no trigger-happy gunman. Even the fact that a sentence of fourteen years penal servitude was imposed on him a couple of weeks later by the Special Criminal Court for attempted murder did not lessen this feeling. The better one grew to

* *The World of Brendan Behan*, ed. Sean McCann (London: New English Library, 1965), pp. 67–70.

know him the more the impression grew that basically he was a very gentle person who in his senses would not hurt a fly.

During the fifteen months or so of the sentence which he spent in Mountjoy I, as Governor, got to know him very well. One could not avoid noticing his presence around the place for he was a character, a complete extrovert. Gay, witty, amusing, always in good humour, and his strong voice with its slight stammer could often be heard above all others in the exercise yard or from one of the 'D' Wing landings.

When he began to write, which he did almost immediately, he came to see me frequently to look for extra visits or letters and for help and facilities for his writing, and, of course, I gave him all the assistance I could. His appearance on the Governor's parade was always welcome for he never failed to be refreshing and entertaining. He talked a good deal about his Borstal experiences and spoke with respect and affection of his Borstal governor, Mr Joyce, 'The Squire' as he was known to inmates, and his wife, and told me of many kindnesses he had done him.

When he had written a few things including a play, called, I think, *The Landlady*,[1] and some short stories and sketches, I arranged that Sean O'Faolain[2] should read them and come to Mountjoy to meet the author. I was present at Sean's first visit which took place in my office. They had a long chat during which Brendan was assured that he had undoubted talent and was strongly encouraged to persevere to continue with his writing. He continued to write incessantly while in Mountjoy and, of course, in Arbour Hill, where he and his companions were transferred in July 1943, and later at the Curragh.

When I first knew him Brendan had a good grasp of Irish from his schooldays. He must have worked hard at it in the different prisons for on his release he could write and speak it as fluently as English. Irish classes were carried on in 'D' Wing but Brendan was not one for classroom discipline and was just as likely to disturb or distract a class as to be part of it. However he improved his knowledge of it in various ways, and he must have benefited considerably from the help he got from a fellow prisoner, Sean O'Briain, a teacher and a native speaker from Ballyferriter. He had a prodigious memory and even in Mountjoy would recite long passages of poetry and prose from his favourite Irish authors.

Brendan was anything but a model of neatness and cleanliness and his cell was easily the untidiest and dirtiest in the Wing. I used to tell him that he kept the second dirtiest cell I had ever seen; the worst was that of a friend and fellow-prisoner of my own in Mountjoy in 1921 who afterwards became a TD[3] and Parliamentary Secretary. He could on occasions though appear spick and span; especially at Sunday Mass – which he never missed – and when going on special visits, such as Seán O'Faoláin's.

He left Mountjoy, as I have said, in July 1943 and was later released in the General Amnesty of 1946. But, alas, that was not the last we saw of Brendan Behan as a prisoner. He returned in 1948 for a month for the nonpolitical offence of assaulting a Garda.⁴ He had no kindred spirits to pass the time with now so he worked hard for the month at his old trade of painter. He was back again in 1954 when he got seven days for being drunk and disorderly. He had no longer the trim, slim figure of 1942; in the intervening years his weight had increased by five stone to 200 pounds. In the course of his arrest his ankle was injured and he arrived with his foot encased in plaster. I gave him a blackthorn stick which I had to help him walk about and also a loan of my own copy of *War and Peace*. He had not finished it when he had to leave; he promised to return it but somehow it never came back. He hadn't quite forgotten about it though for a couple of years later when writing about Mountjoy for one of the English Sunday papers he remarked 'I must send the decent man back his *War and Peace*. I hadn't got around to reading it myself, and now I suppose I never shall.'

Brendan's largely wasted life and cruel early death were a great disappointment to me and to many who knew him in his early days and who realised his wonderful potential as a dramatist and story-teller. He achieved fame as well as notoriety, in the ensuing years, but all that he produced was, in my view, only a small fraction in quality as well as quantity of what, in other circumstances, he was capable of.

In his prison days when he didn't need drink to inspire him he probably wrote most of his best work; he may have revised and rewritten much of it later but I consider that it is to the imposed and self-imposed discipline of those four years that we owe most of what he has left us.

NOTES

On 5 April 1942, the day of the annual IRA commemoration of the 1916 insurrection at Glasnevin Cemetery, Behan was arrested and sentenced to fourteen years for shooting a policeman. He was sent to Mountjoy Prison, of which Sean Kavanagh was Governor. In 1946 the sentence was commuted and Behan was released from prison.

1. *The Landlady* was based on his memories of his grandmother (Granny English) and her cronies and the atmosphere surrounding Russell Street. In *Confessions of an Irish Rebel* Behan says (p. 199), 'I was also writing bits of poems and articles and a second play, *The Landlady*. . . . The play I wrote in longhand, and my cousin, Seamus de Burca, typed it for me, but it was never published.' Behan later rewrote this play, translated it into Gaelic, and sent it to the Abbey Theatre. It is not certain that he sent the whole of it, for only one act survives in the Abbey Archives, though in a covering letter to the managing director of the Abbey Theatre Behan stated that he had sent the other two acts. Part of the manuscript, however, was found later. See P. H. S., 'Behan's First Play', *The Times*, 15 July 1970, p. 8; and Colbert Kearney, *The Writings of Brendan Behan* (Dublin: Gill and Macmillan, 1977) pp. 62–5.
2. Seán O'Faoláin (1900–), Irish writer.
3. Teachta Dála (Member of Parliament).
4. Policeman.

In Jail with Brendan Behan*

SEAN O'BRIAIN

My contribution to the volumes which will be written for posterity about that wonderful character that was Brendan Behan comes not from literary or artistic acquaintance but as a fellow prisoner in Mountjoy, Arbour Hill and the Curragh from 1942 to 1946.[1]

He came into us in Mountjoy in 1942. A group of us had been there for more than a year before that. It was in the Circle, beside the now famous 'Ould Triangle' that I first met him in jail. The 'Old Triangle' was no myth. It was a large steel triangle hanging on a stand. Instead of using a bell, a warder struck it with a steel bar, and made it go 'jingle jangle'.

On that morning of our first meeting in jail Brendan, then in his teens, appeared wearing a black heavy overcoat several sizes too big for him. He was slim and well built and marched along cocky and light-hearted with the tail of his unbuttoned coat trailing on the ground. He looked as if he would fit in the pocket of the coat.

'Barr na maidhne, a Sheairi,'[2] he said, 'and how are the balls of your feet? – What sort of an ould station is this?' (All in one breath.) 'Not bad,' I said, 'better nor the Glasshouse anyway.' ' 'Tis not the station that matters', said he. ' 'Tis the station-master.'

It was in those days that we who lived with Brendan came to know the real lovable character that he was. There was no drink, even the smokes ('snout' as he himself would say) were scarce at times.

He was at his best in those years, and I can affirm that he did not need drink or fame to make him a fine character and a fine writer. Day by day we 'punched in our time' – there was no complaining or no whining.

We made fun and plenty of it, and it was during those days that Brendan's true character made itself evident. That gallant, reckless Brendan that never did a mean turn. He was 'the heart of the Roul', as he might put it himself, and was always in a gay and laughing mood. He loved confusion and never took things too seriously.

He was loved by all of us his comrades and by Commandant Michael Lennon, the Governor of Arbour Hill, who himself was an exceptionally

* *Irish Press* (Dublin), 21 May 1964, p. 8.

fine man. Brendan had a great gradh³ for Mick Lennon which lasted until his death.

Brendan wrote a good deal in jail. He stayed in his cell sometimes – lying down on his bed with a blanket over him. As he finished a page he would peel it off – fling it in the air and let it land where it might – on the floor or anywhere at all, and seldom if ever did he collect the papers of any story together again.

Often when I had nothing to read I went to his cell and collected a bundle of scattered leaves, took them with me and sorted them. I know that he wrote one play and several short stries and I don't think they ever saw the light of day outside of jail.

Brendan loved 'the old Tong-u', as he used to call it. He used to recall singing an Irish song for a few 'oul ones' sitting on the steps in Russell Street and one of them says to the other, 'That's a lovely boy and Mrs Jewel the drling and isn't the Oul Tong-u very sweet.'

Often in later years he would quote a few dozen lines of *Cuirt an Mhean-Oidhche*⁴ for me as we stood on the street. Very few people in Ireland knew as much of the *Cuirt* as Brendan did.

I had a near complete copy of the *Cuirt* – over 1000 lines, and I would say that there were very few lines in it that Brendan could not quote. We had plenty of time to learn it.

When Brendan studied Irish and came to speak it very fluently as he did, 'Niorbh me focal an ughdair i mbeal an amadain a bhi aige.'⁵

He truly loved the language and the literature. He had a great gradh for the *Cuirt* especially for an tOileanach and the stories of Sean-Phadraig O Conaire. He went far deeper into the subject than his gaiety would suggest, and he loved to talk and learn about life on the Blaskets, Dun Chaoin, and Ballyferriter.

One morning a few days before Christmas about ten years ago I met him in Grafton Street. 'Come on,' said he, 'I want to have my breakfast.' We went to a nearby cafe.

'Where have you been for the past month?' I asked him. 'France–Spain–North Africa', he said. 'They were made with you there', I said. 'They were', said he, 'I broadcast on Radio Algeria and I finished up by singing your ould favourite "The Ciarraigheach Malluighthe" for them.'

Before we left, he took a roll of notes from his pocket. 'Are you all right for Christmas, Sean? – Don't be short while I have anything. Now, turn about, fair play (a favourite expression of his) I must go home to Kimmage and give me oul lady a few quid.'

I have heard it said that he looked for notice and publicity. This is not true – in the sense that it has been stated. He liked company and fun and commotion. It was part of his genius always to be starting things and keeping them going always with the best of good humour. He did not have to copy anybody or anything. The whole pleasant manifestation was original, always coming naturally from within himself and always you felt that he was enjoying himself.

These wonderful traits and natural gifts of wit and good humour did not change in after years. To us who knew him so well he did not change. It was his own natural and magnetic personality that attracted people.

Nothing was put on when wealth and fame came his way – neither was there any of the good old natured Brendan thrown away. I had often been in his company during those years of wealth and fame, and the old charm and personality were there unchanged – the love and appreciation of the simple things in life.

I can recall one occasion when I saw Brendan display a number of his natural talents all at one time. On a fine summer day in Arbour Hill a group of us were lying down or sitting with our backs to the prison wall – well inside the outside wall, of course.

Brendan came along and stood there. Somebody asked him, 'Brendan, do you know anything about the Invincibles'.[6]

'You mean Joe Brady and Skin the Goat? Wasn't my grandmother an poor oul Joe Brady's oul one great buddies, before and after. And sure my grandmother – she had it from the inside, of course – she often told us the whole story.'

There he stood, in his pants in the sunshine, no shirt or shoes on, his tangled uncombed hair falling down over his forehead and a grand smile on that youthful face. He started off. Whatever story he got from his grandmother was the basis of a drama that must have lasted over the next half-hour.

The dramatist, the author, the poet with the wonderful imagination, and the actor himself were playing the Phoenix Park executions – an original play if ever there was one. He was never stuck for dialogue. He spoke and acted Joe Brady and 'Skin the Goat'.

He made up the play as he went along. Then he came to 'the job' itself. There he did 'Skin the' the jarvey – standing by the horse's head.

In Brendan's improvised play, Joe Brady comes back to where 'Skin the' is waiting. 'Joe Brady', says he. 'I think I seen that man moving.' Joe goes back and finishes the job. 'That's right', says Skin the. 'A dead cock doesn't crow.'

It was not at the gruesome details of that part of the story that we laughed next day. It was his telling of the story – never hesitating for a sentence – sometimes inventing very serious conversational passages – plenty of witty cracks and Dublin humour all mixed together.

He was very good at portraying real live characters – putting them in a play or in a story. But then he added a bit of Brendan himself for good measure. This he did in his plays and stories, and that bit of Brendan himself he added on was the extra turn of wit and good-natured fun.

Brendan gave me an author's copy of each of his books and wrote a few words on the flyleaf of each. I think it worth while quoting some of these inscriptions because they show what his attitude was to jail life.

Dia leis an sean-aimsir.[7] (*The Quare Fellow*)

I bpríosúm teann níorbh annamh dúinn spórt agus greann.[8] (*The Borstal Boy*)

Ta suil agam ná haithnionn tú an iomarca ciaróg anso.[9] (*The Hostage*)

He just treated the years in jail – the rough and the smooth – as a part of life, something that never got him down. 'Spórt agus greann.'[10] As I remained a close friend of Brendan's until the time of his death, I can say 'Spórt agus greann' was what he liked at all times.

The inscription on *The Hostage* is, I think, interesting from another aspect.

I knew, and I know well, who a few of these characters were – they were real live characters – as in *The Quare Fellow*, for example, 'Neighbour' and 'Dunlavin' were real and we knew them.

One morning, a few years ago I walked along Upper O'Connell Street with him. We started off for a session that morning that lasted a few hours. During that time we drank four or five pots of coffee in a hotel lounge. As we were going into the hotel, there was a group of American tourists getting themselves organised for a bus tour of the country.

One group stopped him, as we went in: 'Aren't you Brendan Behan?' 'Yes, and you are welcome to Ireland', he said. During that morning, groups of Americans kept coming to our table to talk to him and tell him they had seen him on TV in their own country.

One lady abandoned her tour to stay and listen to him. So well she might. To see him being nice and polite to visitors who were delighted to meet him – to hear him tell them stories and sing songs for them was to see the real Brendan come shining through – an Irishman one could be proud of. This was a generous-hearted man who was not changed by wealth or fame.

This was the man who did the busker to help musicians and ballad singers in their endeavours to entertain theatre queues in London, Paris, New York. He would have done the same in his native Dublin at any time of his life, just because it was simple fun and amusement for himself and for everybody else.

One other thing should be recorded. I have never heard him say a derogatory word about Ireland and I have not read of his having done so abroad. He loved to shock people, especially those he thought too smug and content.

On the other hand, he was very honest and always ready, at home or abroad, to praise progress in Ireland – more and better houses for workers, better working conditions for people – particularly in his native Dublin. These were the things he loved to see and he took a genuine and serious interest in them. He was one of the most pleasant men I have ever known.

NOTES

Sean O'Briain, a Kerry schoolteacher who first met Behan in prison and who was to become one of his closest friends. He had been interned some months previously. It was in O'Briain's company that Behan acquired the ability to converse in Irish with something of the ease and copiousness of a native speaker.

1. In July 1943, the political prisoners in Mountjoy Prison were moved to Arbour Hill Prison and later to Curragh Camp.
2. 'Top of the morning, Sean.'
3. Affection.
4. *The Midnight Court*, a bawdy aisling (vision poem) written by Brian Merriman in 1780.
5. 'It was not a case of "words of wisdom on the lips of a fool" [proverbial].'
6. The 'Invincibles' were a Dublin anarchist group who had assassinated Lord Frederick Cavendish and Secretary Burke in Phoenix Park in 1884.
7. 'God be with the old times.'
8. 'In a tight prison we often had sport and fun.'
9. 'I hope that you do not see too many of those bugs here.'
10. 'Sport and fun.'

I Knew the Real Brendan Behan*

SEAMUS G. O'KELLY

I knew Brendan Behan from the word go. Like so many other great Irish writers, he came out of the Republican movement. His father, Stephen Behan, was an IRA man who fought on the Republican side in the Civil War; his maternal uncle, Peadar Kearney (author of our National Anthem, *The Soldier's Song*),[1] took the Free State side.

Behan liked to tell that his father's first sight of him was through a cell window, when his mother held him high in her arms outside Arbour Hill Military Prison.[2] He was then about two weeks old and the Civil War was raging. Sean T. O'Kelly, afterwards President of Ireland, was Stephen Behan's cell companion that morning in 1922.

* *Irish Digest* (Dublin), LXXVIII, no. 12 (June 1964) 67–70.

I KNEW THE REAL BRENDAN BEHAN

In 1931 the IRA and Fianna Éireann had been declared illegal organisations. George Plunkett, son of Count Plunkett and a brother of Joseph Mary Plunkett, one of the seven signatories of the Proclamation of Easter Week, was Chief Scout of Fianna Éireann. His assistants were Sean Mooney, later stage manager of the Abbey Theatre, and myself.

With the help of poetess Norah O'Kane of Derry, we published a little magazine called *Fianna Éireann*, and one of our chief contributors was Brendan Behan.[3] He could turn out a story like lightning. What stories: adventure tales, in which the hero was always an Irishman, always fighting for the independence of Ireland. Behan was then only ten or eleven years of age.

To us in the Fianna he was not only a decided asset, he was also a decided liability. He had a tongue that could curl the hair of your head, and it worried George Plunkett, who was a deeply religious man. I often saw George bless himself devoutly after he had heard a spate of Behan language that would do justice to the toughest soldier in or out of uniform.

'Truth on our lips, purity in our hearts, and strength in our arms', is the motto of the Fianna. Did Behan live up to that motto? I maintain he did, despite his lurid language. He certainly always told the truth.

One notable incident involving Behan happened at Bodenstown, County Kildare, in 1934. We had over 200 Fianna boys on parade to the grave of Wolfe Tone[4] that Sunday evening. They came from many parts. Behan was with the Dublin contingent.

He was no more than thirteen or fourteen, but big for his age. He was a squad-leader. When the ceremony at the graveside had concluded, we returned to Sallins railway station. There was an hour and a quarter to wait for the train to Dublin, and many of the processionists were wetting their whistles in the village pubs.

I was standing on the canal bridge talking to George Plunkett and the Adjutant-General of the IRA. Over the bridge came a Fianna boy in uniform. He was blind drunk. Of course he was Behan. George Plunkett was scandalised. I just had to laugh.

We court-martialled Behan next night for 'disorderly conduct whilst drunk'. But he did not take the proceedings seriously. George Plunkett read him a lecture about 'the noble aspirations of Fianna Éireann and the disgrace he had brought upon us'. Behan just laughed. And he laughed again when we expelled him.

But on the following Thursday night, when I attended a parade for new recruits to the Dublin Brigade, who should I see lined up on parade but the bold Behan himself. He winked at me.

Behan was under age for the IRA, but as he was big he got away with it. In 1939–40 he was prepared to go in on the 'ground floor' and risk his life for his ideals.

I did not know that Brendan was going to England on the IRA bomb campaign in 1939. He was arrested in Liverpool shortly after he landed, and charged with 'the possession of explosive substances'. At his trial, he demanded prisoner-of-war treatment, declared bluntly that he was a soldier of the Irish Republican Army, and stated his profession: 'Housepainter – the same as Hitler.'

The British judge was astounded that a boy of sixteen-and-a-half could make such a brilliant speech, and he said so when sending him to Borstal. That term of correctional imprisonment made a vivid impression on Behan. It was in that period he grew up, and his experiences led to the publication of his now famous *Borstal Boy*.

My next contact with Behan was when we were attempting to reorganise the Irish Republican Army in the 1945–49 period. To raise funds we decided to hold a Barnes and McCormack commemoration concert (on Sunday, 7 February 1947). Barnes and McCormack were two IRA officers executed in Birmingham for their part in the 1939 bombing campaign in Britain.

We needed a one-act play for the programme, and were toying with the idea of producing a sketch relating to the 1798 Rising. We were discussing this at Sinn Féin Headquarters, 16 Parnell Square, when Brendan Behan walked in. He listened for a minute or two, then said: 'Forget about '98. Why not a play on Barnes and McCormack?'

'For the good reason that there isn't such a play', I retorted.

'I'll write one', said Behan.

'You'll write one!' I exclaimed. 'And the concert fixed for Sunday week! What about the rehearsals; when do you think they must begin?'

'I'll have the play in two nights', said Behan. And have it he did. It was called *Gretna Green*, and it dealt with the reactions of three typical Irish characters who waited outside the jail gate in Birmingham on that February morning in 1940...waited for the execution of two brave soldiers of Ireland. The characters were two men and a woman. The play was mostly dialogue; there was very little action.

Behan agreed to play one of the parts. He attended all the rehearsals, but on the evening of the concert refused point-blank to go on stage. 'I'm a writer', he said, without batting an eyelid – 'not an actor.'

That put us in a jam. While we sweated it out, someone fortunately thought of Jimmy Doyle, a lad who had been at all the rehearsals and who knew the lines by heart. He agreed to take the part at three hours' notice. With Jimmy Doyle, the actors were Thomas MacDonagh Byrne, a Liverpool Irishman who had been interned with us in the Curragh, and Máiréad Ward, of Derry.

Gretna Green was the first Behan play produced. He had written others, but to the best of my knowledge the play we produced in the Queen's Theatre was the first-ever Behan production.[5] I am proud to have been, to a large extent, responsible for it.

We lost money on the concert. That particular Sunday was the most inclement of the whole year. It had snowed all through Saturday night, and the snow continued until about one o'clock next day. By the time we opened the doors of the theatre it was freezing hard, and the place was half empty for the concert.

Halfway through the first part of the programme (Behan's play went on immediately after the interval), Brendan turned up dead drunk. He was in no way boisterous, however, as was usually the case when he was loaded. We had no difficulty in keeping him in order, and he saw the play from the wings. He was delighted and he slapped everybody on the back. It never struck him that we were sorely disappointed because of the small audience.

Behan was always generosity itself to his old comrades; he hated cant and humbug. There can be no doubt that he was in the Fenian tradition. Out of that tradition emerged the world-famous writer, and any criticism of his work that ignores that tradition and background will do him less than justice.

NOTES

Seamus G. O'Kelly, Irish journalist.

1. Written in 1907 and set to music by Patrick Heeney. It was not printed until 1912, by Bulmer Hobson in the *Irish Freedom*. For a note on Peadar Kearney see p. 29.
2. Stephen Behan was jailed in Kilmainham Jail, not in Arbour Hill Prison.
3. Behan contributed 'A Tantalising Tale' to the June 1936 issue of this periodical.
4. Wolfe Tone (1763–98), Irish revolutionist and founder of the United Irishmen.
5. No copy of this play survives.

The Catacombs*
ANTHONY CRONIN

Most of this company assembled in McDaid's[1] every day under the benevolent aegis of one of the great barmen of all time, Paddy O'Brien, and almost every night the entire assemblage moved on to the Catacombs. . . .

Most of what went on in the Catacombs was in fact ordinary social boozing. Where there is booze, it will usually prevail over other matters. The Irish for a musical gathering, a concert, is *cuirm cheoil*, the combination

---

* Extracted from *Dead as Doornails: A Chronicle of Life* (Dublin: Dolmen Press; London: Calder and Boyars, 1976) pp. 4–13. Editor's title.

of words indicating a necessary connection between song and drink. That is what we had in the Catacombs. Nearly every regular frequenter had a party piece. One had thousands. This was Brendan Behan.[2]

When I first went to McDaid's and took up residence in the Catacombs, Brendan was in Paris, whither he had gone with Gainor Crist and a Limerick man who had come into a small legacy and was disposed to spend it, if such can be imagined. His doings there were much storied and talked about and his return was much heralded. It was a wet Sunday morning when he eventually arrived in the pub. He had his father, mother and brothers with him and there was a large company assembled, but as we walked up Leeson Street towards the Catacombs at three o'clock closing, he fell back deliberately so that we walked together. Friendship, like other forms of love, takes immediately or not at all. In the course of that otherwise dismal Sunday afternoon we became friends and discovered we were confreres.

Brendan in those days was far from being the gross ogre whose picture became so familiar years later in the English newspapers. He was fat, it is true, for his height and age, but his girth combined with his personality gave the impression that he was somehow merely bursting at the seams. Nor was the porcine effect, to be produced later on by the contrast between his general grossness and his tiny hands and feet, apparent: one was struck instead by the sort of expansive and inflationary possibilities he managed to extract from the contrast, like an operatic tenor who can seemingly expand parts of his anatomy at will.

At this time he worked, when it suited him, and when he was not on his travels, at the house-painting which was his father's trade, but he had published a few poems in Irish and a documentary piece about one of his terms of imprisonment in *The Bell* – he belonged, he said, to 'that large and respectable body in the community that had once had an article in that magazine'. Both then and later he would pose when it suited him as much more of an orthodox working-class product than he really was. In fact there were currents of literacy, liberalism and unconventionality on both sides of his family which many a product of the lower middle-classes like myself might have had cause to envy. And on one side there was a strong theatrical tradition. (His uncle[3] was a music-hall song-writer who had written the National Anthem.) If the realities of working-class life were known to him it was also true that he had never been among the great unacquainted submerged; there was plenty of acquaintance and tradition about in his growing-up; and indeed it was, to some extent at least, the show-business element in him that contributed to his destruction in the end.

He lived for the most part in his parents' house, out in the grey spaces of Crumlin, a working-class housing estate dating from the 'thirties, better than some of the more recent experiments in ghettoisation, but not a very cheerful place all the same. However, he was nomadic by nature and it was frequently too far from him to go in the small hours, so he stayed wherever he was welcome, and often in the Catacombs. Sometimes in the days to come he would share my palliasse in the wine-cellar and on these occasions we would talk long in the mornings, and then when the pubs were open venture forth into the streets, in search of company, drink and diversion. These days became more frequent as my resolution, such as it ever had been, weakened, my new acquaintance developed, and my hold on the job loosened in the clouds of hangover. Eventually I gave it up altogether and became fairly happily jobless, though beginning to publish poems and ill-informed critical comment in the backs of such magazines as there were.

You could not in fact have a better companion in a day's idleness than Brendan. He was a kaleidoscopic entertainment, but he was also fecund in serious ideas. He had a line in bemused wonderment about the activities of the world which was only partly an affectation, for he was genuinely naïve in certain ways and genuinely full of questionings. And he knew too when to drop the act and show himself capable of intimacy. The salt which makes penury palatable, ironic comment on all forms of possession and ownership, sometimes quite savage, he had in abundance. He had also in those days the remarkable gift of being able to realise and humorously illuminate the other person's circumstance while comically examining his own; and he was a good ally, fiercely contemptuous of all who disapproved of one's way of life. 'Fuck the begrudgers', he used to say, the implication being that envy lay at the root of most such disapproval.

He talked a lot in those days about his homosexuality, though I have since met others who knew him then and who claim they never heard of the matter. Mostly when he spoke of it, it was not as a difficulty but as a distinction. Sometimes he averted to it simply to shock. In the presence of a bishop and a curate for example, if that unlikely eventuality can be imagined, he would declare that he fancied the curate, or perhaps even the bishop, in order to shock the one and embarrass the other. He used to say wryly that De Valera's housing reforms had ruined his ordinary sexual development; that the move from the cosy slums out to the windy spaces and semi-detached houses of Crumlin had come at a crucial age and had been disastrous. On the landings and in the dark hallways of the tenements you could always get a grope or a squeeze and at fourteen he was just getting the hang of things and acquiring the necessary casualness of approach when the move came along, the casual courting opportunities among childhood acquaintances vanished and the elaborate approaches and settings-up which all sensitive, shy adolescents find difficult became the order of the day. This history was not advanced as a justification or a pathology nor, to do him credit, were his prison experiences. 'No worse than boarding school', he said he supposed, and in terms of my own experience, we agreed he was right.

It was agreed also that whatever the accidents or the latent tendencies involved one would probably have suffered in any case from the Irish syndrome. Apart altogether from prisons or boarding schools, 'life' would not have lived up to certain literary notions. 'Normal' adolescent development, 'normal' adolescent ecstasies were a myth. Something had gone wrong somewhere along the line, as it was pretty well bound to: though you could of course be cheerful about your flaws or your freedoms and suggest that it had gone right. This feeling was perhaps particularly strong in our generation. You could, and most people did, blame the Catholic religion, of which, incidentally, in the early days – he was to become rather maudlin about the matter later – Brendan had a ferocious hatred. The war, with its impediments to ordinary living, had something to do with it. So had boarding schools. And prisons. Indeed perhaps government housing estates.

It is almost impossible for sensitive, intelligent, over-imaginative people not to make a hames of their development anyway and then only two responses are really open to them; they can believe themselves the ultimate oddity, or they can suggest that everybody else is lying. There are always those of course who lay claim both to sensitivity and simplicity of development; who allege that in spite or because of their poetic imaginations they slipped into life and cunts as to the manner born. Patrick Kavanagh was later to invent a word to cover this sort of literary pretence along with other related ones: 'bucklepping'. As far as we were concerned the buckleppers were liars.

In public Brendan's manner was rabelaisian, jocose, knowledgeable. In private he would admit to difficulties and bewilderments about which he was in fact much funnier. Unfortunately for him, his writing – with the possible exception of *Borstal Boy* – when he eventually got round to it, was a public matter also, and as a way of sorting himself out through the rigours, honesties and ironies of art, it was largely useless to him. That was part of the debacle.

Whatever the truth of his assertions about his basic homosexuality may have been, I do not ever remember him striking up any sort of a liaison, and though there were considerably less admitted homosexuals around in our age-group in those days, there were enough. Nor did he give any surface impression of being queer: of course, contrary to popular belief, most people who are do not: the word covers a multitude of sins and states anyway.

Apart from being queer, he claimed that he suffered from what he called 'a Herod complex', a preference for youth, named so after Herod's fancying the daughter rather than the mother. He fancied only boys of about fourteen to eighteen, he would say; and in the right circumstances these declarations were usually made publicly, humorously and loudly enough to destroy any prospect of success. Once when we were sharing the wine-cellar together he made advances to myself: perhaps he felt he had to. The matter being cheerfully disposed of was never heard of again, through all our wanderings and bunkings.

He complained, however, of strange ignorances and naïveties where 'ordinary' sex and the female were concerned; and was bitter about those who, not being privy to his real preferences, prescribed more orthodox sex as a corrective to our way of life. When reproached once by a progressive lady we knew for not having a regular girl-friend, Brendan replied that it was every bit as un-Marxist to reproach a man for not having a fancy woman as it would be to reproach him for not having a motor-car. For a long time afterwards he used to refer to her suggestion that all his ills and malaises would disappear if he had more sex as 'Dr so-and-so's remedy for the human condition'.

But even about the physical side of homosexual relationships he would admit to bewilderments. He came across something in Enid Starkie's biography of Rimbaud which apparently bothered him and led to much speculation; and he spent days in the National Library reading various accounts of the trial of Oscar Wilde to find out precisely what practices Oscar had engaged in – the only time I can remember him ever going near the place.

In saying all this I do not mean to suggest that Brendan was more than ordinarily ignorant, naïve or innocent about sex. Quite the contrary in fact. And if one were to take some of his boastings for gospel one would have to assume heights – or depths – of sophistication rather rare at the time. These boastings were not of the ordinary kind, however, suggesting mere conquest and procured licence. There was in them an element of picaresque braggadocio which was meant to suggest cynicism and villainy on his part. He did, at one time, have a penchant for such boastings and surprised me by asserting that he got money from a woman I knew for performing what was to him a particularly onerous, not to say unpleasant, sexual service for her.

However that may be, and behind all the boastings and the jokes, what is certain to me is this: Brendan, when I knew him first, had a much more complex awareness of himself, his diffidences, failures and complications than he chose to present even then, and more especially later, to the outside world. He knew he was complicated and he chose to deal with the complications in the best way possible: ironic confession, humorous self-disparagement, mock surprise, combined of course with a satiric savagery about the pretensions of other people. Unfortunately very little of this appears later on in his work or his alleged work, whichever it happens to be. Here the complications and their confessional shadows are constantly at the mercy of bravado, show, pretence. And in the public figure as well as in the writer, for the two are now inseparable, it is the same. He is the great liver, who has drunk it to the lees at all stages of the game, the great avatar of booze and sex and 'life'. Fatal of course, the more so because part of our nature impels us to try 'to become what we sing'; even though, the more our pretences take over, the more we secretly know how much we need 'the deep counter-minings of art'.

In public, comic drama was Brendan's primary mode of being and his enormous talent for it was constantly employed in enactments of one kind or another, created anywhere there was an audience, from the cold morning kitchen of the Catacombs to the partially empty McDaid's of the mid-afternoon. Some of these were merely satirical in intent and involved imaginary scenes between people we knew; but he had too a strangely coherent if very mixed mythology, peopled by miscellaneous patriotic and literary figures, and in the miniature dramas involving these an extraordinary talent for the grotesque took over, so that the originals attained a new surrealist dimension.

'The Childhood of D. H. Lawrence' was a very elaborate performance, often repeated with many variations, in which Lawrence's drunken father comes home to find the boy reading a book and keeps up a running stream of monstrous abuse of the child while getting into the bath and having his back scrubbed, Brendan playing scurrilous father, anxious mother and patronising little boy in various postures and with accents varying from broad Yorkshire to badly cultivated middle-class English. 'The Boyhood of John Ruskin' was created as a sort of companion piece one winter night in the Catacombs when there was very little to drink, and it took the sensitive Ruskin and his doting parents on a tour of Europe in which sulkings and reconciliations, aesthetic wonderments, raptures and incomprehensions alternated. How Ruskin came to find a place in his mythology I do not know, but his reading, being a matter of chance, was strangely various. 'Maud Gonne at the Microphone' was usually performed with a towel over the head by way of a veil and it consisted of fruity recollections of Yeats in a quavering, aged, but, of certain undertones, deeply expressive voice. 'Mr Cosgrave's Visit to Mountjoy' involved the former President of the Free State in a scene with a patriotic lady who to her chagrin is not arrested in a general swoop. She puts a camp bed outside the gates of the prison, gets into it and goes on hunger strike. Goaded by questions in the Dail about the ill-treatment of other Republican lady prisoners who are on hunger strike within, Mr Cosgrave arrives at the prison in a motor-car to see for himself. The disappointed lady rises up in her camp bed and calls after him, 'Imperialist! Lackey! West Briton! Liar! Arrest me! Arrest me!' To which Mr Cosgrave turns round and replies, 'Madame. Imperialist I may be. Lackey I may be. Liar I may even be. But I am not a collector of curiosities.' The rich part of the performance consisted of the lady attiring herself suitably for her vigil, setting up the camp bed, composing herself on it, and refusing all offers of refreshment.

These vignettes were, where possible, embellished and illustrated by song; but he loved song anyway and was happy to sing anywhere and in almost any circumstance. He had a resonant baritone, perfect pitch, and, again, an enormous theatrical sense, whether for the rendition of scurrilous comic pieces or passionate patriotic and left-wing ballads – often the two merged into one. According to what was needed by the song, the lips would curl, the eyes flash and roll and the tiny, sensitive hands clench or unclench in passion, or reach out in mock unavailing yearning and despair.

It was, in all its elements, an original form of *cabaret intime* and it was a highly developed art. Given the proper circumstances he might have used it to feed the exhibitionist in himself that eventually devoured him and the unsatisfied actor who interrupted his own plays, desperate to appear on stage himself and be, for every moment of the performance, the centre of love and attention. It was not an ignoble art – far from it. It was spontaneous, and as his later addiction to the tape-recorder apart from anything else shows, he was an essentially spontaneous creator, who needed company in the act. It drew from its audience and depended on a confidence in affection given and received which might have been the ultimate reassurance for one who so feared to go it alone. It might certainly, ephemeral or otherwise, have been a better outlet for him than the tape-recorder. Perhaps there was a better, and certainly a happier, artist of another kind lost in Brendan.

NOTES

Anthony Cronin (1925–), Irish barrister-at-law, poet and broadcaster.

1. A famous tavern in Harry Street, off Grafton Street, Dublin's main boulevard of chance and converse. See Mairin O'Farrell, 'A Dublin Literary Pub', *Hibernia* (Dublin), July–Aug 1964, pp. 12–13.

2. When Behan was released from Strangeways Prison in July 1947, a party was given for him. 'The party was held in the Catacombs, a flat in the basement of a large Georgian house in a Georgian square in Dublin. It was rented by a tall, willowy Englishman called Cecil, a very kindly person in his own way and a great favourite of my father and mother. The lady who owned the Catacombs was a painter and she let the flat to Cecil rent-free, apparently because he posed for her pictures' – Brendan Behan, *Confessions of an Irish Rebel* (London: Hutchinson, 1965) p. 137.

3. Peadar Kearney [O Cearnaigh] (1883–1942), Irish poet, songster, and patriot. See Seamus de Burca, *The Soldier's Song: The Story of Peadar Kearney* (Dublin: P. J. Bourke, 1957); and Peadar Kearney, *My Dear Eva: Letters from Ballykinlar Internment Camp 1921*, ed. Seamus de Burca (Dublin: P. J. Bourke, 1976).

To France with Brendan Behan*

ANTHONY CRONIN

We had only a few shillings and it was a serious matter whether to buy a Sunday newspaper or not. Eventually we decided to buy a *Sunday Times* and as we sat over two pints and the divided paper we discovered that George Orwell was dead. 'Listen to this, Brendan', I said, and I read him the closing passage of Cyril Connolly's famous obituary: 'But the gardens of the west are closed, and there is no place now for the writer to wander. . . .' A look of intense fury came over Brendan's face. 'Arrah sweet and holy Jasus, would you mind telling me what fucking gardens of the west did you and I ever wander in?' he asked.

Yet in fact that summer we did go for a sort of a walk in the gardens of the west together, even if it wasn't of the idyllic kind Connolly had in mind. One day, as we lay on our bunks in 'The Gurriers', Brendan asked me if I would like to come to Paris. He had published a very short story in *Envoy* and George Morrison, later to be the creator of the well-known newsreel collage *Mise Éire*, had offered him forty pounds for the right to make a small film of it. Forty pounds, he admitted, wasn't a whole lot for a protracted stay for the two of us, but he had a scheme in mind which had immense possibilities. If we played our cards right we might get to spend a year or two on the Continent. Pressed to explain, he tittered to himself in a way he had and said that we were going 'to snatch the Pope's ring'. Then he said darkly that what he had in mind was political. Finally that he would unfold his plan when we got to Paris. It was the sort of thing that if anybody in Dublin got to hear of it we were 'fucked from a height'. I might as well come along to Paris anyway and make up my mind about the rest when we got there.

Well, I had a reason of my own for wanting to get to Paris, apart from the very good one that I had never been there; I was always game for a jaunt in good company; and in those days I was always glad to get out of Ireland. I agreed. Time, like Brendan, was to be merciful in its disclosures.

A couple of nights later we got seats on an Aer Lingus plane to London.

---

* Extracted from *Dead as Doornails: A Chronicle of Life* (Dublin: Dolmen Press; London: Calder and Boyars, 1976) pp. 27–61. Editor's title.

Brendan was equipped with a fairly sizable cardboard suitcase and a sort of duffle bag. I wondered at the size of the luggage, as, later that night, I was to wonder at the number of dirty shirts, legs of pyjamas, disreputable underwear and odd socks he had brought, and at the inclusion in the suitcase of the remains of a suit which was certainly no better than the one he had on. Even if we were planning on a two-year stay, I thought, we should be able to pick up things as we went along. I did not know that in the place he had in mind there was supposed to be a shortage of wearing apparel as well as everything else.

Besides the luggage he had the forty pounds, our tickets to London having been paid for by Ralph Cusack.[1] I had a small zip bag with a shirt or two and four or five pounds besides. Brendan therefore had nearly all the money; and he had also all, or nearly all, the French, which was little enough.

We were slightly drunk getting on the plane and as soon as it was off the ground he applied the Voltairean test to God's existence, rising in his seat, clenching his small fists, glaring at the roof and challenging the deity to prove his power by causing the machine to crash. It was not logical that the test should be more conclusive when applied in the more perilous circumstance of being airborne in a man-made contraption than it would if we had been like Voltaire in the middle of a field, but you never know. Fortunately he did not seem to be overheard either by the deity or by the two elderly priests behind us for whose benefit the performance was put on.

In London we stayed the night with an Irish doctor of my acquaintance, sleeping what sleep we slept on the floor of his Swiss Cottage flat, and in the morning we got the wrong bus for Victoria. We stood on an island in the middle of the Strand, I remember, unable to get across, while the traffic roared past, Brendan hurling curses at the double-deckers with raised fists, reviling the English and their ways, engaged in a titanic contest of wills with all the might of the Empire's capital. Finally we got a taxi, in which I, that was supposed to have lived there, was attacked for my inadequate knowledge of London. It was the first time that the man-of-action-thwarted-by-inadequate-lieutenant streak in him showed up; but it was not to be the last, and in France he had the advantage that he spoke, or fancied he spoke, the French, had been there before and had the money.

At Newhaven we ran into what looked like trouble. Brendan was a deportee from England, released from Borstal originally only on condition that he did not return to its shores. Fairly stiff penalties would attend on the discovery that he had done so; and though it was unlikely that the authorities were at that time still on the *qui vive* for him or anyone else in his category there was a good deal about us to attract attention. Anyway, we had no sooner put our tawdry baggage down on the counter for examination by the ordinary customs man than another official in plain clothes came over, said something to him, and asked politely if he could have a word with us. We went a little way up the counter with him and he examined our passports closely. Then he asked us to turn out the contents of our pockets. Unfortunately Brendan carried a painter's trade-union card which was made out in another name: he was not a proper, dues-paid member of the union in his own right. The official, who had not seemed to attach any importance to the name Behan, remarked on the discrepancy in names between card and passport. Behan proffered an involved, hurried but skilfully contrived explanation to the effect that he was a stepson and that in Ireland a stepson commonly used his mother's original name for certain purposes and his father's for certain others. This was received with the sort of silent interest only authority can assume.

Then it was my turn. Among my bits and pieces happened to be a letter from David Marcus, then editor of *Irish Writing*, about the proofs of some poems he had accepted. Our friend's eyes positively lit up.

'You are a poet, Mr Cronin?' he asked.

I assented to the description in some stumbling form or other. He gazed upon us both for a moment with smiling, considering lips, then handed back what he held and motioned us graciously to proceed.

It was a moment of great relief and we were pleased also to see that the boat flew the French flag, but as we boarded it Brendan turned and complained. 'You might have told the limey bastard your disreputable friend was a poet too', he said.

We crossed Paris in sunlight, on the back of a bus, from the Gare du Nord to the Luxembourg, a route that took us round the Place de la Concorde and past the Tuileries. Nobody could ever forget such a first sight of the city, but this isn't that kind of travel book, nor, either, an autobiography, so suffice it to say here that Brendan enjoyed my enjoyment to the full. He had, after all, a proprietary interest in the place. . . .

We did not, I am afraid, succeed in establishing ourselves sexually or socially in any snug little circle of beauty and booze. We snatched at what offered of course, but for a man who had been there before Brendan seemed pretty short of acquaintance. Perhaps there really wasn't any bohemia of our sort to enter. Most of the people we did meet were Americans. They lived in hotel rooms like ourselves and they were all meditating great books. Some of them were to write best-sellers but the manifestations of the new, post-Hem and Scott Paris were not of great interest. I remember thinking one night when we were ejected from a folksong cellar somewhere round the Place St Germain that the audience did not compose, as they would say nowadays, our scene. We were not to know it then, but we were witnessing the birth of the new bohemia, which would not even pay lip-service to any form of art other than the most rudimentary kinds of music.

Meanwhile, of course, there was Brendan's grand design to be meditated. He unfolded it on the first day and it took my breath away. Like most grand designs it was bold and cunning, simple and tortuous all at once. In case I did not know, we were in the middle of the Marian Holy

Year. The Faithful were exhorted to make pilgrimages to Rome while the year lasted and encouraged by great remittances of the time they would have to spend in Purgatory to do so. We too would head out for the Holy City, begging for food and shelter like mediaeval palmers. The decent pious people of France and their priests would fall over themselves to provide two devout Irish pilgrims with bed and board. There would be free lodging and hot scoff at every turn of the road. We would have a few weeks' luxury in the French countryside, perhaps a little tour in Italy itself, but that was not all he had in mind. We would traverse Northern Italy, go as far eastward as seemed a plausible, and then make a dash for Czechoslovakia. We would cross the Czech frontier, declare ourselves to be refugees from Western Capitalism and abandon ourselves to the mercy of events. We were not, it was true, as eminent as we might be, but we were published writers; we would be among the first such defectors from the West; and surely to God they would find some use for us, in their radio stations or whatever they had.

My notions of geography were a little clearer than Brendan's and I could see he was skimping the last stages. Besides, my ideological feelings were not as orthodox, or indeed as strong. I did not like the sound of the Czechs. And would not they be rather puzzled by the idea of refugees from the West, where after all there was supposed to be freedom of speech? To this last Brendan replied that at least we would have had a jaunt. Somebody would have to repatriate us and probably in a blaze of glory. He was admittedly a little dubious about the reaction of the Czech authorities; indeed he was dubious about the Czechs in general, describing them in the next breath as 'Russians with Manchester accents', but they would hardly be likely to mistake us for spies.

At length we agreed to postpone the Czech side of the journey for further consideration and to make use of the Holy Year along the lines suggested. We would head out, try to get to Rome, and see what, in the contemporary phrase, 'gave' there. It might be that monasteries and like institutions in the Holy City itself would put pilgrims up for nothing, and that by ringing the changes on the possibilities we could get a summer out of it. Certainly, as pilgrims, we ought to be able to make it; we would see a bit of historic-and-whatever-else France and Italy; and if we had to be repatriated in the end by the Irish Embassy we would at least have got value for their money. What, in any case, else could we do? We were down to our last few pounds, and Paris, in spite of its traditions of literary and artistic poverty, was not proving a great source of possibilities. . . .

It was time to go. South or east, Mother Church or Communist Party, it was all one to me, 'Nous nous marchons', I said one day in the Deux Magots under the impression that it meant 'we must march' and that a general had said it. It became our slogan and Brendan used it for years afterwards to indicate that it was time to leave one bar for another.

We took the Métro to Orly and walked out a bit. A large van stopped and after some negotiation the driver, who wanted money, seemed unimpressed by the fact that we were piligrims and said he was going to Marseilles, lowered the back and indicated a small space already occupied by a thirsty and hungry looking Alsatian. No dog-lovers, we refused. Then the driver of a battered vegetable lorry picked us up and took us through the verdant forest of Fontainebleau and all the way to Sens. We made it eventually through the cooling twilight to Auxerre, where we slept beneath a wall on a steep grass bank sloping down to the river, the Cathedral above us under the stars, the big *camions* roaring through the night. We had covered the best part of a hundred miles and felt we were in the provinces. I said Belloc's poem 'When Peter Wanderwide was thrown by death itself beyond Auxerre' as a sort of night prayer for the pilgrims.

In fact the pilgrimage proper only began the following day and it was almost immediately obvious that it was not going to live up to expectations. The response of the French to the statement that we were 'deux Irlandaises en perinage à Rome', which was the way Brendan put it, was at best indifferent. They did not show the same interest or enthusiasm, he remarked bitterly, 'as our own people would have done if any of them were passing through Holy Ireland on a pilgrimage to the North Pole'; in fact, not to put too fine a tooth upon it, 'the fuckers wouldn't give you the steam off their piss'. However, lifts could be got, though not always in the required direction, and not because we were pilgrims; and on the night after Auxerre we found a parish priest who allowed us to sleep on wooden forms put together in some sort of a schoolhouse. He was the first of a line of more or less sympathetic clerics. 'The priests are with the people still', as Brendan put it, echoing an old Irish patriotic song.

This was in Autun, the city where Talleyrand was bishop before he went off to survive. We didn't know this of course, though in fact we behaved like orthodox tourists here for once and climbed a terribly steep hill on a terribly hot day to visit the Cathedral, which was cool at least, whether twelfth century, as I said, or thirteenth, as Brendan, who had the French, insisted. We were remarkably ignorant of most things, indeed a more unprepared, unlearned, and therefore largely blind pair of travellers it would have been hard to find. So far from having a guidebook to give us any historical or other information about places on the way, we hadn't even a map, and were in Autun only by accident. Our ignorance did not prevent us from arguing, however, in the heat or in the rain.

A pattern of days established itself. We worked south, as far as we could, eating bread, tomatoes, cheese and sausage, drinking much wine and a little milk. At evening we would seek out a *curé* wherever we happened to be and Brendan would say his piece about 'deux Irlandaises' etc. If this worked, which be it said again for the reverend gentlemen it very often did, we got put up on floors in draughty parish halls, in outhouses; even, as with some truly delightful worker priests in Lyons, in a bed for two nights. If it didn't, we stayed either in the cheapest *auberge* we could find or slept out, as once on some municipal benches opposite a bakery which opened while it was still dark and perfumed the air all about with the most exquisite scent of fresh bread.

Of course we had neither tents nor sleeping-bags, cooking utensils, water-bottles or stoves. We were dressed as we had been in Dublin and the baggage we carried contained nothing that was of the remotest use to men camping out. Compared to the professional hitchhikers of today, even to such youth-hostellers as we encountered then, we were as two dudes in the American West.

Still, we edged on, erratically and not too hurriedly, through little towns which smelled at dusk of soup and sewage, through Chalon-sur-Saône, where it rained ('a dirty kip, like a little bit of old Brum'), Mâcon, Villefranche, where they were firing off guns ('to keep the rain away from the grapes'), Lyons, where in a café with the worker priests Brendan took to the Ricard ('the nearest thing to absinthe you can get'), knocking it back like so many *poètes maudits* before him had knocked back the real stuff. He explained to them aspects of his political philosophy: 'Communism will not come terrible like an army with banners, but like a Corporation dustman carting off the rubbish of the ages.' In Grenoble he insisted on going up in a cable-car to see what he said was Mont Blanc in the distance. I had already had my first glimpse of the Alps from on top of an uncertain balanced heap of coal in the back of a speeding lorry. They were the largest mountains I had ever then seen and lightning was playing along their mass. To make things more terryfying, we were in a blinding rainstorm, which increased the difficulty of hanging on to the coal, as well as the discomfort of it, until the driver stopped and insisted that there was room in front for all three of us and the bags, which when he got in there originally Brendan had declared loudly there was not.

In Grenoble we found a café full of drunks, men and women who composed some sort of family party and took us home with them to sing 'Chevaliers de la Table Ronde' and other songs familiar in the Catacombs ('It's well known in Holy Ireland that you would never see a Frenchman drunk'). At Briançon we were reluctantly admitted into a youth hostel ('My father was a founder of the youth movement in Ireland – he was too, ye sniggering Judas, leastways he was in the Fianna'). And after Briançon, within a few miles of the long-awaited Italian frontier, we quarrelled.

It was a silly business, about one of the bags which had been left behind in a café; but it was incredibly hot; we had walked a long way out of town to begin with and then had to walk back for the bag; and we were both hung over. Anyway there was some shouted recrimination and insult. Brendan then for the first time divided up the money, which amounted to very little, and headed back for town. I stood alone by the side of the road for a while and then I went after him. I searched the empty cafés in the noonday heat, but I had left it too late. I decided out of some stubborn principle, and because there seemed little else to do, to go on into Italy. . . .

After he left me, he said, he had made his way without much difficulty back as far as Lyons. There he got to drinking the Ricard again. When he was penniless, or nearly so, he came across a Foreign Legion barracks which had a recruiting office and he promptly joined up. He was a member of the Legion for one night. P. C. Wren, it appeared, did not know what he was talking about. If you went to them in the morning 'in a decent and civil manner', they speeded you on your way without even asking for the return of the bounty money. Whether this is true or not I do not know. Probably what happened was that the Foreign Legion found it had met its match. Some aspect of the protean Brendan had disquieted it, perhaps even characteristic verbal advances to a young comrade.

In any case, as time went by he became increasingly proud of having been a member of the corps, and the time spent under the tricolour hearing the bugles blow was suitably lengthened. Three years later I was sitting in a pub in London with the poet W. R. Rodgers. He began to reprove me, as he frequently did, for my then way of life. Why wouldn't I be adventurous, he said, and go away and join the Foreign Legion for a while, like Brendan Behan? The main agony, in most company, is caused by misconceptions which it is impossible to set right without appearing strident.

Anyway, after his term of service with the colours he had made his way back to Paris where he had been for a while, found a kip, borrowed some money and spent it. Then he went to the Embassy, got his repatriation money, and spent that too. Now he had nowhere to go.

We spent the remainder of that night on the embankment. In the morning I had a terrible toothache. Brendan was most solicitous, hunting up aspirins and buying me brandy with the last few francs. Then he suggested that I should go to the Embassy and get my repatriation money too. Meanwhile we decided that we would move into the Hotel d'Alsace down the street from the Grand Balcon. It had a reputation for being liberal with the credit and it must have been a longstanding one, for it was here that our colleague and compatriot Oscar Wilde had died a little over half a century before. He was far behind with the rent and had replied to the landlord, when told he must either pay or go, 'Certainly, either I or the wallpaper must go.' It was from his darkened room there too that he had sent Robbie Ross out for a last bottle of champagne, saying, 'I fear, Robbie, I am dying as I have lived – beyond my means.' The thought of Oscar's difficulties was somehow comforting, though it seemed to me that we were now somewhat lower down in the circumstantial scale than he had ever got. Before we left Paris for the first time we had made a pilgrimage to his grave in Père Lachaise and asked his protection on our knees by the graveside. Brendan later wrote a poem in Gaelic, perhaps the best of all his poems, which takes the inscription on the wall of the Hotel d'Alsace for its epigraph: 'Oscar Wilde, Poète et Dramaturge, né à Dublin le 15 Octobre, 1856, est mort dans cette maison le 30 Novembre, 1900.'[2]

The place did not appear to have changed much since 1900; they let us in for the time being; and I went to the Embassy. Instructed in the drill by Brendan, who waited on a bench in the boulevard, I was civilly enough received, given some Afton Major cigarettes – a brand which was to crop up again in our subsequent adventures – and told to come back in the afternoon. We walked round the area to pass the time and when I went back I was given ten pounds, or enough to get us both back to Ireland if we hitched and crossed the two seas by boat, supposing Brendan was willing to risk the passage through England. We discussed this and decided that the risk was minimal. Accordingly it was agreed to leave the next day.

We went back to the hotel, paid the bill up to the following morning and then went out to have the famous Alsatian sausages and wine by the tumbler at Le Petit Source which were everybody's main source of sustenance. We were in fine fettle, having money, a night in clean sheets and a journey over land and sea to look forward to.

Naturally we went on drinking. Then something odd began to happen. We went into a succession of small cafés round the riverside of St Germain. In each one Brendan insisted on buying drinks for the workmen at the zinc, talking his French, singing his songs and making his jokes. My remonstrations were met with anger and impatience, so I gave them up. Finally we wound up in a small place with a two-o'clock licence where there were about six men at the counter, one of whom unfortunately had a fiddle. Brendan ordered glasses all round and then began to buy wine by the bottle. To show both knowledge and generosity he asked for a particular *appellation controllée* wine of which they seemed to have a lot, and which certainly cost a lot comparatively. At two o'clock the proprietor put up the shutters and closed the door. The man with the fiddle played; everybody sang; and bottles began to appear with the speed of light.

I was now slightly drunk, miserable and angry, but every time I made a protest Brendan would ignore it and immediately order another bottle. I suppose I could have called a halt and walked out into the night with what money was left, but I knew there would be a scene and in the midst of all the jollification and bad French I was weak enough not to want to appear angry or upset or mean. Once when I tried to pay the remainder of the bill and be done with it Brendan spoke volubly to the proprietor who, instead of producing the bill brought out two more bottles. Yet he was not enjoying himself; that I could see. Behind all the pseudo-generosity, the songs and toasts and exchanges of national good will, there was something frantic. It began to dawn on me that it was also something destructive, and this was a new side of him. He wanted to get rid of the money and get back into what was certainly going to be the gutter. . . .

Sometime during the course of the day, however, Brendan came up with another of his startling original ideas, almost comparable to the pilgrimage, or the political sanctuary, or the foreign legion. We would hitchhike to Rouen, from which port the boats owned by the Irish shipping company sailed regularly. On one of these we would stow away. When the ship was irrevocably at sea we would reveal ourselves, appeal to the racial compassion of all concerned and having successfully elicited it, arrive in Ireland of the welcomes hale, fresh and hearty after a salubrious sea-voyage....

And so ended The Pilgrimage To Rome, The Flight Behind The Curtain, The Service Under The Tricolour and The Days Before The Mast. Not to mention, it seems to me now in retrospect at least, an era in a relationship. I know that life has a habit of marking transitions of feeling on the calendar in a way that is false. Looking back we associate such transitions with journeys, seasons, public events that have really nothing to do with them. For some time we continued more or less as before, though both of our circumstances were changing and drama, of a sort, was in the offing. But I see him differently as from that time, and certainly most of the rest that I have to tell about Brendan Behan is considerably darker, though it includes the days of the fame that many must have envied. So far as I am concerned, much of what follows is nothing less than nightmare. It is true that I ceased to see the whole picture and did not know the whole story, but much of what I did see is neither pleasant to the memory nor gratifying to the reflective faculty.

NOTES

For a note on Anthony Cronin see p. 29.

1. Ralph Cusack, a writer and artist who had left his bulb-farm in County Wicklow on his doctor's orders for a farm in South of France. When Behan got married, Cusack sent him ten pounds as a wedding gift, with an invitation to visit him.
2. In *Brendan Behan's Island* (London: Hutchinson, 1962).

Brendan Behan in Paris*

SINDBAD VAIL

I met Brendan somewhere in the very late 'forties. Big and burly as you know, putting on the Irish to ridiculous extremes and fascinating. He had heard that I paid 30,000 francs for a story, which was not much, but it was

* Ulick O'Connor, *Brendan Behan* (London: Hamish Hamilton, 1970) pp. 138–9. Editor's title.

a token and no other little magazine did that. He came to our little office with thirty manuscripts and demanded 90,000 francs on the spot. He was broke and living from hand to mouth. It never occurred to him that I wouldn't take all his manuscripts and pay him in advance. That sum just about covered the printing bill for an entire issue. Anyway I think I gave him 30,000, which went somewhere in those days. It's too late to regret that I did not keep all his manuscripts, but most of them were illegible and even boring. We saw each other frequently, he always dropped by when he wanted a small loan or drink or food. I don't recall talking much about writing, he used to ramble on, sing Irish songs, tell dirty jokes and try to get off with a very pretty American girl who was helping me.

NOTE

Sindbad Vail was the editor of an *avant-garde* magazine called *Points*, to which Behan made some contributions.

Brendan*

JOSEPH COLE

The most pervasive myth fostered by the I-knew-Brendan school of journalists is of a Brendan Behan who was invariably the centre-piece of any company he chanced to be in, and that his wit, good humour and lovable drunken antics were enchanting to his (often captive) audience. This is a journalistic trick, and a good one as far as it goes, but it cheats in so far as Brendan was not always in the leading role in these incidents. As often as not, he filled in a bit part which only his subsequent fame caused to be built up (in the minds of those writing about him) into the star role. I shall depict a Brendan Behan as I remember him, sometimes the most important person in a group, other times, not. In every incident and scene I have endeavoured to put down on paper the truth as I remember it, hanging the consequences.

I first met Brendan Behan in the summer of 1950 at his parents' house in Kimmage, a working-class suburb of Dublin. Sean Furlong, a man of indeterminate age, gave record concerts of classical music in the front room

* Extracted from *Books and Bookmen* (London), XIII (Nov 1967) 34–5. Repr. as 'Brendan, I Hardly Know You!', *Quadrant: An Australian Bi-Monthly*, LIX (1969) 46–50.

(or parlour, for those who prefer the old name) of the house. Everyone knows by now that Sean is a stepbrother of the Behan side of the family, but it was all very confusing in those days, particularly as neither the Behans nor the Furlongs saw fit to explain the familial tie-up when making introductions. Not that they often did introduce each other to the newly initiated, for they seemed to assume that the stranger must, somehow, have heard of this famous family and would instantly recognise any member of it as he or she entered the room. Very few of us did. For one thing, we were too young and weren't conversant with the latest political sensations; and, for another, our minds were so occupied with the love-affairs of early youth that politics took, at best, second place to the consuming lust of the moment. . . .

On a particular day that I recall quite vividly, he had a mainly quiescent audience composed of Liam Maguire, the bohemian, poet manqué; Bill Gannon, the anarchist; Alfie Venencia, a Shavian in politics and lover of symphony; and myself. Carmel Behan, the 'baby' of the family, popped in and out of the room whenever the mood took her. This was obviously severely trying for Sean, but her wide grin never drooped on meeting his fierce, thick-lensed glare. (Come to think of it, when any of Sean's enthusiasms were interrupted, questioned or challenged, he bore an uncanny resemblance to a certain kind of lean ascetic priest who *knows* that everything he says is correct.)

We had moved sluggishly into the second movement of a symphony, the title of which I simply cannot recall no matter how hard I try: I suspect this to be due to an elaborate seduction I was planning and which occupied most of my thinking time, a familiar experience to normal youths of every era. At a very interesting stage (or phase, if you like) of the music (and my devilish plan), the door of the room was thrown open with a resounding crash. I looked behind me, wondering how Carmel had summoned the nerve to make such a dramatic entrance, but instead of Carmel I saw a man in his late twenties. He had a large stomach which he carried in front of him with all the pride of a pregnant Yoruba tribeswoman; a magnificent leonine head that shook slightly from a cause I could guess at; and an imposing Caesarean nose that was, alas, cancelled by a small, pettish mouth.

'Where's that bloody book of plays by Wilde?' he asked nobody in particular, but we all knew that the question was directed at Sean Furlong. He rolled with a seaman's gait over to the bookcase and stared at it angrily.

Sean did not answer, but his thin lips compressed disapprovingly and his eyes began emitting danger signals behind the thick spectacles.

Not having found the book, the roly-poly man rounded on Furlong. 'Has Rory been at this bookcase?' he demanded.

'How should I bloody well know?' snapped Sean, exasperated beyond endurance by this unseemly intrusion on his golden hour of music. Then, gritting his teeth, he stopped the record-player, to which none of us – with the single exception of Alfie Venencia – was listening. I noted that Venencia had not even looked around at the man, but had continued to listen to the music (with hand pointedly cupped over ear) from the moment he had entered the room: and now that the music had been cut off, Venencia sat with his back still to the intruder and stared bleakly at the blank wall opposite.

Eagle-beak (as I mentally dubbed him, after the manner of unsure youth) stuck his stomach out as far as it would go and waddled out of the room, but managed to get in the following for Sean's benefit before he reached the door: 'If that fella wants an education, he should go to the bloody public bloody library for it! I'm not Andrew Carnegie, y'know!' *Bang*. The door was slammed to so violently that the window rattled. Sean was also rattled and said that the record-playing session was at an end. 'That', said Venencia bitterly, 'was Brendan Behan.'

In the late forties and early fifties, there was a house in Lower Baggot Street, where rooms could be rented by the day or night for lectures, meetings, or for any other lawful purpose. Patrick Swift, the artist, had a flat in this house; a fact I offer quite freely as it has no relevance whatever to my story.

On a particular night in early autumn, a group of four or five youths, including myself, were walking down the steps of this large house. We had just come from a lecture, and were full of what we had heard, which might have been anything from 'The Sex Life of a Rat' to a reading of Apollinaire's poems. It was our intention to saunter in the direction of St Stephen's Green, discussing what we had heard, and end the night in Grafton Street over a cup of coffee, and probe into the true significance of whatever nonsense we had spent two hours listening to, with added fury under the influence of Nescafé.

We had not taken many steps, however, when out of the penultimate shadows attending a shop front there lurched a monstrous figure. Black, wavy hair tumbled down over wild eyes. Its aspect was menacing, its gait, unsteady. There could be no doubt about it – we were face to face with Brendan Behan, and he was drunk.

He saw us, probably recognized some of us, and roared: 'More pimply-arsed students, b'jasus!' This was a reference to our having attended the lecture rather than to any academic standing which one or two of us could claim. No one had any intention of asking him to join us, a fact he must have sensed, for he joined us unasked and sickly welcomed.

Soon, what had hitherto been a group of peers, rapidly changed into a school of small fish in attendance on a whale – with Brendan filling the big role, of course. Not that we really minded (once having got used to the idea that we couldn't shake him off), for we were at an age when Brendan's rumbustious behaviour and braggadocio seemed like genuine rebelliousness against the restrictive social standards set by the Irish Establishment. And we were all in favour of *that* kind of rebellion.

All went well until we reached the Shelbourne Hotel in St Stephen's Green, when Brendan was suddenly inspired to sing a perfectly lewd song. Lewdness in itself is not found insufferable by the tolerant people of Dublin, but blasphemy is, and this no doubt was the reason Brendan chose to sing this particular song. We were lucky, I suppose, that it happened in St Stephen's Green, this central and highly respectable part of Dublin, where people, even if they heard and disapproved, would not be provoked into an attempt to correct matters with fists, boots, broken bottles, studded belts and other standard debating equipment of Catholics in the less privileged sections of the city.

I took the great liberty of pointing out to Brendan, when once he paused for breath between stanzas, that he was probably hurting many an old lady's susceptibilities with his song. I didn't think it necessary, or even wise, to mention the possibility that it might also give umbrage to any young punks who just happened to be within earshot, thus affording them the excuse (which would most likely stand up in any subsequent court case) of using the concealed weapons that generally only appear in dance hall or back-street pub. That would only have encouraged Brendan to sing the song from the beginning again. And probably *louder*.

I think that this must have been the first time he had really noticed me, or thought of me as an actual *person*. He stopped walking and asked, amiably enough: 'Whaz yer name, son? You look like one of the *Herrenvolk* to me. A proper Hun bastard, in fact!' This I imagined at the time (and later found to be true) was based on my physical appearance; in particular on my square head, pale complexion and one-inch-high fair hair. I told him my name.

'Cole? COLE!' he roared at the top of his voice. Several people who were passing by stopped momentarily, and then hastened on. 'That's a bloody *Saxon* name. The greatest enemies the Celts ever had!' I must have looked suitably contrite for the bloody conquests of my distant forbears, because he placed a heavy, avuncular arm around my shoulders, and said with conscious magnanimity, 'Never mind, butty, the wars are over.' Our little group started off again in the direction of the coffee-house. And, just to show there was no ill-feeling, Brendan sang his outrageous song twice more before we parted company with him at the corner of Grafton Street.

The relief that showed on everyone's face was, alas, to prove somewhat premature. We had not walked very far, when a frightful bellow broke through the namby-pamby atmosphere of this sedate street, causing several soaks from some nearby literary pubs (who had just been turfed out, as it was closing time) to rear up like startled mares and ending, one supposes, several discussions on how to make a dishonest living out of literature.

'JOE COLE! COAL-HOLE! POLE! Wait! I wanta say something. . . .' Brendan was lumbering after us, down this street that some fool in a fit of patriotic euphoria had once dubbed 'The Bond Street of Dublin'.

'Go to him, for chrissake!' hissed Jim Fitzgerald (who was in later years to win renown for his production of stage plays in Dublin and London), 'or we'll have the fuzz from here to Gardiner Street down our throats!'

It had to be done, or we would all (including Brendan) end up in a paddy-wagon. I ran back up the street, fully conscious that I was being sacrificed for my friends' peace of mind, and glorying in it.

When I reached him, he was out of breath and leaning against a window that sold, among other temptations, caviar at twenty-seven pounds a stone jar.

'Listen, Joe Mole', he wheezed, breathing Guinness (which he drank in those, his poor days) into my face. 'Listen, china...I got to apologise! I'm sorry if I offended against your religious suscep...sus...sus...oh, bollocks...your religion. Take my word on it! There's them I would *like* to offend in this shaggin' city of hypo-hypo...*lousers*, but you seem a decent young fella for all that you look like a concentration-camp guard.'

I said, 'There, there, now, now, no sweat', and made other reassuring noises, all of which he waved aside like so much rubbish.

'Now you listen to me, Joe Dole...When I'm in Belfast, I sing the Irish National Anthem to the friggin' roof-tops – but when I'm in Dublin and tanked up, I sing the "Orange Sash", or anything else that will bestir the equally sluggish bastards down here. All I wanta do is to start them *thinking*. Do you unnerstand, Joe Noel?'

I understood only too well, but what Brendan did not understand then (nor at any later date in his life) was that the great majority of people in Dublin and Belfast were perfectly satisfied with their non-thinking, non-critical state of mind. Furthermore, they would certainly react violently to any external stimuli aimed at changing this situation. The Cold War had this effect on Ireland, and only with the Thaw were minds and energies freed so that the people could listen to voices beyond their own shores and act accordingly.

'Maybe I went a bit too far tonight,' he muttered, and seemed to be about to add something else, but changed his mind. He lurched to the middle of the footpath, waved a vague goodbye, and staggered off in the direction of the park.

A day or two later, I heard that he had tried to force his way into the Conservative Club in York Street and was ignominiously bounced out on his ear by a natty little British-officer-type, who sported a Douglas Fairbanks (Jr) moustache. Stories of this kind about Brendan proliferated in the saloon bars of Dublin, and such was his reputation for drawing trouble to himself that none of them, not even the most fantastic, seemed improbable or impossible.

Night Out in Dublin*

JOSEPH COLE

It was closing time. The barmen in McDaid's were shouting 'Time, gentlemen, *please!*' with an automatic insistence that intimidated nobody. Drinks continued to be sipped slowly and sensually, and the barmen's end-of-day ritual was, as usual, an unrelieved failure. Yet it would be the barmen who would win in the heel of the hunt, for it was within their power to cut off supplies from behind the counter, forcing us to leave. But that would be later, perhaps fifteen minutes later, and in the meantime there were things to be said...

It had been an unusually quiet night. Few of the regular customers of this pub just off Grafton Street had shown their faces, and it was assumed – by Brendan Behan, anyway – that they were frantically busy, as he put it: 'Artising, poetising, novelising, playising, or just enjoying themselves in non-creative sex.' This had left the stage clear for Brendan who, as the only celebrity present (though at this time he was celebrated more for his promise than for his achievement), was lionised by a worshipful company of students from University College, Dublin. They bought the drinks. Brendan talked. They listened. This was the etiquette that had to be observed by any students wishing to remain in Brendan's court, and it had been adhered to scrupulously that night. It was a fair arrangement. Brendan was not mean with money, but in those days – before *The Quare Fellow* had been heard of – he was usually penniless, and rightly felt that if he was to extend himself entertaining 'a shower of pimply-faced students,' then the least they could do in return would be to keep him well oiled.

The students were always appreciative. As well they might be, for no one in Dublin could provide them with a comparable night of enjoyment. Not in a pub, anyway. And these particular students had a greater need than most of their fellows from other colleges in Ireland of meeting a full-blown social anarchist like Behan. It was said at the time (and the time was that of the Cold War–McCarthy sit-upon) that UCD was a hell of a dull place in which to study, with freedom of thought and expression on such a short academic chain that even the theological students of Maynooth College were filled with compassion for their fellow Catholic students in Dublin.

Brendan had sung songs for them, songs they had never heard before. He

---

* Extracted from *Meanjin Quarterly*, XXVII (Sep 1968) 309–21.

had sung them in Irish, English and French, and though many of these songs were demotically bawdy, they were also of undeniable antiquity. This placed anyone who might have felt like protesting in an unfavourable position, for no one in a literary pub wishes to be thought a philistine as *well* as a hypocrite. The students were charmed. He had also delighted their immature minds and titillated their youthful prurience with anecdotes about the great and the famous in Ireland, destroying flattering public images built up with imagination and loving care over many years with one or two shocking, iconoclastic sentences.

It was therefore understandable that not one of the company – and least of all Brendan, who enjoyed such occasions – wanted the night to end so soon. 'Let's do the *bona fide*?' he suggested, when all the glasses were empty. Everyone was game.

The *bona fide*, as it was commonly referred to by Dubliners, was the law that allowed a man or woman to continue drinking after the official closing time, providing only that the drinking was done in a pub not less than three miles from his or her place of residence. There are those who might be tempted to argue points of law with this definition, but that was how I, and countless thousands of other drunks, understood it.

When Brendan assembled his troops outside McDaid's, preparatory to moving on the nearest *bona fide*, he was slightly nonplussed to find that, besides the students and myself, whom he had expected to see, there was Dominic, whom he had certainly not expected to see. Dominic, who had assiduously avoided contact with Brendan and his pigeons all night, now found that he was alone; his own party, consisting of Lucien Freud (that was who he said it was), having gone his own way. After his initial start of recognition, Brendan's reaction to the situation was atypical: like the upper-class English gentlemen of whom he constantly declared his loathing, he simply acted as if Dominic had neither shadow nor substance, and ignored what was obviously not there. It was no secret in Dublin that Brendan and his younger brother preferred each other's room to each other's company.

We walked away from McDaid's in a close bunch, turned crookedly into serpentine Grafton Street, and crossed over to the bus stop on the St Stephen's Green Park side. When a bus drew up some five minutes later, no one was greatly surprised to find that approximately half of the passengers were also making for Templeogue. It was quite easy to pick out those who were doing the *bona fide*; they were the ones who, although stinking drunk, had not yet subsided into a stupor like the others....

A road sign flashed past my eyes. TEMPLEOGUE, I read. Templeogue is a residential district of Dublin, quite rural in some parts, and very attractive by night or day. But we were not there in search of aesthetic pleasures. Templeogue was the statutory three miles from all of our homes, and moreover, contained the pub popularly known as the Morgue. It acquired its odd sobriquet due to an old law which declared that any man found dead on the streets of Dublin should be taken immediately into the nearest public house. Now it so happened that in the early years of this century a tram-line passed quite close to this particular pub's front door, and, as a natural and dire consequence, the drinking establishment was seldom without at least one *literally* dead drunk on the premises. It soon became known as the Morgue, and the name has stuck to it ever since.

The door was opened cautiously to our importunate, but not wholly unexpected, pounding. An elderly man poked his head out. 'Are yez bono fido?' he asked, this being the customary challenge. 'Get outa me way, yeh old louse-bag, and let me pass!' roared Brendan, pushing his way into the pub. The door-keeper yelled after him, 'The hard man, Brendan! May yer elbow never grow weak!'

'Poor old bastard!' said Brendan, when he had found seats. 'He was one of the few who really *did* fire off a bullet or two in 1916 – and look what it's got him!' He turned to the student whose privilege it was to buy the drinks. 'The greedy old pig will have a pint of Guinness', he hinted, and glared balefully at the old man who was smiling inanely at him.

With his drink within finger-gripping distance, Brendan relaxed. For the first time that day he seemed content to allow others to do the talking, even if the talk did consist of some arrant nonsense about Joycean symbolism, which came from an athletic-looking student who had only recently received from the United States the latest book (written by a professor of psychology) on this literarily unimportant subject. Brendan was in his element, and was obviously happy. All was almost right with the world. *Almost*, because this was the time that Dominic chose to demonstrate some breathtaking, skilful guerrilla tactics on how to draw attention away from Brendan and to oneself.

When, for example, a student asked Brendan what he thought of Wilde as a playwright, irrespective of his reputation as a wit and social gadabout, Dominic interposed a lightningly-quick composed piece of doggerel verse, which began,

> It's said that Oscar was low
> Because he was a queer,
> But so was Bosy, even though
> His daddy was a peer.

Not the kind of thing that would have gone down well at the local Literary Circle, perhaps, but in that place and at that time of night it was considered by some to be a stroke of genius. These students noticeably warmed to Dominic. The rest – those with the sloping shoulders, the bony wrists, the intolerant glare in the eyes, the constipated pallors – moved closer to Brendan, as chickens which have sensed a hungry fox in their vicinity will move closer to the hen-house.

Brendan himself showed no sign of being amused by Dominic's wit. On the contrary, he cast many a controlled but potentially explosive glance in his brother's direction. Which was understandable when you come to think of it, for the students had been 'his' to begin with; but Dominic, by using his obstreperous device, had drawn off a considerable number from his sphere of influence.

Not long after this opening shot of Dominic's, one of his newly-won students displayed distressing signs of wavering in his loyalty to the younger Behan. He actually turned his back on Dominic, and spoke to Brendan. 'You must know a million folk-songs, Brendan,' he said, in that ingratiating way some people have with those whom they secretly consider to be their inferiors, 'but which one is your favourite?'

Dominic's timing was as perfect as ever, for just as his big brother opened his mouth to pronounce judgement (or whatever it was he was going to pronounce), he burst forth into an excellent imitation of an American Mid-Western barn-dance caller, which was as folksy as anyone could wish:

> Oh, catch your granmaw by the hair,
> Now throw her UP in the air.
> When she falls – let's be fair,
> Don't you trample on the old grey mare!
> Doh-zy doe . . . .

It went on for several more verses, at the end of which Dominic had not only won his wandering student back to the one true faith, but had also gained about three-quarters of the people in the pub, who showed their appreciation with prolonged applause and piercing whistles. Dominic was jubilant, as well he might be, for upstaging Brendan was not an everyday occurrence. Brendan raised his bulk slowly, swore at a glass that was knocked over by the end of his jacket, and walked with ponderous dignity in the direction of the urinal. . . .

It must have been near one o'clock the following morning when we left the Morgue. Whether we quit it voluntarily or were given the bums' rush, I cannot recall. But it was at this point that my eyes became mobile again, and I found that I was able to grasp and retain all that was happening round about me.

The first thing to register was that we were crossing the road, and that the far side seemed a long, long way off. The bus stop was over there – somewhere – over-hung with the leaf-laden branches of trees that reached out for freedom from a high, incarcerating wall.

Brendan must have become bored with the students, or else he had decided that they had been sufficiently diverted for the money they had spent on him, because now he left them and walked beside me.

'I *hate* students!' he growled. 'There's not a man-jack among them who won't grow up into a bloody, complacent, smug little member of the bourgeoisie.' He spat on the dusty road. 'Guinness doesn't agree with me like it used to do, b'jasus! Do yeh think I have the right mouth for slobbering over champagne, eh?' It was a rhetorical question, and he did not wait for an answer. '*You* hadn't much to say for yourself tonight', he accused. 'I know I told yeh to keep your gob shut, but yeh needn't have taken me so literally. Jasus – it was like sitting beside one of the Sitting Dead all night long! What were yeh *thinking* about all that time?' And he eyed me in mock wonder, as if it was inconceivable that anyone should want to think when in such a merry company. 'I'll bet you were thinking of some little bint – did yeh know that *bint* is Hindi for "daughter" – or sheila, as the Kangaroos say. Or maybe it was a boy you were thinking of – with the way the sexual revolution is going these days, a man doesn't know which way to turn!' Brendan was obviously in a mood for shocking, but I was not falling for that old bait.

I shook my head and sighed. He leered at me, and I realised that the sigh (which had really been brought on by a momentary lightness in my head when I had shaken it) had confirmed his supposition that I was in the throes of some sexual frustration. Brendan was as incorrigibly romantic as my maiden Aunt Fanny.

After a short pause, during which I did nothing to encourage any further talk about sex, he asked, 'Ever been to Paris?'

'No. Should I have?'

'Don't talk like a shaggin' fool!'

I knew of course that Brendan had been to Paris not once but many times, and that he was known there as the Irish Rabelais. A story circulating in Dublin about this time concerned one such incursion. Like most anecdotes about Brendan's eccentric behaviour, it was probably apocryphal, but it was none the worse for this. As told around the pubs in Dublin, the story had Brendan as the honoured guest of an Irish couple who were more or less permanently resident in Paris. The husband was a well-known artist, and he had been on the best of terms with Brendan for many years. The time was summer. Not just any part of summer, but August, when every Parisian of discernment and franc-wealth leaves the sweltering city with all haste. Leaving it, apparently, in the care of earnest Americans, savage Irish and Scots, stolid English, and other assorted non-Latin idiots.

One day, when the sun was really searing, Brendan complained to his hosts that he was being French-fried, and that he had not expected such treatment in a civilised country. They advised him to go up to the roof of the house, which was flat, and where it might be cooler. He did this, but soon discovered he was no better off there. A thought struck him – would it not be better if he were to divest himself of his clothing? There was only one way to find out, so he stripped naked and lay down again. This, alas, also proved a less than satisfactory solution, for now the seething sun had unhampered access to skin normally protected from the Irish mists by heavy-weight clothing, and which in consequence was vulnerable in a baby-pink way.

He stood up again. Looking about him in raging desperation, he saw a large tank, which was partly hidden by a projecting wall. He hot-footed it over to this tank, and was enchanted to find it was full to the brim with tantalizing, sweet-smelling, clear water. Driven almost mad by the heat— he must have been, or else he would have given the matter a second thought—he plunged into the tank of water.

He was happily splashing about when Dudley (I think this was the name of his host) arrived on the roof. Like most artists, he was not much given to taking physical exercise as a remedy for other excesses, and as a result was breathless and perspiring. He was also fuming. The reason for his agitation soon became clear as he explained to Brendan, with great emotional output, that the function of the tank was to trap rain-water which was then used in the drought-prone season, and that that season was *now*: it was positively *not* for cavorting about in like a frenetic porpoise. And, furthermore, he would be *pleased* if Brendan were offended to the extent of packing his toothbrush and finding somewhere else to kip.

It was said that when this story was told to Brendan, he laughed till the tears came. Typically, he refused to confirm or deny it.

'Ah, Paris!' exclaimed Brendan, kissing his finger-tips and blowing kisses to the night air, for all the world like an Italian who has just seen a pretty girl cycle past him on a windy day. He also tried to do a twinkle-toed dance, but his great bulk and the alcohol in his blood-stream made the effort impracticable. 'Now that's a city everyone should live in when they're young or very old. It's no place for the middle-aged...coming to think of it, where the hell is?' We were still crossing the road unhurriedly, and a car flashed past us, hooting in shocked anger.

'Look', he said, not even bothering to glance after the ten horse-powered machine that had come within inches of trampling us into the ground. 'Next month is May, and I'm fucked if I can think of a better month to be in Paris – unless, of course, it's June, July, August...' And he went through the whole calendar until he reached April. 'I've been thinkin' that it's about time I showed my interesting face over there again, so how about you stringing along with me?'

'How about money?' Never having been embarrassed with too much of the stuff, I was naturally conscious of its absence being an obstacle to any physical movement or pleasure on my part.

There was genuine surprise in the look he gave me. 'Now isn't that just bloody true to form!' he exploded. 'You not only *look* like a bleedin' Teuton, but you shaggin'-well *think* like one, too!' Then he assumed a mock rhapsodical tone. 'Ah, if only poor auld Oirland had more of youse and your thinkin' kind, shure and bedad, we'd be like Swedan, Switzerland – or maybe even Germany itself – in next to no time!' I took a mental note that the rise and fall of his voice was reminiscent of the mollifier with the scheming whine in *The Playboy of the Western World*, the odious Widow Quinn.

'And are youse after thinkin' what that would mean?' he continued, drawing his jacket over his head to represent a shawl: he was well into his impersonation of an old woman from the tenements of north Dublin. 'No? I'll tell yez! A par-e-dice on teary-infirma, with everything in its place and a place for everything. Millions of little manikins and womanikins living their mingy lives in hire-purchase splendour in far-flung suburban semi-detached villas. Today, Ireland, tomorrow, the world! *Ireland, Ireland, über alles*...'[1] Although I felt that the last part of his act was out of character for an old woman wearing a shawl, I still felt like applauding.

We had reached the bus stop at last. This was the inauspicious moment chosen by one of the students to formally introduce himself to Brendan as the son of a well-despised Irish concoctor of innocuous novels, the kind of novels that are not banned inside Ireland and are not read outside it.

Brendan rounded on the unfortunate young simpleton. 'Who asked *you* to interrupt? – you acne-faced runt! And that goes for your auld fella, too...if he *is* your auld fella, which I very much doubt. I hear tell he's going around calling himself a "nov-hil-ist" to anyone who'll listen. If maggots had wings, they could fly! I'll tell you what he is – he's an obsequious arse-licker of the bishops and gombeen men. The old bastard wouldn't earn a crust of bread if it wasn't for the shaggin', bogman-imposed censorship in this crucified country. Bad cess to him and all his piggish tribe. What do you mean by shoving your long nose into my private conversation with Joe Cole...'

The student retreated, his face flushed, before this entirely undeserved onslaught. I felt sorry for him. At the same time, I must admit to finding myself in complete agreement with Brendan's critical estimation of his father's character, and of his position in the literary world. He *was* a lousy writer, and he *was* a sycophantic groveller before the almighty swine in the land. A genuine bred-down Irish Establishment pom, in fact.

Brendan was still vibrating with anger, when I asked, 'Well – how *can* we live in Paris when we haven't a deuce between us? It's nice being you! All you've got to do is to drop in on Tom, Dick...'

He stopped me with an impatient wave of his hand. 'I've *never* sponged on any of me friends in me whole puff. Get that straight!' A vague gesture of his small, fat hand. 'They may have occasionally *invited* me to stay awhile in their homes, but I never pressed me comp'ny on them.'

'All right, then. Tell me – has anyone invited you to Paris this year?'

'N-no, not that I can say.'

'Well, then...?'

'We'll live by poncing.'

'PONCING?'

'Yes, y'know – *poncing*. Defined as living on the immoral earnings...'

'I *know* what poncing is!' I interrupted. 'I went to school with a kid who took up poncing as a career in his fifteenth year, for christsake!' This was true, but I did not bother to add that the last time I had seen this boy he had been wearing a beret to cover the ravages of VD: actually my informant, another boy, was wrong; it couldn't have been VD, and must have been 'crabs'.

'Have *you* ever ponced?' I asked.

'Don't talk wet! Of course I have. The last time I was over there, to be exact. It's bloody easy. Especially for a good-looking young stud like you. I'll bet all the tarts of the Left Bank would tear one another's hair out by the roots to get at you.'

'Great! What are we waiting for? I only hope I can live up to your plans for me.'

'You'd do it?'

'Natch!'

He looked away, his face becoming shadowed by the overhanging branches of the trees, but not quickly enough, not before I had seen the ineffable disgust distort his tough features. That was the last I ever heard of poncing in Paris from Brendan.

'Hey Joe – Joe Cole!' It was Dominic, and he was making an uncertain line in our direction. One foot was on the pavement, the other was in the gutter. His body inclined forward at an angle, as if moving ahead of, and independently of, his legs. A black lock of hair flopped wildly over his right eye, and his left hand was reaching out for us, although he was still some twenty yards away from where we stood. Then, when he was within six feet of us, he suddenly straightened up as if shot by a silver bullet, collapsed in a heap, and rolled into the gutter.

There were several things I did not know about Dominic at this time. One was that he was apt to fall down and sleep for several hours when he drank beyond his capacity. This being my first experience of this tendency, I was naturally shaken by what I assumed to be a fainting spell, or possibly worse.

I bent over him, and gently slapped his face a few times. 'Dominic! DOMINIC – Stand up for godsake, Dominic!' And I treated him to another couple of powder-puff slaps.

Just then I was struck on the left shoulder by what felt like a falling tree, and was knocked sprawling into the gutter beside Dominic. I looked up, still dazed, and saw an apparently outraged Brendan glaring down at me.

'Don't you *ever* hit my brother like that again!' he snarled. 'I suppose you thought you were interrogating a Russian-Communist-Jewish-Commissar, eh? Bloody Hun!'

He looked speculatively at his younger brother, who was sleeping quite peacefully in the gutter, and added: 'Only his big brother has the right to hit him, b'jasus!' Following his rails of thought with the train of action, he bent over Dominic and administered such hearty backhanders that the sound of the fraternal slaughter was heard clear across the road in the Morgue. It brought out one of the barmen, who shouted over at Brendan, 'Stop killing that poor man now, or I'll call the polis, so I will!'

Fortunately there was no need for letting the bulls out of their pens that night, for Dominic recovered rapidly under Brendan's therapeutic technique, and was standing upright when the bus arrived a few minutes later.

NOTE

1 'Ireland, Ireland, above all.' On the lines of the German National Anthem, 'Deutschland, Deutschland, über alles'.

At Kelly's Pawn Office*

DOMINIC BEHAN

'Why are yeh all dressed up at this hour of the mornin'?' asked Da. 'Are yeh not goin' to your work?' We were standing outside the parlour door, and I put a finger to my lips, bidding him speak softly. 'I'm goin' somewhere today and I don't want the other fella to know.' My father hunched his shoulders, as much as to say, 'Between yeh it is', and as he opened the hall door and the weatherboard struck the stone step my mother came out of the kitchen and whispered, 'Don't be makin' so much noise. Poor Brendan has a sick head.' Da laughed, and left with a glance over his shoulder at Ma, and the valedictory, 'Poor Benjamin, while I'm away to my nice warm work he'll have to lie all day in that cold ould bed.'

I went back into the kitchen and, taking a roll of notes from my back pocket, I counted four single pounds into Ma's hand. 'There yeh are now. I don't think I owe yeh anything. I'm goin' away for the weekend but when the other fella gets up, tell him nothin'.' 'Ah,' she said, 'poor Brendan. And him the one that loves to hear a bit of news.'

When the streets were well aired, Ma knocked on the sanctuary and whispered through the door to Brendan that breakfast was ready. 'Have yeh the paper?' he asked. 'I have,' Ma replied, 'and the nicest little mushrooms yeh ever saw.' 'Good,' said Brendan, 'I'll be there in a minute.'

'They were the curse of the famine', he said as he sat to the table. 'What's

* *My Brother Brendan* (London: Leslie Frewin, 1965) pp. 79–82. Editor's title.

that?' asked Ma. 'Mushrooms', he answered. 'When yeh saw more than the usual growth in the fields then yeh knew that the potatoes had been hit. I see', he said, looking at the paper, 'a fella has been elected on the fifteenth count. That sort of thing makes a mockery of proportional representation. Will yeh lend us a quid?'

Mother was neither shocked nor startled, but she put on a show of surprise. 'Where in the world would I get a pound on Friday mornin', Brendan? Yeh saw me yerself tryin' to make a manage on the ten shillin's I got from Tommy on me ring yesterday morning? Are yeh mad or what?' 'I heard yeh gettin' yer money from Dominic this mornin'.' She looked at him and covered up her mouth. 'Yeh could hear the grass growin'. But I've too much to do, Brendan. By the time I release Da's suit and a couple of other things there'll be little left of either of their wages.' He waved an end to the conversation. 'If yeh don't want to give it to me, that's that.'

He read silently with glances over the top of the paper at Ma. 'Nice mushrooms', he said. Mother sat counting her debts. He read for a while. 'I'd nearly risk a famine for them, begod. Tell me, Mother, did yeh ever hear a song that goes...The praties they grow small over here?' Unfair tactics, Ma would rather live in the workhouse than not sing. 'Don't I know every song in Ireland that was ever written? When my poor father had lost everything and we were in the shabbiest basement he used to write the songs in chalk on the wall so that we'd never forget them.' And in a big voice of her father's she loudly declaimed, 'With a rifle as a redcoat, yer son yeh wouldn't spurn? I'd blow yer brains out on the floor, said Mick of Carrickbyrne.'

At the end of a blood-curdling account of what the Irish would do to the Saxon, in which Ma's song likened the battle to a harvesting, the Redcoats being the corn, the Fenians the reapers, Brendan said, 'I'm goin' to pawn my typewriter, and I'll give yeh the pound off that. If not I'll pay yeh when I get the money from "The Confirmation Suit".'[1]

'Oh,' asked Ma, 'did yeh sell that story?' 'I did, begod,' replied Brendan, 'and for good money.' 'It won't go to press as it is, will it?' Ma asked. 'Why not?' he replied. 'Well,' began my mother, 'I thought I'd remind yeh. That suit wasn't made for you, Brendan, as yeh said in the story. Don't yeh remember it was made for Rory? Sure yer granny wouldn't allow anything on you that didn't come out of a tailor's shop. She'd have died first.' 'Ah, Mother, for Christ's sake gimme the quid and let me out of this. I've never heard such rubbish. There's not a haporth the matter with me memory. I know bloody well that the suit was made for Rory. It just makes the story better when I say it was made for me, that's all.' He looked at the clock. 'Christ!' he muttered. 'I'll be late. They'll be gone without me. Is that clock fast?' 'Right to the very minute,' said Ma. 'Maybe half an hour on but no more.' 'Who'll be gone without you?' Brendan laughed as he pulled the tie round his waist, and shoved Ma away when she tried to stuff his shirt into his pants. 'That precious little gem of yours and his cronies. If they think they're goin' to leave me here while they go to a good drinkin' county on their own...well.' He held up his cheek to be kissed as he took the note from her hand, then grabbing his typewriter he ran for the bus with hellos and goodbyes for all who passed.

Paddy Collins and I waited with Eddie Connell for Christie O'Neill to arrive at McDaid's. The pub opened its doors at half past ten and the manager, Paddy O'Brien, asked, 'By god, you fellas are here early enough. Not go home last night?' 'Did John Ryan leave a cheque here last night for me?' I asked, as he pulled three pints and left them to settle. 'He did indeed,' replied Paddy. 'Twenty quid. Oh, by the way, Dom,' he took me to the corner of the bar, 'yeh know there's a little...' I pulled him nearer and said, 'I'd sooner leave it till next week. If that's all right?' He clapped his hands and said cheerfully, 'Oh, as right as rain. Now then,' as he put up the drink, 'who's the victim?'

Brendan alighted from a no. 50 bus at the corner of Westmoreland Street and made his way to Kelly's pawn office in Fleet Street. 'How much will yeh give me on me typewriter, John?' he asked. 'What yeh always get, Brendan, three quid.' 'All right, then, give it to us.' A young, shabbily dressed woman waited on her receipt. Discreetly the man handed her the ticket and a ten-shilling note. Outside he heard her saying, 'Will yeh leave that bell alone. Can yeh not keep yer hands off anything! Mother of the Devine God but between the two of yeh I'll be up in the asylum.' Brendan took the money from the pawnbroker and shoved it into his pocket. He overtook the woman at the bottom of the stairs and smiled at her two children. 'Ah fuck it!' he said to himself, and without a word he pressed the three single notes into the woman's hand and fled back into Westmoreland Street.

NOTES

For a note on Dominic Behan see p. 7.

1. 'The Confirmation Suit', Behan's last short story, was published in the Easter number of *The Standard*, 1953. It was reprinted in *Brendan Behan's Island* (London: Hutchinson, 1962) pp. 147–53.

'Get the Rozzers'*

ANTHONY CRONIN

The years from now until the first production of *The Quare Fellow* and his subsequent marriage were to be, in general, bad ones for him, and as a consequence of the rejections he suffered – some of them self-invited – he began to behave in distressing and obsessional ways. He could not take no for an answer and confronted by a rejection or coldness of any sort he would react with an extraordinary verbal violence, shouting abuse and not infrequently foaming at the lips. His victories depended either on the other party's terror at the spectacle of rage he then presented, or on their mere embarrassment at the degree of noise created and the kind of public attention attracted. Since a Dublin pub audience is highly pleased to have a public show of any kind put on for its benefit, Brendan could depend on their encouragement for the discomforture of the victim, who could only cower or scarper, thus leaving him the field and, in that sense at least, the victory.

He had certain terms of abuse the damaging significance of which was known only to himself. But since the bystanders cared only for the show he did not have to be too accurate or witty, though of course he was frequently these things too. One of Brendan's special prides, amounting almost to an obsession, was the fact that he was a Dubliner. All those who had the bad taste to be born elsewhere were 'Kulchies' – called so of course after the town of Kiltimagh, pronounced Kulchimah, in County Mayo – or bogmen, because of the prevalence of bogs in rural Ireland. They were supposed to possess traits of character, particularly avarice and cunning, from which those born in the slums of Dublin were singularly free. Kavanagh, the peasant poet, the archetypal countryman, was to become a special target for this line of abuse; and because his long poem *The Great Hunger* was concerned with sexual frustration in rural Ireland and its symbolic countryman, Maguire, occasionally masturbated, he became without any justification other than a work of the imagination – a common process – the Monaghan wanker' and was eventually so referred to in the Paris little magazine *Points*, where one of Brendan's few published pieces dating from this time appeared. (The issue of *Points*, with its bright yellow

---

* *Dead as Doornails: A Chronicle of Life* (Dublin: Dolmen Press; London: Calder and Boyars, 1976) pp. 69–73. Editor's title.

cover, became in the end almost as familiar as the typescript.) Hailing from
the County Wexford as I did, I too was finally a Kulchie, though in fact
Wexford is as different from the County Mayo as Berkshire is from Banff.

But I go ahead of my story. In spite of 'The Bridewell Revisited'[1] and
other matters, our relationship had by no means foundered. We had a
quarrel or two, but they passed over. His obsession with Kavanagh and his
attempts to force himself on his notice had not yet grown to the pitch they
were to arrive at later – there was as yet no ranting in the streets – and if we
were no longer daily companions we continued to associate companionably enough.

He was not, it is true, as much fun to be with as he once had been, but he
was not unconversable, as he was to become. I had left 'The Gurriers' and
moved into a room in a house in Hatch Street. It was a bare enough
apartment, with only a stretcher bed and a table and some books, but it
was of noble Georgian proportions. When Brendan stayed, as he still did
sometimes, he slept in a sort of nest of old newspapers in a corner, and
unless Peadar was on the phone editing *The Bell* we still issued forth
together in the mornings to see what the day might offer, much as we had
always done.

One incident from this time I remember, though whether it is evidence
of the general frustrations he was suffering, or of the fact that his principles
remained uncorrupted throughout, I cannot say.

It was Christmas, and we came out of McDaid's about nine o'clock to
find that it was raining. The Christmas lights were on in Grafton Street,
there were more people than usual about, and a bunch of carol-singers was
standing at the corner with coat collars turned up, still sweetening the
damp night air.

They carried placards advertising their charitable intent – something to
do with the St Vincent de Paul Society, or the Legion of Mary or the
Morning Star hostel for down-and-outs. As we stood in the rain
deliberating the next move, Brendan began to mutter. As I have said, he
had in those days a ferocious hatred of the Catholic Church in all its
manifestations. We decided to go to Keogh's, which is in Anne Street, and
moved towards the corner. The carol-singers were still hard at it, tenor and
alto, bass and treble, but as we passed them Brendan suddenly seized one of
the placards and proceeded to tear up the cardboard and smash the lath
while roaring 'Chairman Mao Tse Tung will soon put a stop to your
fucking gallop, ye creepin' Jesuses ye.' The singing ended on various notes
while he flung the fragments across the road towards Mooney's, bellowing
away. There was a moment's hiatus everybody, including myself, being
taken by surprise, and then a couple of bystanders rushed him. He was off
like a hare, up Grafton Street and towards Stephen's Green, with about
four fellows after him. Fear lends wings to the feet and Brendan kept his
distance. At the top of the street he dashed into the roadway and succeeded
in gaining the far side well ahead, the others having followed with more

respect for the traffic. I crossed over too, but with even more circumspection. Brendan pounded on towards the Harcourt Street end.

The inner side of Stephen's Green was in those days lit by ordinary street lamps and there were pools of light with intervals of darkness in between. The pursuers ran on until suddenly it was evident that there was no quarry in front, then stopped unevenly, regrouped and began to argue among themselves. I stopped too. It was, as Brendan would say, the best of my play. After peering into the bushes inside the railings, they began to straggle back and, hoping not to be identified as the companion of the atheistic communist, I went on and even met them, walking as casually as I could, though of course in fear and trembling. They were still hotly debating and occasionally peering, so I passed unrecognised, whistling a little tune.

I had almost reached the far corner when I heard my name called. It was Brendan, crouching inside under a dripping laurel bush.

'Did you climb those railings?' I asked in surprise.

'Of course I did. Why wouldn't I? Didn't I fucking paint them?' he answered petulantly.

I had to be content with the logic, though it was an astonishing feat to have swung himself over in a dark interval and in the time available.

'Well you'd better climb out again now,' I said, 'because I badly need a drink.'

He climbed over, this time with, it seemed, immense difficulty, and blowing like a grampus. I watched, powerless to aid or hinder, until at last he dropped down beside me. We had both forgotten by then about the outraged populace.

Suddenly there was a rush of feet from quite close by and a shout of, 'There he is, the rotten bastard.' Brendan was off again, this time towards the Russell Hotel, but they caught us in the middle of the road. There was nothing for it but to turn and fight.

Whether it was the shock of our sudden *volte-face* or not, after a few rather ineffectual punches were exchanged they gave ground before us, and I learned again what a little determination will do in a fight, a thing an intellectual is always, alas, inclined to forget. In the confusion we got up the steps of the Russell and burst into the lobby on top of a startled porter and some guests.

'There's a mob out there,' shouted Brendan, already beginning to bolt the glass-panelled door. The surprised porter came over to have a look for himself. There were in fact four fellows standing outside on the pavement, gesticulating and shouting, but apparently regarding the hotel as some sort of sanctuary, and uncertain as to what to do next.

'Get the rozzers', said Brendan in tones of command. 'I'm a Dubbelin man. I'm a citizen of no mean city and I'll show these bogmen that there's law and order in this town.'

By the time a police-car arrived the mob of four had apparently given up hope of getting us and drifted off. Brendan told the sergeant he had been attacked for no reason at all in the streets of his own city by a crowd of murderous countrymen he didn't know but suspected to be members of a rural-based organisation of fascist tendencies.

Unimpressed, but equally incurious, the police drove us round the Green and dropped us at the corner of Merrion Row. We went to O'Neill's. Brendan expressed no word of apology, remorse or regret, but he seemed a bit shifty, and at one stage he flattered me by saying 'You're handy with your dukes', which, like all successful flattery, attributed to the opposite party an aptitude he did not possess but would like to.

NOTES

For a note on Anthony Cronin see p. 29.

1. Behan had given Cronin, in his capacity as Associate Editor of *The Bell*, the typescript of 'Bridewell Revisited'. It was in fact an early version of the first fifty pages or so of what was subsequently to be called *Borstal Boy*. The story was not accepted for publication, and Behan took its rejection badly.

The First Play*

MARY LODGE

The national dailies and evenings had been carrying references: 'A play', they said, 'by Brendan Behan,... *The Quare Fellow* at the Pike Theatre, for a limited run...'

There was some elaboration. The *Evening Press* suggested tentatively that readers of Brendan's weekly column in its sister paper, the *Irish Press*, would have little doubt as to his potentiality as a dramatist.[1] He could, was the view, well afford to begin where Sean O'Casey had left off. All he needed was theatre-workshop experience.

The *Irish Times* reminded its public that Brendan had already appeared before them as a journalist, a novelist, a poet, and in two languages, Irish and English. Now he had chosen yet another genre – drama.

His stage was to be minute, twelve feet by twelve feet. Its setting was a converted Georgian coach-house, known as the Pike Theatre, in Herbert Lane. The site was remote enough to draw the waggish comment, 'Be sure to get specific street directions, or you'll lose yourself somewhere along the River Dodder!'

* *The World of Brendan Behan*, ed. Sean McCann (London: New English Library, 1965), pp. 80–7.

But the small unpretentious theatre, brainchild of producer Alan Simpson, and his wife, Carolyn Swift, had in a mere year of existence won a reputation for discerning selectivity. Simpson Productions had achieved a certain cachet. They were exciting, stimulating, that bit different.

Explained Miss Swift, 'we saw ourselves as a revolutionary force stirring up the theatrical lethargy of post-war Ireland. The name was picked for two reasons, one as practical as the other is symbolic.' The pike, a long spiked pole used in the anti-British rising of 1798, stands for resurgence, and the terseness of the word made it perfect for advertising.

Carolyn Swift, the Pike Theatre, Brendan Behan, dramatist, they are inextricably joined. It makes no difference that he is dead and Herbert Lane quiet of an evening. A short distance away, in a simple austere office, a dynamic, versatile, English-Irishwoman, leafs through a much thumbed scrapbook and remembers...

How did the Pike come to having the staging of *The Quare Fellow*? It had been submitted to the Abbey, who rejected it, and to the Edwards–MacLiammóir Company,[2] who weren't interested. On its rounds, however, I learnt from Miss Swift, it had been read by MacLiammóir's niece, Sally Travers, who thought there might be something in it for Alan Simpson.

The Simpsons got a copy of the manuscript eventually, and an unprofessional bit of work it was too. 'It had', chuckled Carolyn Swift, to whom was to fall the task of editing, 'obviously been typed by several different typewriters, in varying stages of decay, on paper of dubious origin and catholic size! The construction was loose and rambling. In Brendan's mind one good gag led to another. But dialogue and humour of that quality could not fail to hold an audience.'

Acceptance by the Pike may have been Brendan Behan's big break, but the Pike, in the person of Carolyn Swift, remembers him as its most tractable author ever. He impressed with his humble attitude to suggestion. He agreed immediately to change from one act to three, and that 'the quare fellow', Dublinese for a condemned man, and recurring frequently in the text, would not only make a more arresting title, but cost less in printing.[3]

Prospective improvements were drafted and passed on. In a matter of moments there would be a couple of lines of brilliant dialogue, an apposite gag in each. 'And what is more,' she added with a proud affection, 'any of my phrases good enough he let stand.'

She loved him for his obvious thrill at seeing his play taking shape on a professional stage. 'He used to nudge the person sitting next to him and say, "I wrote that." While he liked to hear a full house laughing at his jokes, he wasn't interested in impressing the conventional first-nighter. He wrote for the worker out on the town for an evening.' His pride, in fact, was not in the play itself, but in what it could do for people.

Other Pike dramatists with a first play on the boards considered it déclassé to show any emotion. They must appear blasé, as if this was an everyday occurrence in their lives. 'And it goes without saying', commented Miss Swift, with a touch of acerbity, 'that every word is pure gold and mustn't be touched.' But Brendan Behan retained to the end his spontaneous naïveté.

Rehearsals got under way, and the Pike management set itself the task of gathering together an all-male cast of twenty-nine, reduced by doubling to twenty-one. The actors were a glorious hotchpotch of the professional, the amateur, the student. A further worry was the danger of libel. Brendan's gift for vivid reportage gave a dangerous verisimilitude to his pen portraits of the prison staff and inmates.

Indeed at the end of the run one Dublin management was to refuse the play on that ground alone, and Carolyn Swift tells an enlightening anecdote of another. 'Oh, no, they couldn't possibly consider such a play. The author's brother had worked for them as a gallery spot-operator, and had been fired for selling the *Daily Worker* to the patrons in duty hours.'

Brendan enjoyed rehearsals and was a frequent attender, adored by the cast. He posed, however, according to Miss Swift, a problem in proportions, being so large and the Pike so small. Then he was given to loud roars of encouragement, 'good man yourself', to individual actors. A by-product of the lack of space in the Pike too, incidentally, was that any old 'lag' friends of Brendan's in the auditorium were overcome by the illusion of being back inside!

As the opening night drew near, the author's excitement mounted. It was all too much for him, and the remedy was obvious and there, literally, for the taking. He went on the bottle, and appeared in the theatre at intervals, as often as not accompanied by a bemused, amiable, and utterly uncomprehending boozing partner.

'And at the dress rehearsal', went on the assistant producer with a laugh, 'he had no sooner arrived than he fell asleep. I had to detail someone to sit beside him and kick him awake every now and again. He was snoring so loud that the players couldn't hear their lines.'

But it is an ill wind, and the point was well taken. On the big night, it was the task of manager Tom Willoughby, in between sporadic appearances as the prison governor, and his wife Rosamund Stevens, the theatre's public relations officer, to keep the neophyte dramatist in a delicately balanced state of inebriation. As Miss Swift explained, 'we had no licence in the Pike, and if Brendan got too dry, and set out to rectify it, heaven only knew how he'd come back, if at all! So the Willoughbys had a bottle in the box office and instructions to keep him happy, but upright.'

As a result, it was a docile, almost shy, Brendan who came on stage at the final curtain in response to cries of 'Author', 'Author', and hitching up his trousers, captivated everyone with a spirited rendering of Sean O'Casey's 'Red Roses for Me'. Later he was to appreciate that it didn't do his audience any harm to feel he might make an appearance. But Miss Swift considers him incapable of the deliberate publicity stunt.

Some of her first night memories may be that bit hazy. 'I don't remember too much about it', she confesses with a disarming twinkle, 'I was out in the front of the house prompting. In fact, I was hanging over the fly rail. One of the cast, it would be kinder not to mention his name, was a bit deaf and he was only happy if he could see me mouthing the words.'

But there is nothing hazy about her memories of Brendan Behan, man and playwright. The two first met in 1947 at an informal gathering in sculptor Desmond MacNamara's studio. The 'literary lion', not long out of jail, was writing short stories for *Envoy*, and the odd poem in Irish. She was a little apprehensive, 'not of Brendan himself, but that he would sneer at my middle-class background, and English voice. I needn't have worried. If people were genuine, he didn't give a damn what else they were.'

The shy quickly became his friends. He went out of his way to meet them half way and make them feel at home. On the other hand, those who tried to patronise him made a big mistake. He had a fantastic facility for making them appear cheap and shoddy.

Carolyn Swift speaks of him as straightforward and sincere. She ranks his character high as a factor in the international repute of his writings. Where Dublin gags and allusions lost in translation, character delineation did not. 'He depicted in the round,' she pointed out, 'no one is ever all black or all white. Personal bias wasn't allowed to interfere with objectivity. He wrote composite portraits of the people he knew, in a witty unprejudiced manner.'

She has no recollection of hearing him refer to his writing in the abstract. He wasn't one of those 'what am I trying to do' types. The form was more 'Wasn't that a great success!'

Talk about Brendan Behan and sooner or later it has to come up, his exhibitionism, his drinking, and that seeming 'skulduggery' where legal contracts were concerned.

Exhibitionism and a certain histrionic quality were a part of his make-up. Miss Swift accepts this, and more important, understands it. 'He was a born actor and raconteur. He was only exhibitionist in a particular way. I have seen him for instance, when he thought no one was looking, cross the street to give a half-a-crown to a kid. He had a quality of childish innocence that drew the young to him. They felt he was a person they could play with. My own daughter, Maureen, was on a school outing when she heard of his death, and she cried all day in the bus.'

The complacent, the self-satisfied though, were there for the shaking. 'There was nothing he enjoyed more than to amble into the lounge of the Shelbourne Hotel, on a Sunday afternoon, when Dublin's prim ladies were decorously sipping tea, and say something outrageous, just to see the effect!'

Much of his drinking was for conviviality. He met his friends in the pubs and that was the social life he liked. He drank too for 'Dutch courage' before a TV appearance.

'Take a look at his family background', insisted Miss Swift, emphatically. 'As I see it the sole difference between Stephen Behan, father, and Brendan, son, is that, in the case of the elder, drinking capacity was limited by a weekly wage packet of about fifteen pounds and the obligation to be on the top of a ladder, painting, the next morning, while in Brendan's case, an advance payment of £200 was not unusual, and there might be no commitments for four or five days.'

Circumstances had changed, and he had failed in the adjustment. This applied as well where contracts and fees were concerned. Where, in Carolyn Swift's opinion, he might have been a perfectly competent and business-like house-painter, the mechanics of big-time publishing mesmerised him. Ten pounds in the hand meant far more than the promise of a stout cheque. 'Pay him in cash', she concluded humorously, 'and he would fall in with any suggestion.'

Brendan Behan, drunken, rumbustious, Dublin house-painter, had his following, and the theatre was full that Friday evening in November of 1954.[4] Amongst the audience was a nineteen-year-old Dubliner, born and reared. He remembers it vividly. 'I went along to that back street garage of a theatre. It was a tatty place, with coffee at the intervals, and served by those inevitable stage-struck pretty girls.

'We all knew Brendan slightly, and had some idea of his background. He was the sort of fellow, who, if he announced he was coming to your house you got a bit nervous. Later you asked Lord and Lady this to meet him!'

The Dublin of that first night he would have a Dublin of compromise. 'Today', he suggests, 'we are, or like to think we are, more cosmopolitan. At any rate opinion is not a thing to be frightened of.' He is convinced that nobody in the Pike that evening had any idea that they were in at the birth of a great play. 'They didn't know how to take it.' He said firmly, 'You felt they were just waiting for the final curtain to rush after a knowledgeable body and ask how to react!'

His theatre-goer of a decade ago was the man with a steady job. How could such a person ever hope to understand Brendan Behan, wildly talented, but given to behaving in a crazy way, drinking, and using four-letter words.

He describes the curtain coming down to shouts of 'Author', 'Author', in refined tones. 'It was that sort of audience, Simpson had a Protestant middle-class heritage. The Behan family, and the Behan pals were there, of course, but much more in evidence was the young man about town out for a lark. I saw some discerning people, and the odd literary figure or two.'

Provocative incidents I gathered were at a premium. All he could report was the effort of a fellow member of the Sandycove Swimming Club to oust him from his place after the interval, 'on the grounds that if he had to stand any longer, he certainly wasn't waiting for the end!'

And what did an impressionable young man think of that strange play? 'I was lifted out of my seat by the implacable inevitability of the death sentence. I wasn't expert enough to see the objections to the dramatic format. Structurally it was on the lines of a joke book.'

The controversial author he thought of as a kindly enough man when sober, but with a streak of viciousness that came out when he was drunk.

The professional critics were not exactly of one mind either. Gabriel Fallon of the *Evening Press* tells an entertaining behind-the-scenes tale.[5] It appears that the *Irish Press* Editor, anxious to do his columnist proud, asked the late Dr Lennox Robinson, Director of the Abbey, and a member of the board responsible for the selection of its plays, to do the review.[6]

Came the interval, and what more natural than for Mr Fallon to turn to his companion with the query, 'Well, Lennox, how are you liking it?'

'My dear fellow,' was the laconic reply, 'how can you possibly expect me to enjoy a play I turned down?'

And Lennox Robinson was consistent. The following morning's *Irish Press* read, 'Walter Pater has said very truly that we are all condemned to death but with an untimed reprieve.

'Again and again in poem and play and in short story, the subject of the man condemned to death and the subject of the hangman and the subject of the victim have been treated.

'Oscar Wilde treated the subject poignantly in his *Ballad of Reading Gaol*; Thomas Hardy treated the subject from the angle of the hangman in a short story, and the hangman's point of view has been simply explained in a one-act play.

'In *The Quare Fellow* which had its first production in the Pike Theatre last night, Brendan Behan has taken as his theme this macabre subject – for it is macabre.

'But he treats it flippantly. Behind all his excellent vivid backchat we should feel a shudder, a black cap, quicklime, but he never makes us tremble. A canary is going to expire from lack of water. We feel nothing more poignant . . . .'

In complete contrast came Gabriel Fallon's effusion. 'An Aristotle searching Dublin for pity and terror would have found them in good measure, primed down and running over at the Pike theatre last night where Brendan Behan's first essay in drama was presented under the title *The Quare Fellow*.

'Prisoner E777 may not have worn a cricket cap nor stepped out light and gay but his departure from life at a rope's end powerfully inspired Mr Behan to write a documentary of prison life in many respects more profoundly moving and more deeply religious than Wilde's *Ballad of Reading Gaol*.

'For even more than poor Wilde, Brendan Behan has a feeling for a permanence above the permanence of one human existence, and sees man's life wholly against the background of eternity. Our academicians of drama may dismiss Mr Behan's work on the grounds of technical immaturity, may suggest cutting this and touching up that but Mr Behan has what most of our academicians lack, an abundance of felt life, and when he finds himself technically, the Irish theatre will have found another, and I think a greater, O'Casey.

'Even when he writes didactically – and his play in essence is a plea for the abolition of capital punishment – all the qualities that go to make a great playwright keep breaking in.

'Although the pity and terror of *The Quare Fellow* are blended with a rich full-flavoured humour which at times provokes riotous laughter, the moral content of the work has the power to compel immediate stillness and bend our attention toward things we give little care to in the lives of our less fortunate brethren.'

The *Irish Times* was careful. 'One of the positive qualities – and there are many – of Mr Behan's play, is its power of provoking thought. Like a modern novel, it rounds off neither character nor situation, but "passes the buck" to the customer.

'The vivid sharpness of the dialogue commands attention and makes one forget, for the moment, the blurred edges of characterisation and motivation; it produces in retrospect something horribly true to life in its apparent pointlessness.

'There is no progression nor development of any of the characters, but that is presumably intentional and they are all at least memorable.'[7]

And the *Irish Independent* left no doubt that while the play was the finest by a new dramatist seen in Dublin for some years, it was not a masterpiece. 'It could well be', went on the criticism, 'the first essay of a great playwright still fumbling with the mechanics of his craft.

'Mr Behan draws characters with insight and sensitivity and his dialogue – rich, racy and humorous – is as authentically Dublinesque and as forceful as O'Casey at his best, and his work gives an almost Chekovian sense of continuance. His construction is weak however, and the very exuberance of his flair for dialogue and character lead him to being too diverse....

'When', concludes the reviewer, 'Mr Behan develops something more of a plot than in his present work which moves simply to the death of the "Quare Fellow" and the throwing of his last letters into his grave, we may well look to him for a truly great play.'[8]

A section of the scrapbook closes. In the words of friend, producer, editor Carolyn Swift, 'it was the end of an era...' She pauses a moment before asking softly, 'Did you know, I sold the Pike the day Brendan died?'

NOTES

1. A collection of Behan's best columns for the *Irish Press* later appeared in book form as *Hold Your Hour and Have Another* (London: Hutchinson, 1963; Boston: Little, Brown, 1964).
2. The Dublin Gate Theatre, by Hilton Edwards and Micheál MacLiammóir.
3. The original title of the play was *The Twisting of Another Rope*.
4. *The Quare Fellow* had its world premiere at the Pike Theatre, Dublin, on 19 November 1954.
5. Gabriel Fallon, 'Behan's Play Should Not Be Missed', *Evening Press* (Dublin), 21 Nov 1954, p. 3.
6. L[ennox] R[obinson], 'Acting Was Superb in Behan Play', *Irish Press* (Dublin), 20 Nov 1954, p. 9.
7. '*The Quare Fellow* at the Pike', *Irish Times*, (Dublin), 20 Nov 1954, p. 9.
8. N. L., 'Premiere of Play by New Dramatist', *Irish Independent* (Dublin), 22 Nov 1954, p. 2.

Making up my Mind*

BEATRICE BEHAN

We were drinking together in a favourite pub of Brendan's in Baggot Street one January evening in 1955 when he surprised me by asking, 'What would you say to a trial marriage, Beatrice?'

Above the noisy conversation in the bar the words came clearly to me. I didn't know whether to take them seriously or just laugh. Before I could reply, he had added, 'Let's shag off together to the South of France and give it a try.'

There was a pause as he called for a pint of stout and a bottle of Guinness for me.

'We'll be married soon, Brendan', I told him firmly, 'or we won't be going anywhere.'

Brendan was a great man for the unexpected. Did he expect me to drink my Guinness and accept his invitation to the South of France without question? Although he erupted in laughter I knew he was serious. He was prepared to settle for a period of living together without marriage. He had more experience of Dublin than I had, and he should have known that to live as man and mistress would be considered a scandal in the society of the time. I could only assume he didn't want to marry me, not just now anyway, because he couldn't face the prospect of losing his freedom.

* Extracted from *My Life with Brendan* (London: Leslie Frewin, 1973) pp. 40–50.

'You know it wouldn't be right, Brendan,'
'To hell with the begrudgers', he said to me. 'We won't fall out over it'.
I loved Brendan, but I didn't believe my love would extend to a life together without marriage. Perhaps I was conventional, but I was not a puritan or I would never have wanted to marry him in the first place. He must have sensed my determination, for he asked me casually to fix a date in February, the month of his birthday,[1] for our wedding.

'If you had suggested a ceremony in a registry office,' I remarked, 'it mightn't have sounded as absurd as your other idea.'

He grasped his pint and looked at me sternly.

'I want you to know that all belonging to me are Catholics, Beatrice, and if we're to be married it will be in a Catholic church.'

I had been meeting Brendan regularly for just a few weeks. If he was late for a date I would stand outside the pub, reluctant to enter on my own, but content to wait until he turned up. He wasn't a romantic bachelor; he preferred drinking to dancing and pub-singing to party-going. 'I like pubs because I like people,' he would say. And with the people who gathered around him in a pub he talked endlessly.

I was never bored by his stories of Dublin and its characters. But he could be cruel as well as charming, and when somebody irked him he would lash him with his tongue.

'What does the Dalai Lama think about you and me, Beatrice?'

This was his sardonic reference to my father, Cecil ffrench-Salkeld, who was born in North-west India on the borders of Tibet, one of two sons of Henry Lyde Salkeld, a Cumberland man in the Indian Civil Service. Cecil's mother, Blanaid ffrench-Salkeld, my grandmother, was widowed at the age of twenty-eight when her husband died of typhoid fever. She brought her two boys to Ireland and they settled in Dublin.

'I hope you don't mind, but I'll have to tell him about the wedding, Brendan.' He didn't argue the point. . . .

The few friends who knew that I was soon to be married were anxious not to hurt my feelings, as if that mattered now. They would remark, cautiously, 'Are you sure you're doing the right thing?' They were well-meaning and honest, yet I suspected they couldn't comprehend that I, the reserved Beatrice ffrench-Salkeld, was about to marry this outspoken man whose background differed so greatly from my own.

Brendan was conscious of this difference. Not only was he suspicious of the middle and upper classes, but he derived malicious pleasure from taunting them. When we were alone I would ask him about his own upbringing.

'That's the past, Beatrice', he would say.

'But I'd like to know, Brendan.'

Eventually he talked about his childhood days in a closely-knit community in the gas-lit northside streets of Dublin where drink, laughter and song provided a release from want and suffering. One day as we walked through a landscape of tall tenement houses he told me he had in fact been born in Holles Street Hospital, south of the River Liffey.

'So you're really a southsider,' I teased him.

I could see this was a truth he took no pride in because he considered southsiders a race apart. He could laugh at his tough boyhood.

'You had to be a hard chiseller, Beatrice, to hold your own. I gave as good as I got. I quit the Christian Brothers' school at fourteen, but I was always inquisitive.'

He told me that at the age of six he could read aloud Robert Emmet's[2] *Speech from the Dock*. 'That chiseller isn't reading it at all', his relatives insisted. 'He learned it by heart.'

Brendan never forgot that early insult.

As we passed the old family house in Russell Street, I asked him if he had been spoiled as a child.

'Never by the Ma and Da. But I was Granny English's favourite. D'you know she gave me my first sup of porter when I was a kid? My oul' wan used to say the granny started me on the downward path. There was a saying in Russell Street that to get enough to eat was a struggle, but to get drunk was an achievement. Myself and the granny once turned up at the Hospice for the Dying with an oul' fella we wanted to have admitted. I'd say it was the first time the Hospice had to throw out three people for being drunk, a grandmother, a prospective patient and a kid of six.'

I wasn't trying to excuse myself when I told him, 'I'd like you to know the Salkelds were poor, too, in a genteel kind of way.'

'The fighting poor of Dublin are my people,' he retorted.

But despite our backgrounds Brendan and I had much in common.

We both enjoyed walking in the Dublin mountains and swimming in the bay. In my teens I had joined An Oige, the youth-hostelling movement, and spent every weekend tramping through the countryside with my friends Pauline Parker and Nuala Maher. I once went with a group of hostellers to Scotland. Another time I toured Holland on a bicycle. And I had holidayed in Italy and Corsica.

If Brendan had learned his Republican ideals from his parents I had grown up among people who weren't hesitant in talking about nationalism. . . .

Cecil talked to Brendan on his own terms, and I sensed that Brendan understood my father's fears. I owed much to my father. In those early days in Glencree I first met artists and writers. Not far from our cottage lived Francis Stuart, the novelist, and his wife, Iseult, daughter of Maud Gonne, and their children, Catherine and Ian, who became my playmates, as did Pegeen, Liam O'Flaherty's daughter. Liam O'Flaherty recalled that at the age of five I received him graciously at our door and recited a poem for him. Joseph Campbell, the poet, lived nearby and sometimes visited our cottage, as did the folk writer, Padraic O Conaire, who set up his tent in the valley.

When we moved to Dublin, a move which saddened me because I had come to love Glencree, our home continued to be a meeting-place for writers. Their unpredictable ways led me to accept Brendan's world, although I could not pretend that I understood this world fully, just as I had to admit that there was an enigmatic side to Brendan's nature. By his very exuberance Brendan tended to be the dominant partner in our relationship, and the world he lived in seemed to embrace much more than the world of my friends. Theirs was discreet and conventional, Brendan's was spontaneous and full of surprises.

But a woman, caught up in the anticipation of marriage and a new life, longs to tell her friends about her man. My happiness had to stay hidden and I could only assume that Brendan's demand for secrecy was born out of his days in the IRA.

In another way, keeping our secret brought us closer together. My only worry was that he might find himself in trouble with the police again and would spend his wedding day behind prison bars.

NOTES

Beatrice Behan, artist and Brendan's widow, was the daughter of the well-known Irish painter Cecil Salkeld.
1. Behan was born on 9 February 1923.
2. Robert Emmet (1778–1803), Irish nationalist leader.

A Memorable Occasion*

SEAMUS DE BURCA

On one memorable occasion Brendan appeared in the shop[1] bareheaded – did he ever wear a cap? – and in a new overcoat. The overcoat should have warned me. He called me to the basement with an air of mystery. He turned towards me and pursed his mouth. He was abashed. 'To be honest.' he said, 'I was married this morning.'

'Congratulations', I said, shaking his hand warmly for the second time.

He put his second hand over mine and sighed. He had let me into a secret. One knew instinctively when Brendan wanted to hold the stage alone. I said nothing.

* *Brendan Behan: A Memoir* (Newark, Del.: Proscenium Press, 1971) p. 4. Editor's title.

'I hope,' he began again, 'I hope I am as loyal to my wife as you have been to yours.'

I started to preen myself, imagining the scene in Kildare Road when Chrissie[2] had retreated with my portable.[3]

'Now lend me a fiver', Brendan said, quickly dropping my hand. This was one five pounds I was glad to give him. He left the shop without speaking to another person, and without even telling me the name of his new bride. Even the press missed Brendan and Beatrice's wedding; at this time he was still able to live a normal private life.

The priest from Clogher Road called to Kildare Road to give Brendan the 'letter of freedom' to marry. As he sat diffidently in the parlour, he said, 'Do you know I was awfully nervous coming to this house.' The Behans had the name of being Leftist, and good Catholics blessed themselves passing the house. Brendan roared with laughter, putting the priest at his ease. 'My dear Father,' he said, 'you weren't half as nervous of coming to my house as I was of going to yours.'

NOTES

Seamus de Burca (1912–), Irish dramatist and director of theatrical costumiers in Dublin; son of the actor–playwright Patrick J. Bourke and cousin of Brendan Behan. He has just completed a book on the Queen's Royal Theatre, Dublin (1829–1969).

1. In Dame Street, Dublin.
2. De Burca's wife.
3. Brendan had borrowed de Burca's typewriter and de Burca's wife went to 70 Kildare Road to demand it back.

A Terrible Man*

SEAMUS DE BURCA

Jimmy Lynch was an assistant in Lipton's provision shop in Baggot Street in the 'fifties, after Brendan and Beatrice took up residence in Herbert Street. He got to know the Behans very well, and they did most of their shopping in Lipton's. Brendan often gave Jimmy an IOU for fifteen or thirty shillings but he always scrupulously paid his debt. Jimmy recalled how the women queued in the shop after the ten o'clock Mass in

* *Brendan Behan: A Memoir* (Newark, Del.: Proscenium Press, 1971) pp. 34–5. Editor's title.

Haddington Road. It became a kind of ritual, the women standing in line with pious faces, large prayer books and missals. On one occasion, Brendan's head appeared in the doorway, and he shouted the length of the shop at Jimmy.

'Do you know what I was wondering, Jimmy?'

'No, what?' Jimmy answered back, falling into the trap.

'If we get the Six Counties what will we do with all these foggin' Catholics?' And Brendan disappeared, laughing.

'He was a terrible man', Jimmy said.

NOTE

For a note on Seamus de Burca see p. 69.

*Borstal Boy**

JOHN MURDOCH

I played an indirect part in having *Borstal Boy* published. Brendan had tried various people without success and he asked me to read it in typescript during Horse Show week in 1956. The uncensored version was much more hilarious and outrageously funny than the final product. For Brendan found it difficult to restrain either the written or spoken word. He never wrote to please or displease anyone and he was not interested in making an impression. It must be said that in that first typescript of *Borstal Boy* there was a superabundance of oaths and swear words but no blasphemy. On one page I counted a certain four-letter word twenty-six times.

As a work of its kind this autobiographical novel was a masterpiece and the cleaning-up process did not detract from the merit of the story. I wrote to Charles Eade, Editor of the *Sunday Dispatch* in London recommending that he should serialise *Borstal Boy*. This was done and the series appeared in September and October 1956, bringing in a substantial weekly cheque to Brendan at a time when he was really hard-up. Fortunately for Brendan, Charles Eade did not fully appreciate the public appeal that *Borstal Boy* would have and he published it only in his Irish edition.

About a year later it was suggested that Brendan should try selling the same story to *The People* because the London executives of that paper were

* *The World of Brendan Behan*, ed. Sean McCann (London: New English Library, 1965), pp. 62–6. Editor's title.

not aware that it had already been serialised in the Irish editions of their rival. This idea worked and the Editor of *The People* ran the story in all editions. This not only meant a substantially bigger cheque for the author but it also attracted the attention of London publishers. So *Borstal Boy* appeared as a book with tremendous success in 1958. As a writer, the Dublin house-painter had arrived. He painted and papered no more although he retained his trade-union card right up to the time of his death.

Delivering the weekly cheque to Brendan for his *Borstal Boy* series in the *Dispatch* gave me an opportunity to see another aspect of the author's mental make-up. The cheque was sent to me from London to be handed to Brendan because at that time he had changed his address to a basement flat in Waterloo Road. I made three such deliveries, gaining much in experience in the process but on the discredit side, suffered much from a shocking hangover.

Beatrice, his wife, was not at home and there were empty bottles and tumblers all around the kitchen, on my first visit. Brendan had been entertaining some of his cronies and a good time appeared to have been had by all.

It was about noon on a bright sunny morning when I knocked and the response was a deep raucous voice to 'come in'. It was Brendan's voice and it sounded throaty, dry and crackling. 'Come in', he roared again when I was in the kitchen. The voice came from a small darkened room off the kitchen. There I found Brendan in bed in his shirt. The bedclothes were tossed into a heap on one side and some were on the floor. Brendan laughed and broke into 'The Bold Fenian Men' as he lay in bed. I could see that several upper teeth were missing. He was quick to explain that this was due to the ordinary process of dentistry and not through being involved in a fight.

Despite the hilarity and the good humour, Brendan was obviously suffering from an excruciating hangover; his half-closed eyes were slightly bloodshot; his face was flushed and he gave occasional groans. But when I produced the envelope with the cheque, it had an electrifying effect on the patient. Brendan was certainly not an avaricious person, but he clutched the cheque like a hungry child grabbing a crust. With a bound he was out of bed. Within seconds he had his trousers on; stuffed his sockless feet into laceless shoes without stooping and threw on his jacket as he was leaving the kitchen. Unwashed, unshaved and with an open-neck shirt, he grabbed me in a vice-like grip by the elbow and within a couple of minutes we were in Searson's of Upper Baggot Street.

Searson's it had to be because Brendan was barred from the nearby Waterloo House and from Devine's at the corner and Mooney's opposite did not cash cheques. Resistance on my part would have been as impossible as trying to stop Niagara Falls.

Brendan breezed into the pub like a king, distributing greetings in Irish and in English to imbibers all around. He stuffed the cash for his cheque carelessly into his pocket without even counting it. Brendan called for a pint in a cheerful mood. Presumably not to waste good drinking time and to keep things moving, he called for a glass of malt while waiting for the pint to be pulled. It was a matter of slick timing. Brendan had knocked back his glass of whiskey and had broken into a bar of a rebel song when the overflowing pint glass of Guinness arrived.

He had a voracious appetite for hard-luck stories. Within fifteen minutes he was called aside by three different characters for a whisper and each time he parted with folding money. There was no haggling. When I left in response to a phone call, Brendan was entertaining a whole party. He was in an uproariously funny mood; singing songs; reciting ballads; telling amusing stories of his Borstal days, mimicking Irish and English accents – and buying drinks.

That became a regular Behan routine until an argument started and then it happened so often that fists would fly and Brendan would be unceremoniously thrown out and told not to come back. Until he became famous as a writer, he was barred from entering many pubs in Dublin. But when Brendan became internationally known many of the publicans regretted their action. Several of them tried to induce him to return for Brendan always had the money when he had established himself as a writer and his entertainment value attracted customers.

When the next *Borstal Boy* cheque arrived, I had to consider the matter of delivery with a little more strategy. But it happened on this occasion that I had been asked to get an interview with him as well. In Searson's I was told that Brendan had been barred. He was not in Mooney's, but walking down Baggot Street I spotted him ahead of me on the far side of the street. Brendan was sober enough. As he sauntered along he was stopped by a character with another hard-luck story with the usual result.

He handed out money to ragged shoeless children. Then he stopped at a convent and knocked. He gave money to an elderly nun who opened the door. Before reaching Larry Murphy's a woman stopped Brendan and said something in a low voice. He parted with more folding money. 'Her husband is in jail for Ireland', he told me. It was all part of Brendan's other world – the part that so few knew about, even though the recipients of his charity might not always have been deserving cases.

It was on that particular visit to Larry Murphy's that he coined a dialogue to illustrate his contempt for the boastful phony. And when Brendan used his wit to poke sarcasm at an individual or an attitude of society he could be most devastating. We were listening to an elderly character boasting about his part in the 1916 Rebellion and making exaggerated claims.

Brendan's version ran like this: he overhears remarks in a snug between two voices.

Voice Number One, gruffly: 'Where were you in 1916?'

Voice Number Two, softly: 'I wasn't anywhere in 1916; I wasn't born until 1920.'

Voice Number One, sarcastically: 'Oh excuses! Always excuses!'

He used this happening frequently in his writings.

There was a similar situation in McDaid's of Harry Street where a loud-mouthed individual was addressing imbibers on his achievements as a freedom-fighter. This time Brendan had a different approach.

Exasperated, Brendan Behan got up from his seat, walked over to the individual at the counter and roared at him, 'You are far too young to have died for Ireland!'

He always had a high regard for the true Republicans and the IRA men and he never ceased to help them in a very practical way when possible.

NOTE

John Murdoch, Irish journalist and friend of Behan.

Ex-IRA Man Returns as Poet*

EDWARD GORING

Brendan Behan, the poet known as the Dylan Thomas of Ireland, was back in England yesterday – a free man at last. This ex-IRA-man, who was banned from Britain in 1939, has returned for the London premiere of a play he wrote based on his years in jail.[1]

Gaelic-speaking Behan has spent eight of his thirty-three years in prison for IRA activities.

When he tried to return to Britain six years ago he was arrested at Newhaven and deported to France. His last attempt to visit this country three years ago also failed.

'I was surprised and delighted when the British Embassy in Dublin said I was not likely to be arrested this time', he said last night.

Yesterday he made a 'sentimental journey' to a Borstal establishment in Suffolk. He was sent there for three years for possessing explosives in Liverpool.

'Heath the murderer was there and objected to my bad language',[2] laughed Behan.

* *Daily Mail* (London), 17 May 1956, p. 3.

He laughed, too, when he recalled the fourteen-year sentence he received for shooting at two detectives in Dublin.

'The judge sent me an electric coffee-pot as a wedding present', he said.

'I joined the IRA at the age of fourteen and worked for them in Liverpool, Dublin, Belfast and Cork. I don't think I would like that sort of thing – shooting at policemen – now.

'I have finished with the IRA. But I still have many friends in the movement.'

His play is called *Quare Fellow*. It is being produced by Theatre Workshop at the Theatre Royal, Stratford, E., and opens next Thursday.

NOTES

1. *The Quare Fellow* was first produced in London by Theatre Workshop at the Theatre Royal, Stratford East, on 24 May 1956.
2. Neville Heath's savage crimes (he had sadistically beaten two women to death) had appalled England at the time. Behan's reference to him was a good touch. To have been a prison-mate of his and to have shocked him with bad language made Brendan a pretty naughty boy indeed.

The Years of Fame Had Begun*

ANTHONY CRONIN

I was sitting in *Time and Tide* one morning, with, as luck would have it, a hangover ebbing and flowing inside my head, when I had an unexpected telephone call. In order to cool the ardour of certain would-be reviewers of the sort who want to come round every day and eventually to come and live with you, I had asked the girl on the switchboard to enquire for the time being who was calling, a thing I had never done before. In this case she told me that the caller would say only, 'Tell him it's Brendan.' Because the tides of hangover were at that moment beating against the walls of the skull, I did not immediately realise who it was. So I told her to ask again. And, unfortunately, after she had done so, and the same answer had been given, I was still unyielding. Then I got it. My heart sank. I had, if you can

* *Dead as Doornails: A Chronicle of Life* (Dublin: Dolmen Press; London: Calder and Boyars, 1976) pp. 161–4. Editor's title.

have such a thing, visions of diatribes, justified ones too, because if this was an overture and I knew who it was, not taking the call must have seemed what Brendan would describe as 'the act of a bollocks'.

To begin with I was right. When he was put through he said among other things that he was 'a real writer, not like some other people that were supposed to be writers and sat in offices all day'. He did his writing 'with ink and paper, not with telephones and dictaphones'.

There were no dictaphones in *Time and Tide*, but I bore with this, for old times' sake. Then he asked me to meet him for a drink. He was in Ward's Irish House in Piccadilly.

Ward's Irish House is an underground bar, suited to a race of tunnel-diggers. Brendan was with his wife and a friend and an illicit bottle of Irish whiskey. This was parked under the table in the alcove where he sat, and poured from every now and then, into the glasses provided by the house for the first drink. The procedure unnerved me. The barmen in Ward's may have been Irish, but I was used to limey legality.

I remember little of the conversation, if there was any conversation. The tides of hangover raged and frothed and I think I may have said a few stupid things. I remember saying something about his having a chip on his shoulder.

Then calamity struck, obliquely, as calamity usually will; and as is usually the case, the extent of the damage was not revealed till later.

Brendan told me he had a play coming on. This was *The Quare Fellow*, though I knew nothing about that. He asked me would I like to go to it.

I asked him when and where it was being produced.

He said, at Stratford.

I said, 'Oh, that's too far away, Brendan. I'd have to take a couple of days off from the paper to go down there.'

Strange though it may seem for a London literary man, which, after my fashion, I was in those days, I had never heard of Miss Joan Littlewood's theatre at Stratford East in the East End of London, and for some reason I thought that a production of some sort was in the offing at Stratford-on-Avon. Stratford East is of course a good way from the normal haunts of West End man, but it is not a day's journey.

Anyway, soon after, the pub closed. There had been no open breach, but there had hardly been anything else either. Still, in spite of my response to the invitation, which must by now have been rankling, when we got outside, Brendan asked me if I would come down to Fleet Street to the Press Club where apparently he had the entrée. I had a perfectly good club of my own up the road, the Caves de France, and it crossed my mind to suggest it, but I didn't, and so we parted.

A couple of forenoons later I was sitting in the York Minster with two friends when Brendan came in. He had one or two people with him and a bundle of newspapers under his arm. *The Quare Fellow* had been produced at Stratford East the night before and apparently it had been an uproarious success, but not having seen a newspaper I didn't know that either.

I half-waved. Perhaps he expected me to get up and congratulate him – I don't know. If I had read about the play's production and success I would, and indeed, should, have done.

He walked over to the table, apparently selecting with some care one of the papers from under his arm. Reaching us, he flung it down in front of me, knocking over my glass. It was the *Daily Express* and it carried quite a spread about him.[1] He had evidently taken some care that this should be right side up, legible and visible to me. There followed a diatribe, long and detailed, about some university contemporaries I had published in *The Bell*; about my bogman and bourgeois origins; and, for some reason, about my relationship with Kavanagh. Then he picked up his paper, collected his companions and, surprisingly, walked out of the pub.

My friends, to whom the diatribe had been wonderful but incomprehensible, asked me who that was.

'His name is Brendan Behan', I said.

'Ah,' they said, 'the famous Brendan Behan.'

For unbeknownst to me, the years of fame had begun.

NOTES

For a note on Anthony Cronin see p. 29.

1. John Barber, 'A Hangman Calls – A Jail Waits', *Daily Express* (London), 25 May 1956, p. 7.

A Celebrated Interview*

BEATRICE BEHAN

It was almost June and I wanted Brendan to come away to Connemara, away from the strain of the past months in London. But no sooner had we returned to Dublin than Duncan Melville, the press agent for Theatre Workshop, called us. Would Brendan go back to London to be interviewed by Malcolm Muggeridge[1] for the BBC? Brendan had not appeared on television before. He was nervous at the idea, but Duncan assured it would be good publicity for his play and improve its prospects of transferring to the West End. Brendan agreed and decided we would go by air. What was

* *My Life with Brendan* (London: Leslie Frewin, 1973) pp. 86–9. Editor's title.

the point of the long journey by sea and train for a single interview?

Brendan disliked making plans in advance, but I thought that we should book our 'plane seats at least the night beforehand. The only seats available were on a dawn flight from Dublin Airport. We got up at four in the morning to take a taxi to the airport. Duncan had suggested on the telephone that we should publicise the play by photographing Brendan standing beside a wartime bomb crater, pretending he had just blown it up.

'For Jaysus' sake, are you mad?' Brendan wanted to know. 'I don't want to be associated with that kind of activity.'

As we came down the steps of the aircraft, Brendan placed a floral hangman's noose, given him by the cast of *The Quare Fellow*, around his neck.

We went straight to Duncan's flat for breakfast, but Brendan soon became restless and we moved on to the Press Club which reminded me of an air-raid shelter. Brendan held a journalist's union card and felt at home with journalists. He loved to talk to them, and he was in talking form now.

When we arrived at the Garrick Club shortly before four o'clock he was boisterous, but not drunk. He had not eaten since breakfast, although I pleaded with him to have a steak, realising the ordeal ahead. We met Malcolm Muggeridge, and Brendan, still wearing his floral noose, began drinking Scotch because there was no draught beer. Malcolm impressed me as a gentle person and Brendan seemed relieved to learn that he would be his only interrogator. They discussed the format of the television interview and then Malcolm excused himself to go to the studios at Lime Grove. Brendan stayed drinking at the club. I knew the dangers of Brendan's whisky drinking, but although he had drunk a lot of Scotch and, by any standards, was noisy, he was not drunk.

We took a taxi to the studios where I sat for a long while watching Brendan and Malcolm rehearse the interview.

Brendan asked a producer, 'Do you think would it be all right to slip out for a couple of pints?'

'If you leave the studios, Brendan,' he was told, 'we may never track you down in time for the programme. Why not have a drink on us in the entertainment room?'

Brendan did not seem enthusiastic.

'Then why not something to eat in the canteen?'

'I don't want any of your fucking canteen food,' he replied truculently.

The entertainment room presented an array of bottles. We were introduced to Richard Dimbleby, and Brendan improvised a Dimbleby commentary on a royal tour. Dimbleby wasn't amused.

Brendan was drinking his way through a bottle of Scotch. I couldn't reason with him any further. To me this drinking was tangible proof of his anxiety about the interview and his impatience at being confined. I wondered at the BBC's refusal to allow him to go out to a pub where at least he would have found a casual atmosphere. But in the entertainment room they invited him to 'Help yourself, Brendan', which he did, liberally.

When he staggered from the room to go to the studio I knew he was in no condition to appear on television. He was drunk.

I would not have dared tell Brendan to quit the programme; that would have been as much as my life was worth. You didn't tell Brendan what to do or where to go.

Concern among the BBC executives was growing as Brendan collapsed heavily into his chair. It was my first time in a television studio and I was at a loss to explain my predicament to the harassed young men who bustled around me. I heard someone say, 'They're not *really* putting him on, are they?'

'Malcolm *wants* him on', answered another voice.

Brendan was positioned beside Malcolm. His white shirt under his tweed sports jacket was grimy after the long day in London. He sat slumped in his chair, his shoes discarded. God, I thought, he looks terribly tired. And as he came on screen and Malcolm put the first question to him, Brendan's answer was slurred and incoherent. He dragged on his cigarette and muttered a few words about his Borstal experiences. I knew it was torment for him.

'Did you meet any important people during your eight years in jail?' asked Malcolm.

'I met Neville Heath. He objected to my bad language.'

Muggeridge looked apprehensive.

'I do hope you're not going to use bad language on this programme, because that would be in extremely bad taste.'

My heart went out to Brendan as he made a feeble attempt at a smile.

'All right,' he muttered, 'I won't.'

Further conversation seemed improbable, so Malcolm invited Brendan to sing 'The Old Triangle' and Brendan obliged in a voice which sounded quite off-key.

I dared not to look at the two men directly. To me it was like a bizarre ceremony: a drunken penitent being questioned by a patient confessor. I looked at the monitor screen and noticed the cameras favouring Malcolm instead of Brendan.

I could not help admiring Malcolm's composure. Another interviewer might have lost his nerve, phrasing and rephrasing questions to which Brendan was incapable of replying. I knew the only reason Brendan did not use four-letter words was because he was exhausted.

I was relieved when the interview was cut short and Brendan heaved himself out of his chair and muttered, 'Thanks be to Jaysus that's over.'

He was not put out by his performance, not even when a distraught executive told us that calls of protest were jamming the BBC switchboard. He was only interested in getting another drink.

'Jaysus, you're a gentleman, Malcolm', Brendan told his interviewer. Then he began to sing 'The Red Flag'.

I was told the police had been called. But before they arrived Joan and Gerry[2] burst into the entertainment room and hustled Brendan out. They were appalled, they told me, at what they had seen on their screen and fearful that worse was to come. I tried to explain that if Brendan had been allowed to go out to a pub he would not have drunk so much. He needed to feel free, and you can't feel free in the claustrophobic atmosphere of a television studio. Of course, I was annoyed and embarrassed. Of course, I would have preferred if the BBC had dropped the interview. But it was not my decision. Brendan was under contract to the BBC and it was not for me to argue.

In Duncan Melville's flat the telephone was ringing. Reporters wanted to talk to Brendan.

'My husband is suffering from nervous exhaustion', I told them. 'He has been travelling since four-thirty this morning.'

Brendan surfaced beside me next day as if nothing had happened. The publicity which is the by-product of success delighted him. He went out and bought his usual armful of newspapers.

'Do you know what a bus-driver just said to me, Beatrice? He roared out of his window, "Saw you on telly last night, Paddy."'

'What did he think of your interview?' I asked.

'He couldn't understand a fucking word of it.'

'I'm not surprised.'

'But then he couldn't understand Muggeridge either.'

Neither of us could believe that after a single appearance on television Brendan had become a household name. What could I say to a man whose attitude towards journalists was, 'They've got a job to do. I can't refuse them an interview'?

NOTES

For a note on Beatrice Behan see p. 68.

1. For a note on Malcolm Muggeridge and his recollections of Behan see p. 82.
2. Joan Littlewood, the producer; and Gerald C. Raffles, the manager of Theatre Workshop.

Drunk? Sure, I'd Had a Bottle*

VINCENT MULCHRONE

Irish playwright Brendan Behan, star of the most talked-about TV interview of the year, said last night, 'Of course I was drunk.' The rumbustious, sixteen-stone Irishman threw back his dark, curly head and laughed at the furore caused by his first TV appearance.

His wife, Beatrice, showed him newspaper stories about the protests which flooded the BBC.[1]

Behan was interviewed by Malcolm Muggeridge on his highly successful play, *The Quare Fellow*, now running in London.

Behan's replies to his questioner were indistinct, sometimes incoherent. 'And not a bit of wonder', laughed Behan last night as he viewed the Thames-side scene through the bottom of a pint glass.

'I had a bottle of whiskey – good Irish whiskey – inside me before I went to the TV studios. I went there at five o'clock, and they kept me locked in the place until I went on the air at about ten.

'I had a few drops of Scotch there – but I'd better not say too much about that for I don't want to let the BBC down.

'Anyway, there I was getting a fair sup of the ould stuff in the BBC. What happened then was my fault, not the BBC's.

'I usually drink stout at home, and bitter in England. But last night I'd had plenty.

'So, I made an exhibition of myself.'

The extrovert Dubliner who has spent eight of his thirty-three years in prison for IRA activities, threw back his head and roared with laughter.

'Ashamed of myself? Not at all. I'm never ashamed.'

The BBC said there had been 'quite a number of complaints' from viewers after the broadcast. A spokesman added 'Mr Behan was nervous. He had a few drinks and the heat of the studio affected him.'

---

* *Daily Mail* (London), 20 June 1956, p. 1, where the complete title is 'Drunk? Sure, I'd Had a Bottle, Says the Quare TV Man.'

But Behan said last night, 'Nervous? Not a bit of it. You can put me down as a ham actor if you like, but I wasn't nervous.'

To prove it he sang a couple of verses of O'Casey's song, 'Red Roses for Me', to the delight of the saloon bar.

'I'm sorry', he said, 'if I've let the governor of my old Borstal down and sorry if I annoyed Malcolm Muggeridge – a real English gentleman. And *they*', he added, 'are a rare breed nowadays.

'The first man I saw this morning was a bus conductor who recognised me. He said, "I understood your play, but I couldn't understand you – and I'll tell you something else, I can't understand you now."

'I love the Londoners. London is the greatest city in the world. I agree with Dr Johnson. The man that's tired of London is tired of life.'

NOTES

1. See, for example, 'Had a Load On', *Daily Mirror* (London), 20 June 1956, p. 5; "Tis a Quare Tale Now", *Daily Sketch* (London), 20 June 1956, p. 16; 'A Sorry Morning for Mr Behan: TV Playwright "Didn't Really Mean to Get Drunk"', *Daily Express* (London), 20 June 1956, p. 9; Philip Phillips, 'Mr Behan Himself – The Quare Fellow', *Daily Herald* (London), 19 June 1956, p. 1; 'A "Quare Fellow" on TV Puzzles Viewers', *Belfast Telegraph*, 19 June 1956, p. 6; 'Such a Strange TV Interview', *Daily Mirror* (London), 19 June 1956, p. 24; B.-R. G., 'A Bigger Helping', *The Star* (London), 19 June 1956, p. 6; 'Black Monday on BBC TV', *Sunderland Echo*, 21 June 1956, p. 4; 'Mr Behan Feels Fine', *Evening Standard* (London), 19 June 1956, p. 4; Leslie Ayre, 'Opening the Windows', *Evening News* (London), 19 June 1956, p. 3; Maurice Richardson, 'Television', *Observer* (London), 24 June 1956, p. 8; 'Defiant Gesture', *Glasgow Evening News*, 19 June 1956, p. 4; John Harris, 'The Quare Fellow Says " I Was Drunk"', *Daily Herald* (London), 20 June 1956, p. 4; Peter Black, 'Teleview', *Daily Mail* (London), 19 June 1956, p. 12; 'The Quare Fellow', *Northern Whig* (Belfast), 20 June 1956, p. 2; 'The Way It Goes', *Sunday Express* (London), 24 June 1956, p. 11; Harry Mitchell, 'Television: BBC Last Night', *Evening Chronicle* (Manchester), 19 June 1956, p. 5; and Cyril Aynsley, 'Man on TV "Had a Few Drinks"', *Daily Express* (London), 19 June 1956, p. 1. See also 'BBC Reply on Artists' Drinks', *Daily Telegraph* (London), 23 June 1956, p. 9.

Brendan Behan at Lime Grove*

MALCOLM MUGGERIDGE

Characteristically of this crazy time, it was appearing drunk on television, not his plays and writings, which first aroused public interest in Brendan Behan. As I was the interviewer concerned in this hilarious episode, I should like, now that the poor fellow is dead, and while my memory of it is still clear, to record exactly what happened. It was the excellent idea of Catherine Dove, then working on *Panorama*, to get Behan to Lime Grove. His play, *The Quare Fellow*, was running, under Miss Littlewood's spirited direction, out at Stratford. Though it had been well reviewed, no West End management had evinced any interest in it. On the morning after Behan's *Panorama* appearance, Miss Littlewood told me in her amusing, dry way, she had five eager inquiries.

I arranged to meet Behan at the Garrick Club in the early evening. He arrived there, in a fairly high condition, with his delightful wife and carrying some kind of a wreath he had acquired in the course of the day's festivities. One or two members peeped in curiously as we took a few noisy drinks together before leaving for Lime Grove. There, in the entertainment room, refreshment continued to be available, and Behan was soon singing, shouting obscenities in his customary style.

The other *Panorama* items were perfect. Woodrow Wyatt was to question two brasshats from the War Office on Civil Defence. They were equipped with the inevitable map and long pointer. Then there was an item about finishing schools, in which a finishing-school headmistress and some of her charges were to appear. At one point they all filed into the entertainment room, heard Behan holding forth, and then abruptly about-turned and filed out again. After they had gone, Behan turned to me and asked with some anguish, 'Didn't I see a lot of pretty girls in here just now?' I explained that he had been dreaming: we were in a place of dreams.

As Behan grew drunker and more boisterous, doubts began to be felt in the higher BBC echelons as to whether he should be allowed to appear at all. I argued strongly that he should. After all, I contended, somewhat speciously, walking up and down a corridor nervously with Leonard Miall,

* *New Statesman* (London), LXVII (27 Mar 1964) 488.

this is the man who wrote *The Quare Fellow*. Let us, then, present him as he really is. Miall in the end agreed, only adding beseechingly, 'If he uses the word c—, don't laugh.' I readily accepted this condition. As it happens, I do not find the word particularly amusing.

On the set it was apparent that Miall need have had no apprehension. Behan was incapable of speaking coherently at all, which perhaps, in the circumstances, was just as well. He took off his boots and muttered something about 'wanting a leak'. To have tried to arrange for him to have one would have been too complicated. I decided to take the risk. When the cameras came on us, I put my first question and, allowing Behan to mumble a little, answered it myself. All television interviews are really like this. Behan's was simply an extreme case. Towards the end of our time, I asked him if he would care to sing. In a thin, reedy voice he managed to give a rendering of a song in his play.

Afterwards, we returned to the entertainment room. I left him there roaring out the 'Internationale' at the top of his voice, with the two War Office brasshats giving every indication of being about to join in. It was the pleasantest and most rewarding evening I ever spent in Lime Grove.

In his subsequent remarks to the press about the interview, Behan was extremely considerate and friendly in his references to me. I liked him, except, of course, that, like all drunks, he was a fearful bore. Drunkenness is a device to avoid having to think of anything to say. As Johnson observed once to Boswell, it leads to a confusion of words with ideas, which is conversationally disastrous.

NOTE

Malcolm Muggeridge (1903–), English journalist and writer.

Behanism*

MYLES NA GOPALEEN [BRIAN O'NOLAN]

It is not unexpected that people should ask this simple question – is he a human Behan at all.

I believe he is. I seen him. I know him for years. Matter of fact, you could say that I reared him, paid his university fees (he never qualified for anything in that quarter but forthwith resumed his studies in the

* *Irish Times* (Dublin), 23 July 1956, p. 6.

competing academy, the university of life), though he always acknowledged his obligation to me, and in his queer way harbours a little respect for me still. I intend no pun when I use that word 'still'.

Perhaps the situation was better put by a plumber I had a pint with two nights ago.

'Do you know that man Been?'

I was cautious. I ventured a guarded 'No', embroidering the nakedness of the syllable with an inquiry as to whether Mr Been was a member of the BRM motor-racing team, then volunteering an opinion that that concern was no damn use, never won races, and was bringing disgrace on the British motor-car industry. My attitude was that of disengagement. I did not wish to be involved with my plumber friend on an artistic issue. From this distance in time, this attitude may look arrogant, conceited, destitute of the humility of the true artist who, properly attired, wears humility as a cloak. The distance in time was only two days. My motive was a smaller, possibly a meaner one. I did not want the Boss to come up and say 'Now, gents, yez'll have to keep yer voices down!'

But the plumber first of all asked me whether I had any objections to himself having his own notions about art. I said NO. My main reason for saying it was that I was sure he would hit me if I said YES. He then said that Mr Been was a tradesman, and his faaather was a tradesman, and damn good tradesmen, and what about it?

I said, 'Nothing about it.'

I relieved the mounting tension somewhat by saying that we were all tradesmen in our own way. I felt terribly like Leopold Bloom, Esq.[1] I told my friend that I could paper a wall, put up shelves, distemper the pantry, give the dog a fried sausage for his breakfast – all single-handed. I could put a new washer into a leaking tap, dig the garden with a patent spade of my own design, mow the lawn (of all things), go to Leopardstown races in a train without paying any fare. But my friend seemed to take little interest in my litany of boasts, none of which was unfounded. He was thinking deeply. Obviously, he despised me. He probably inferred, erroneously, that I lived in Pembroke Road, Dublin. I feared that his next utterance would be terrible. I took the only precaution available in that lethal situation. I ordered two more pints.

I believe, the plumber said, that Mr Been is a class of a pote.

Don't know about that. Most of us have written poetry in our time. And most us are extremely sorry for ourselves on that account.

Tell you wan thing about Mr Been. He wrut a play. Right?

Right.

It was turned down be that crowd in the Mechanics Theatre, th' Abbey, and had to be put on at the heel of the hunt in some sort of somewhere. Now it's in the middle of Lunnon. And they tell me it's going across to America. What's wrong with that?

Nothing at all.

Know what I mean? There's another crowd in this country that gets out a wee book now and again and has a whole crowd over the head of it drinking small sherries in the High Berinian.² Your man just clatters a play off the typewriter and takes the whole world into his lap. What's wrong with that?

Not a thing...

NOTES

Brian O'Nolan (1912–66; wrote also under pseudonyms 'Flann O'Brien' and 'Myles na Gopaleen'), Irish novelist and dramatist.

1. Leopold Bloom, a Jewish advertising salesman in James Joyce's novel *Ulysses* (1922). Bloom is Any Man, plodding through the daily routine of living – visiting bars, restaurants, newspaper offices, hospitals, and brothels of Dublin; he hopes for something out of the ordinary but must be satisfied with the tawdry.

2. The Royal Hibernian Hotel, Dublin.

Fourteen-Pint Behan Switches to Milk*

Brendan Behan, thirty-three-year-old author of the successful play *The Quare Fellow* is in hospital. He told me yesterday, 'I am trying to get rid of a hangover to end all hangovers. This one has lasted ten years.

'The doctors tell me I must cut out serious drinking. Man, it's desperate. I might as well not be alive.'

As we talked in a cream-painted, four-bed ward of the hospital just around the corner from his Dublin flat, the curly-haired, fifteen-stone Irishman sipped a glass of milk.

'I suppose things came to a head when I was in London the other week for the first night of my play', he said.¹

'I had a great party with the stage hands. Only this time I couldn't shake off my usual hangover the morning after.

'Then I was having a glass of malt (Irish whiskey) with a doctor friend of mine here in Dublin last week and he said, "You're sick, man. Come with me."'

* *Daily Mail* (London), 3 Aug 1956, p. 3.

'Before I knew where I was, they had tucked me up snugly in here', waving a pudgy hand round.

Since then Brendan has not touched a drop. How does he feel? 'Thirsty, man. But all they'll give me is tea and milk.'

Over the past ten years Brendan claims he has drunk fourteen pints of stout or two bottles of whiskey or the equivalent a day.

'Now that is over with. And I don't think I'll ever be the same man again.'

'Fitter maybe. But happier? Definitely not. I don't regret one minute of the last ten years, though I must admit I don't remember much of them.'

He hauled a battered typewriter from his locker. 'This has helped to keep my mind off a pint glass', he said. 'And these too', pointing to twelve volumes of Proust's *Remembrance of Things Past*.

Brendan has also cut out sugar, but he is getting double helpings of lunch and dinner – on doctor's orders.

Each night Behan gets a visit from his pretty wife, Beatrice.

She said last night, 'I am glad he is having this rest. Brendan has not been well for some time.'

He hopes to leave hospital after another week. Then he plans to go to London again and see his play from the stalls.

'I really haven't seen it yet. When I do I'll be stone-cold sober.'

NOTE

1. Behan is here referring to the West End production of *The Quare Fellow* at the Comedy Theatre on 24 July 1956, and not to the earlier East End production.

The Woman on the Corner of the Next Block to Us*

BRENDAN BEHAN

I am driven to write by murophobia – the fear of having to paint walls, or doors, or anything else, or having to work at my trade as a house- and ship-painter.

There is no better way of escaping hard work for a boy without capital or a religious vocation than writing.

* *Vogue* (New York), CXXVIII (Dec 1956) 85–6.

THE WOMAN ON THE CORNER OF THE NEXT BLOCK TO US

The first thing you have to do is to get the idea into other people's heads that you are a writer.

I started by going into pubs in Grafton Street and writing for little magazines about being a house-painter. There was one of these magazines called *The Bell* and it went in for this sort of writing, and writing about Donegal fishermen and Monaghan bogmen and Belfast shipwrights.

Any day of the week, in the *Bell* office, you could meet these fishermen and bogmen taking up their manuscripts, and getting away from fishing and turf-cutting by writing about it.

Those of them who could speak Irish I could exchange greetings with, but I could not understand the English-speakers very well. I speak Dublin, Belfast, Cockney, Geordie, rhyming slang, but like Nehru, I have no common tongue with the majority of my countrymen from the interior. Especially when they had a few issues of *Horizon* digested and mixed the names of the English literary great into their speeches:

'Hah sure Aydit is a naice semple wamman at the back avitt, aye shewerly, aye. And more betoken and where would you lave Satchamarverell? And Aveleen Waw has the Ting, aye, an' Sirril, aye, and Graves – aye but you wouldn't be sure a Raine, owenly sometimes.'

I didn't know whether I had the Thing or not. What I did know was that whatever about the pen being mightier than the sword – it's lighter than the stockbrush.

And I envied these bogmen one thing. Half their battle in setting up in this business was won by the time they got on the train for Dublin. They were amongst new people who would accept them straight away as literary men because they had never known them in any other guise. The Dublin people would accept them as literary men all the more readily because they looked like bogmen.

But I had to go back through the roads of Crumlin Corporation Housing Estate, and pass the woman on the corner of the next block to us. She'd shout from the window or from the garden, 'Can you not get e'er a job?'

In the morning she was as bad. I'd go down the road about half-past nine to have a good walk into the city and chew over in my mind a short story for *The Bell*, which by this time was being printed on a paper made of oats or something, so that it looked almost as wholesome as its content, and she'd shout, 'Do you know what time it is? All the men is gone to their work two hours ago. Have you a bad way of lying that you couldn't get up?' And I'd snake down the road hiding from the woman amongst the schoolchildren.

Sometimes there were literary parties and I'd come into my own, as a house-painter, and a proletarian, and I'd come home in the dawn, with my head filled with Portuguese Burgundy and Cork gin, a little unsteadily but happy, the sounds of old ballads and Pisan cantos still in my ears, and hear her, risen on her elbow from beside her sleeping lord, screech from the bedroom window, 'Are you on the night shift these times?'

As it became clear to her that I had no intention of painting any more, and that I had resigned from the building trade, she'd shout sadly after me, as I fled down the road towards Grafton Street, 'Do you never think of your poor mother?' and 'Are you going in with them that will neither work nor want?' That was one evening she saw my name in the *Radio Éireann Programme*, and thought I had become an actor or a commentator on Gaelic football matches.

Since those days I have been asked, and publicly, many awkward questions; did I plead guilty or not guilty, was I drunk on TV, but I fled from them and went back home, myself and Beatrice, and lived in peace – till one day ago Beatrice said I should go up and see my mother.

I went up to Crumlin in a taxi, and cowered down in the back as we passed the house of the woman on the corner. I needn't have troubled. She was in the house talking to my mother.

I pulled out a handful of English gold and suggested we adjourn to the Floating Ballroom for a drink.

She greeted me a bit weakly, but rallied when we got to the pub and asked, 'Do you not think it's a bit early in the day for you to be drinking a glass of whisky?' And after she had a couple of glasses herself, she asked when I was going to pull myself together?

We were joined by her two sons, and she said, 'These is Mick and Seamus, and' – indicating one gloomy-looking youth – 'he's an IRA man, and he's a Common-unionist.'

'Listen', said Mick, 'are you a bourgeois decadent?'

'No,' says I, 'but I'm saving up.'

'Well,' asks Seamus, 'is it true you're going to let down your country by writing for a stage-Irish magazine called *Brogue*?'

'Yis, 'tis', said I, rolling my eyes – my first exercise since we opened in the West End.

My First Meeting with Brendan Behan*

IAIN HAMILTON

Brendan Behan is dead, and I had thought of him as indestructible. Our first meeting was in January 1957. I went to Dublin in the tender care of

* Extracted from 'Among the Irish', *Encounter*, XXIII (Oct 1964) 36–7. Editor's title.

Gerard Fay of *The Guardian* and Brian Inglis of the *Spectator*. While they were off about their business I was after Behan, whose name at that time was quite unknown in England except to the police. Irish friends had told of a roaring boy with a real talent. An autobiographical fragment of thirty-odd pages of typed foolscap had been circulating for a year or two. Get hold of Brendan, Val Iremonger[1] advised me; read the typescript; sign him up; and pray God he'll finish the work.

So there I was on the job, with the enthusiasm of a man new to publishing, a predilection for the Irish, and a certain sceptical caution engendered by much reading of English or Anglo-Irish writers embittered or disillusioned by their experiences among 'the all-drinking, all-talking, all-bitching, non-writing writers of the Dublin pubs'. I looked for Behan and failed. But there was plenty to occupy me otherwise. Seamus Kelly had written a couple of paragraphs in his *Irish Times* column, announcing that I was in Dublin on the hunt for Irish writers and inciting all and sundry to dig out their piles of typescript, ancient or modern, and bring them along to the Shelbourne. I could hardly get out of my room for the memoirs of wars both civil and of independence, and many an engaging old warrior lay in wait in the lobby.

At four o'clock in the afternoon a day or two after our arrival we were sitting in the lounge of the Shelbourne, mulling over some weighty but cryptic remarks about reunification that the Taoiseach,[2] Eamon de Valera, had let fall to us during an interview. Behan suddenly rolled down on us, his wife Beatrice behind him. He had an old briefcase under his arm, and in it the thirty-odd pages of typescript I was so anxious to see. But there had to be preliminaries before I was allowed to look inside: a mutual sizing-up process.

Well then, what was he to me, now that he was there in the flesh, already half a legend, bulky, scruffy, unshaven, a touch musty, a shade elated? Within five minutes I had no doubt at all that here was a person quite unique, a man of a kind I had never met before. I am not referring to his appearance, or his manner, or to what he said, or to that generosity of character and personality which was immediately apparent in any conversation with him, and not at all to his 'outrageousness', that 'stage Irishness' which he cultivated, I think, less to please the English and Americans than to needle his more self-conscious and respectable fellow-Dubliners struggling earnestly against the image imposed on them years ago by comics who had taken their cue from the hostile English caricaturists of the nineteenth century. No, what struck me was this, that whatever else he was, Behan was God-branded. I don't know how else to put it. Among other odours, that of sanctity was predominant. It might have been Coleridge's mariner who was talking to me.

And what was I to him? A bloody Presbyterian Scots chancer on the make, too neatly dressed, with a moustache a little too British-military for comfort, a phony out to tie him up and render him down, if possible, into publisher's profit? Something like that to begin with, I think. But maybe it was only the uncanny feeling that this man could see straight into the depths of his interlocutor. No matter: we embarked on a verbal investigation of the universe which went on non-stop for six hours. Huge volumes of whiskey and stout lubricated the dialogue. It was Behan who set the pace, and his rule was clear: drink for drink. We moved from the Shelbourne lounge to the Shelbourne Rooms, and from the Rooms (when Behan's illustrative snatches of song began to alarm the staff) to a corner of the deserted ballroom, and from the ballroom to O'Neill's in Merrion Row, and from O'Neill's to O'Donohue's, and from O'Donohue's to a pub whose name I've forgotten somewhere off the south side of St Stephen's Green. By ten o'clock Behan must have conceded that there was some decent humanity behind my unprepossessing front, for by that time I was in possession of the briefcase. We parted then for the evening. Fay and I had to go on to a party at Blackrock. When at length I got to bed and opened the briefcase, the lines of spattered typescript wavered and wobbled behind the fumes that my very pores were exuding. But I got the message: those few opening pages were like a crystal of the whole man, who seemed in himself an impossible embodiment of all the extremes of Dublin. It was perfectly clear to me that I had the beginning of something extraordinary in my unsteady hand.[3]

NOTES

Iain Hamilton (1920–   ), English author and journalist.
  1. Valentin Iremonger (1918–   ), Irish poet and diplomat who started his career as an actor.
  2. President of the Irish Republic.
  3. *Borstal Boy* was published by Hutchinson in October 1958. Iain Hamilton was an editor at this firm.

His New Play Is Loaded*

KENNETH ALLSOP

'Now you be having a look for the new play', Brendan Behan shouted to his wife, Beatrice, while he tipped out some whiskey for himself and for me. 'I'm a bit busy.' Beatrice began rummaging among piles of newspapers.

* *Irish Digest* (Dublin), LIX, no. 1 (Mar 1957) 31–2.

The thirty-three-year-old playwright who wrote last year's success *The Quare Fellow* settled back into reminiscing about his life as a political prisoner, signwriter, merchant seaman, playwright, poet, and Dublin roaring boy.

It was late afternoon and we were swimming, slowly and gracefully, towards the end of a long Dublin lunch.

'During my eight years as a political prisoner of the British', Brendan was saying, when Beatrice surfaced from behind the coal scuttle with a wad of different sized, stained sheets covered with pencillings.

'You'll be the mother of a bishop', Brendan congratulated her. 'Well, here it is, back with me.' He held it at arm's length and eyed it like the snout of a loaded revolver.

It is, in fact, a loaded play. *The Hostage*, which Behan had planned long before the Egyptians seized Lieutenant Moorhouse in that Port Said alley, is strangely parallel. It describes the taking of a National Service man as a hostage by the IRA.

'Ten years ago in Strangeways Prison I stopped trying to find political solutions and began being a writer', he told me.

'I don't argue the issues. I mirror what happens to the people involved. This play is about the ordinariness of people – which is an extraordinary thing at such times.

'The only solution I suggest is for people not to allow themselves to be fooled by the Establishments of any side.

'Some people say they've got friends on both sides. I'm proud to have enemies on both sides. I won't talk about Partition and all the killing that's going on up on the border now.

'I can't be indifferent to the fact that young Irishmen on both sides are being killed. Yet, as the case of Lieutenant Moorhouse showed, one man's death can be more significant than the issues involved.'

This house-painter's son, who left school at thirteen (by mutual agreement between him and the headmaster), has felicitously fallen into the garrulous, brilliant company of Wilde, Shaw, Joyce, O'Casey and Beckett, all sons of Dublin.

In the city he is recognised as easily and from as far off as a bus. And a similar watchfulness is observed as his rubber-tyred personality comes thundering into view. He is a buoy of a bhoy.

But beneath his billowing shape are tiny, delicate feet, invisible under bell-bottom trousers, so that he appears to be whizzing along on castors. His face glows like a Galway sunset. He hosepipes his conversation around him, quenching opposition into silence.

Periodically he flies to an isolated cottage on the West Coast, and there rises at 5 a.m. and writes hard.

He is working on an account of his prison career. With five productions chalked up for *The Quare Fellow* and another due in New York, Behan now has more money than ever before in his life.

'Which isn't good for my writing', he said as we walked through a scything Irish Sea wind. 'I work better when I'm skint. Then I shall make an onslaught on London with *The Hostage*.'

He stopped and grabbed my arm. 'There you are,' the ex-house-painter said, 'didn't I tell you I was a proletarian writer? Dublin will never forget my work.'

There on the wall of an hotel were tall black letters, the output of an earlier period. *No Parking* they said.

NOTE

Kenneth Allsop, English writer and BBC commentator.

Half Angel, Half Beast*

JOHN MONTAGUE

'For myself as well as Madeline,' Montague recalls, 'these few years were a joy, despite the occasional awkwardness of dealing with Brendan. I was very fond of him. He seemed to me half angel, half beast. On the one hand a very handsome little man with delicate feet and hands and a quick intuitive mind: on the other, a beast, with a crooked mouth that spat poison at people. Never at me, however, though I had to put manners on him several times. I think he always respected people who stood up to him.

'He was at the height of his powers in 1957, a formidable little bull crackling with energy and affection for the world.'

NOTE

John Montague (1929–), the Irish poet, lived a few doors down from the Behans in Herbert Street at this time. He remembers Brendan as 'nearly happy and working at his best'. Brendan used to drop in to Montague's flat nearly every day to talk French to Madeline, his wife, who was from Paris.

* Ulick O'Connor, *Brendan Behan* (London: Hamish Hamilton, 1970) pp. 190–1. Editor's title.

Brendan Behan Fought for Franco!*

BEATRICE BEHAN

By late March the Mediterranean sun was strong. The garden and terraces hummed with dragonflies and a silver haze hung over the sea. Standing on the patio I could hear the distant tinkle of goat-bells.

To cool ourselves Brendan and I would go swimming from the beach at Figueretas. The locals thought we were crazy; it was still winter to them; but the water was clear and not at all cold.

Sometimes, in the afternoon, we would sit outside Francisco's drinking our Alicante wine and watching the happenings of San Jorge. It was a way of life I had dreamed of; it reminded me of summers in a lazy Irish village. In the evenings we would go down to Ibiza and join the drop-outs and the retired English people in 'Dirty' Domingo's.

Among the English was a former army brigadier who, I sensed, disliked Brendan. He and his wife made it clear they thought Brendan's drinking and bad language was letting the side down.

One evening when we met Desmond and Ayllie[1] at the bar I noticed the town doctor playing a game of chess in a quiet corner with one of the locals. They said he was the largest man on the island; he was powerfully built and well over six feet tall.

Brendan had been told that the doctor had served in Stalingrad with Franco's Blue Division. When the doctor walked across to the bar to collect his drinks, Brendan said in a loud voice, 'You had no fucking business to be in Stalingrad.'

I pretended I hadn't heard him and continued to talk to Desmond and Ayllie. The doctor just shrugged his shoulders and resumed his seat. But Brendan was in an aggressive mood. He continued to shout insults across the room.

Just then the Brigadier and his wife walked into the bar.

'For God's sake,' I whispered to Desmond, 'don't let him draw the Brigadier on us.'

* *My Life with Brendan* (London: Leslie Frewin, 1973) pp. 110–13. Editor's title.

But already the Brigadier, flushed with drink, was bearing down on Brendan, who had started to sing a Republican ballad to rile the doctor.

'Stop that singing at once!' the Brigadier ordered. And to Pedro behind the bar, 'Can't you put this man out?'

Brendan swung round angrily to face his objector.

'I'll sing if I fucking well want to sing.'

He grabbed the Brigadier's shirt front. 'You're the bastard who insulted my friend Henry.'[2] He took a swipe which was apparently aimed at the Brigadier's jaw, but the Brigadier's wife, a small, blonde woman, sprang between them.

'Don't you dare strike my husband!' she cried, her hands outstretched like claws, reaching for Brendan's face.

Then Brendan did something which shocked me. As the little woman tried to scratch his face he snarled and, puckering his lips, spat at her.

I had seen Brendan drunk, abusive, even violent, but this was the first time I saw him spit like a cat.

Pedro was horrified. Above the noise he appealed for order. 'Señors! *Por favor*, please, no more!' But his voice was drowned in the din.

Desmond and Henry joined in the mêlée. The doctor in the corner continued with his game of chess, apparently indifferent to the row that raged around him. He was jolted rudely as Brendan and the Brigadier, locked in combat, went hurtling across the table, upsetting glasses, bottles and chessmen on the floor.

I heard myself say to Ayllie, 'Can't Desmond get him out of here?'

But the doctor acted swiftly. He rose to his feet like an offended headmaster and gripping Brendan tightly by the coat collar flung him out of the bar as though he were an ill-behaved schoolboy.

A few days later Ayllie and I were sitting outside Francisco's, watching Desmond taking photographs of Brendan as he posed beside his barrel of Alicante wine, when a black Mercedes swung into the street and braked to a halt beside the *cantina*. Two men in dark glasses got out. They were wearing lightweight suits and smoking cigars.

Brendan looked at Desmond.

'The fucking cops in my life again. What the hell have I done now?'

The two men walked directly over to him.

'Señor Behan?' one of them enquired.

'That's me', acknowledged Brendan.

'The *Jefe* wishes to see you. Please come with us.'

He asked them if his wife could accompany him.

'Si, la señora también', they agreed.

The locals watched curiously as we stepped into the Mercedes. We were driven down the mountain road to the *jefatura*, the police headquarters in Ibiza. There we sat in a small room for what seemed an interminable time. At length Brendan was taken into another room. I sat wondering when I would see him again. I recalled that friends had warned him to avoid

Spanish jails at all costs. Spanish prison authorities, they told him, had a habit of forgetting about their prisoners and losing the cell keys.

But after about an hour Brendan returned.

'What's wrong?' I asked him.

'I've been given a lecture about gargling and fighting. It's not the custom here and they don't like the *extranjeros* doing it.'

'What will happen to you?'

Brendan shrugged.

'I told the *Jefe* I was *Irlandés* and *mucho católico* and that I love the *españols*. So he just took my name and address.'

When we got outside Brendan told me he was certain the Brigadier's wife had denounced him. Desmond had warned us about the Spanish custom of *denuncia*. All your enemy need do is complain about you to the nearest policeman.

Next morning as Brendan was writing on the patio I heard a knock at the door. A sweating young *Guarda Civil* stood there mopping his brow after the climb from the village. I invited him to come inside and offered him a glass of Alicante wine which he accepted and swallowed in one long gulp.

As soon as Brendan entered the living-room the policeman pulled an official document from his pocket and handed it to him.

We understood the document to state that, contrary to Rule 36 of Spanish law, Brendan had caused a disturbance in a public place and had been fined *cuincuenta pesetas*. When the policeman had left, Brendan having wished him 'Long life', we went down to Francisco's to discover how much *cuincuenta pesetas* amounted to. It was more than three pounds, which we didn't happen to have. So we set off towards the town in search of friends who might lend us some money. Desmond and Ayllie gave us a portion of it and Henry the balance.

We hurried to the *tabacalero* and paid the fine. Brendan was given a long roll of paper, not unlike a toilet roll, with official stamps spaced at intervals. We took this paper to the Governor's office. The Governor was a fat man who joked with Brendan in Spanish and handed him back one piece of the roll of paper, which was evidently the official receipt.

We didn't know then that the Governor had made out a deportation order against Brendan.

It was Desmond who brought us the news. 'I told the Governor it wasn't a very nice way to treat two Irishmen, men who had fought side by side with General O'Duffy[3] on the streets of Madrid.'

'We *what*?'

'Fought side by side with O'Duffy', Desmond repeated with a sardonic smile.

'That Fascist bastard!' Brendan snarled.

'He saved our skin, Brendan. The Governor tore up the deportation order as soon as he heard you had fought for Franco.'

'Well,' said Brendan, 'aren't you the flower of the flock, Mackey?'

NOTES

In January 1958, Brendan and Beatrice Behan went to Ibiza, a primitive island off the eastern Spanish coast just outside the Gulf of Valencia. For a note on Beatrice Behan, see p. 68.

1. Desmond and Ayllie Mackey, an Irish couple from Dublin whom the Behans met in Ibiza.
2. An American who was living in Ibiza.
3. Eoin (Owen) O'Duffy (1892–1944), Irish soldier who was put in charge of the forces of the Irish Free State in 1924. He organised and led the Irish brigade fighting on the side of General Franco in Spain (1936–7).

Brendan Behan*

RODERICK W. CHILDERS

Talking about Brendan Behan is an easy task. He was a wonderful, irreverent, decent person who delighted his friends and scorched his enemies. The first time I met him he was sitting atop a ladder during his lunch break, drinking from a bottle of Irish whisky and reading a book by Camus. It was about 1950. A friend of mine, Ralph Cusack, knew Brendan and asked me to come along to Harcourt Street, where Brendan was painting a sign on the bridge during some general reconstruction work.

There we found this young man sitting on the ladder. I climbed up, introduced myself and accepted a swig from his bottle. We came down and went over to the nearby construction shack. Brendan grabbed the telephone and placed a long-distance call to Sean O'Casey, who lived in Devon, jabbering away for about twenty minutes in a hodgepodge of Irish and English. It must have been shock when the construction firm got the bill – for by the time they did no doubt Brendan was on another job.

Brendan is known all over the world for his writing and drinking, not necessarily in that order. What most of his friends remember about him, though, was his singing and story-telling. He was a troubadour, what the Irish might call a Shanacus. Most people in Ireland, if they were asked about Brendan, would say: 'He was a great story-teller and mimic, a great singer, and fierce with the drink.' He was also kind, a champion of the wretched and the poor, and always vigorously anticlerical...a trait viewed less seriously in Ireland than in America.

He painted houses and the inside of houses right up until about 1955.

---

* *Chicago Today*, III (1966) 50–4.

Prior to that he was only published in a small European magazine called *Transition*. *The Quare Fellow* was his first stage success. He was incredibly generous with his money, standing everybody drinks, talking continuously, and when he got tight, rebelliously. His repertoire of Irish songs stretched from the Napoleonic period through the Troubles and included many of his own inventions. His stories were glorious. There was the one he loved to tell about his part in the Irish Pilgrimage to Lourdes during the Anno Sancto, 1950. Brendan and an American friend, Ronny Thirst, were up against it in Paris. They had been cadging drinks and food for some time and were in a bistro one night, just about to give up. In walked this huge, gaunt Swede, aged about forty. Brendan told the story this way:

'My name is Olaf Svenson. I have a PhD from the University of Oslo. I have an MA from the University of Durham in England. I have a research grant to study the social behaviour of slime moulds, which I have received from the University of Ankara. I have a secondary BA from the University of Catania in Sicily. I am on leave from the University of Gothenburg. I have just been left a very large legacy by a wood magnate, a remote relation from northern Sweden.'

'Well, that's fine. How about showing us a little bit of your old Swedish beneficence.'

'Very well. *Garçon!* Three glasses of champagne.'

'Bottles', says Brendan.

They lived off the Swede with 17 million degrees for about three weeks. Then he disappeared. Next came the Irish Pilgrimage, headed for Lourdes under the command of a Father Flynn, a gentle country priest who had never heard of Brendan.

The first meeting took place, naturally, in a bar. The priest heard Brendan sing 'The Holy City', and asked Brendan and Thirst to join the pilgrimage.

'Well, Father, I'd like to, but we'd feel badly. You know, Ronny and myself have no money at all. I wouldn't like to be living off you. Good God, on a sacred thing like this, you'd want to pull your own end of things.'

'Now, Brendan, don't worry about that. I will only ask you one thing: If you'd be ever so kind as to carry the cross the last part of the way into Lourdes. As you know we're leaving Paris on the train and we get off at a place twenty miles from Lourdes. Our fine body of men and girls will then march the last twenty miles, led by you with the cross.'

'Well Father, just how big is this cross?'

'It's nothing. Just a couple of sticks tied together.'

'I'll do it.'

Then Brendan, with his wonderful sense of the ridiculous, told how they got on the train, rode to this little town, had a few gargles, as he called drinks, and got up the next morning for the last twenty miles.

'I got up early and went down to collect the cross. What did I find? Two monster railway ties, nailed together.

'I started off with these two railway ties toward Lourdes. In the first hour we fell back about a mile behind the main body. By the second hour we were five miles behind, I suppose. Thirst had a bottle of whisky, and the going was slow, real slow. Round about the third hour we sat down on a bridge, and Thirst, with a deep reverence in his eyes, said to me, "Brendan, for the love of Jesus, throw that cross in the river."

'Between the two of us, we managed to heave the cross into the water. It floated away, and we finished the bottle of whisky.

'We got into Lourdes just as the High Mass was about to start. All the groups were at their station except the Irish, who were waiting on the outskirts of town for their cross. I hate to tell you what went on. There were bad words. Real bad words.

'A cross was bought in a religious store – and I carried it the last stretch.

'That night I made up for the trouble by singing "The Holy City" – 135 times. Throughout we had plenty of gargles. There was one thing about the Irish Pilgrimage, they surely knew how to break out the gargles once all the religion was out of the way.'

Another story he loved to tell was the one about going to the greyhound races with two of his chums and a greyhound. This one, like many of Brendan's stories, had several versions, one of which was published in *Brendan Behan's Island: An Irish Sketchbook*. I like this, a different version, the best:

Brendan, a Baptist, and a Roman Catholic set off to a greyhound racecourse outside of Dublin. The race was to be held in a stadium in which an American priest was holding a Rosary Crusade. This is where everyone says the rosary, endlessly, and onward. When the Rosary Crusade ended, the race would start. The essential part of this story is that the dog the lads were carrying was heavily fortified with benzedrine which is, of course, against Irish greyhound-racing rules. They'd given the dog an injection just before they left Dublin and were depending on the Rosary Crusade to be over on schedule at 8 p.m. Everything had been timed perfectly. They had a couple of belts before leaving Dublin and on the way out were in tolerably good humour. All along they saw signs and banners in both English and Irish proclaiming the glories of the Rosary Crusade.

The conversation went something like this:

'What's all this nonsense stuck up here about a Rosary Crusade?'

'Now Brendan, I may be a Baptist, but I respect the majority religion of this country, and in deference to my friend Jack, here, who is a good RC, I will not have you attack the majority religion.'

'You're very right, Ted. We're not going to have any obscenity in this van while I'm in it. We may, perhaps, be participating in a little bit of a shady venture, but I'll thank you, Brendan, to keep your mouth clean while you're with us.'

They rode on like that for a couple of miles. Then, written in Gaelic on a big banner over the road, was a sign which Brendan, a fluent Gaelic speaker, translated.

'Believe it or not, you can say what you like, but the translation of that banner over the road is, "Welcome, O Jesus, to a piece of cheese."'

'Now Brendan, I'm telling you: I'm not going to tolerate any more of this blasphemy. I'm a good Baptist and my friend Jack here is a good RC, and we're not going to have any more blaspheming the name of the Lord.'

'All right, All right. But I don't care what you say. That is what the banner says.'

They got to the racecourse about ten minutes to eight, and the Rosary Crusade was in full swing. Over the loudspeakers they could hear the steady prayers, so they decided to stop in a pub.

'I think it's a marvellous thing', said Ted. 'I really do. I may be a Baptist, but I think it is a marvellous thing the way all those fellows turn out for the greyhound races and say a few prayers beforehand. I'm sure it probably will help them to hand out their money and put it where it belongs. I'm also very pleased to see that our dog is ranked fairly well.'

It gets to be eight o'clock, and the Rosary Crusade is roaring on.

The Baptist says, 'You know, Jack, I don't want to say anything against your religion, but you can have too much of a good thing. That old dog of ours isn't going to have this stuff working forever, you know.'

Brendan says, 'We'd better have another round.'

At quarter past eight the conversation goes like this:

'Who is this bloody priest from America giving all this jaggery about a Rosary Crusade? Jack, for the love of God, let's get it over with. There is nothing like this in my church.'

At half past eight Jack pops off:

'My God, give me an Irish priest any day. Ted, it's these bloody Americans coming over here and carrying their religion to a place where it doesn't belong. It would make you bloody well sick.'

The Rosary Crusade finally ends, and they go to the kennel where the dogs are being kept. Their hound is fast asleep, and even though they were able to wake him up, he ran dead last.

Perhaps Brendan's most moving story is about the day he gave up house-painting and decided to depend for a living on his writings, a truly momentous step for a poor man in the Dublin of the early 1950s.

It happened like this:

'I just didn't get up one morning until opening time (10 a.m.). Then I walked at a leisurely step down through the local shopping district. There was something strange about the streets, something disturbing. It was the women, droves of them and not another man in sight. The firing commenced.

'"Aar yuh on the nyat-shift now, Brendan?"

'"Whan did yuh git the boot?"

'"Bin sleeping it off?"'

He eventually reached Davy Byrne's or McDaid's where there were people who understood. Later he was to return a successful playwright from London and empty the contents of his pockets on his mother's kitchen table – £300 in crinkled balls of paper – and she was to look up at him and say, 'Were yuh down in the mines, Brendan?'

His escapades were not confined to Ireland or America for that matter. There was the time when he gave a St Patrick's Day party in a small coastal village[1] in Spain which ended forty-eight hours later with Brendan and twelve Spanish fishermen in the local jug. There was the time when, shortly after taking off from Paris, one propeller gave out and Brendan made his way to the pilot's cockpit and announced that *he* personally had no intention of dying for an airline. And there were the many times he created havoc in Irish courts by insisting on a constitutional right – to have the police give their evidence in Gaelic and conduct his own defence in that language. (There are only 12,000 fluent speakers of Irish in the whole nation.)

He was at his best when he was sober. In 1957 he developed diabetes. He described his illness at length in a subsequent newspaper article. He came to Baggot Street Hospital and asked me to slip up to Mooney's for a liquid lunch with him. When we were seated he unloaded.

'As you know, Rory, I'm not at all opposed to a gargle now and then. When I have the thirst I drink whiskey, beer, or stout, depending on my pocket. But lately I've been waking up in the middle of the night and found that I'll actually be happy with water. I can assure you this is a pretty serious state of affairs.'

Thirst, as a symptom of diabetes, was to confound his life thereafter, creating an endless series of vicious cycles.

He came into Baggot Street Hospital that same day and stayed for three sober but riotous weeks. The first Friday lunch came and Brendan was automatically given fish by the nurses. He demanded to see Professor Victor Millington Synge, the head of the medical service and a nephew of the playwright.

'Sir, there appears to be in this hospital a sort of weekly solstice, an occasion where you are not allowed to partake of flesh. Now, where I come from, which is the slums, there are only two times when you don't eat flesh. One is when you're too damn broke to buy it. The other is when you're too damn sick to eat it.'

'Give Mr Behan some meat.'

The next uproar concerned a priest's efforts to give Brendan some spiritual comfort, a job the priest performed regularly in all the wards. We were having lunch one day when I heard an enormous commotion.

It was Brendan, clattering into the doctor's dining room, clad only in pyjamas. 'Rory, Rory, save me. The Druids[2] are after me.' We got him back to bed after several exchanges.

On the day of his discharge (on a small daily insulin dose) Synge came to him and said, 'Well now Brendan, I want you to be sure always to carry a couple of lumps of sugar with you wherever you go.'

'Is that in case I should meet a horse?'

Brendan's singing was quite something. He had a lovely, poignant voice, always sang at full blast, walking very slowly around the room, often making up verses with no great difficulty. On one famous occasion, he walked on stage in London, stopped his play, and sang 'Land of Hope and Glory' – with new words. I don't recall it completely, but it started like this:

> I'm Lady Chatterley's lover, game game keeper am I.
> I am Oedipus's mother, I really cannot lie.

It goes on to Oscar Wilde, Whistler, the Marquis de Sade, Sappho, and so forth. Of course, he was brought up on folksongs. His uncle wrote the National Anthem, a fact which made Brendan incredibly proud. He knew all the national songs of the War of Independence and the Troubles. He knew no less than six songs about my own grandfather, who was a figure in the Revolution. He had a wonderfully ribald song about a girl being seduced in front of the lion's cage in the Dublin Zoological Gardens. It was the most unlikely Irish event you could possibly envisage.

He sang in Paris and sang, apparently, quite to the French taste.

Radio Diffusion Française heard him and brought him in to do a record. I'm told they locked him in a studio with several bottles of whisky and a bucket to be sick in and a microphone. He sang, and they subsequently brought out a record of Irish folksongs. I've heard it. It is Brendan at his very best – a mixture of Gaelic and English songs with none of the 'When Irish Eyes Are Smiling' type.

In politics, Brendan, it is sad to say, was a puppy. He frequently spoke up for Mao and 'Joe Stalin' who would undoubtedly have shot him on the First Day. He had absolute unflinching loyalty to the memory of Ireland's fallen and to the latter-day 'heroes' who were in the illegal IRA right up to recent times.

He was rebellious and wild. By the way, as the saying goes, he had a priest when he died.

Brendan was a close friend for many years. In the early 1950s, when he was, as a writer, not yet known, he would come to my apartment about two o'clock every Sunday afternoon and, using my mother's old typewriter, work for several hours. During this particular period he was working on a translation of one of the most remarkable poems in Gaelic literature. This is Brian Merryman's *The Midnight Court*. It is a wild, exotic, Rabelaisian poem completely unlike anything ever done before or since in Ireland. There have been many translations into English, most of them pussyfoot. Brendan translated the words as Merryman meant them. I don't know whether Beatrice, his wife, has it, or whether it is lost. It will never be published in Ireland.

Brendan used to ring up my wife and say, 'Get ten siphons of soda water. I'm off It and I'm coming over to see you.' He would arrive with or without

Beatrice, either within minutes or a day later. The evening was largely a fascinating and uproarious monologue lubricated with incredible quantities of fizz. It was impossible for him not to use an endless stream of four-letter words. I saw him make this effort several times with my father and one felt like throwing in the words oneself to ease the thing along.

He was not a very good listener in company and created apprehension among actors when they knew he was in the audience. I went to *Gone with the Wind* with him and was asked to leave no less than seven times by the usherettes.

There are endless numbers of his stories one could recount but not print because of the people involved: The time he went to a socialite priest (who didn't know him) and confessed an endless stream of carnal sins, naming as his partners all the women in Irish Society with whom the priest was socially acquainted; the time he walked into the New York office of the Aid to Refugees from Spanish Fascism, turned out all his pockets and gave $250 for the cause; the time he offered the English police (who arrested him for agitating for the 'lost Northern six counties') the southern twenty-six if they would only give him a drink.

Brendan's poem on Oscar Wilde ended,

> Delightful the path of sin
> But a holy death's a habit.
> Good man yourself there, Oscar
> Every way you had it.[3]

NOTES

A native Dubliner born in Paris, Dr Roderick Childers is a professor of medicine.

1. San Jorge, near Ibiza.
2. The Celtic priests of Gaul and Britain.
3. This poem, entitled 'Oscar Wilde', is included in both its English and Gaelic versions in *Brendan Behan's Island* (London: Hutchinson, 1962) pp. 180–1.

Encounter with an Irish Genius*

OLOF LAGERLÖF

Who is Brendan Behan? A burlesque and noisy character according to the press, a person who has not spent a single sober moment since he was weaned. This is the description of the Irish writer who for the last few years has had London audiences at his feet, and whose plays have now begun their triumphal progress over the Swedish stages. Even if the critics unanimously praise his works, the press – in Sweden too – with a few exceptions, seems to present him as a cranky character who alternates box-office plays with scandals. As I happen to be the only person in Scandinavia to know Behan, and considering that it was under my roof that he composed the greater part of his play *The Hostage* (which made such a success in Gothenburg and is now running at Uppsala) I feel it an imperative duty to put down my impressions of one of the greatest personalities and noblest men I ever got to know.

It began on a night in mid-May last year[1] as I and my wife chanced to stop at a small Irish inn far down in the south-western corner of the Emerald Isle. We came driving at dusk in a small blue car along the Atlantic coast, where the sea rolled the breakers against the cliffs. The little white house lay as if tossed up on the stony ground with the sugar loaf form of the Great Blasket forming a striking background in the distance. The house had a blue sign on the gable stating that it was an inn.

We entered and saw a stocky man in a soiled sweater. He was having tea with a dark young lady with a thin face, intellectual and attractive. We inquired after a room. The man disappeared for a moment and came back with a grey-haired elderly woman who spoke English with great difficulty. She gave us a room on the first floor. There were only eight of them, all double rooms. When we had taken up our bags we went down and introduced ourselves and found that we were in the presence of Brendan Behan, the famous and notorious Irish playwright. I was confronted with a rather short, stout man with a round cherubic face, an unruly head of hair, kind blue eyes, a sensual, full-lipped mouth.

---

* *Veckojournalen* (Stockholm), Oct 1959, pp. 26, 63–5. Translated from the Swedish by Marianne Levander. This is its first appearance in English.

'You are the author of *The Quare Fellow*, which was such a success in London', I said. 'That's right', he said.

Seized by an instantaneous and somehow inexplicable sympathy I extended my hand to him, and from that moment on it was as if we had known each other from childhood.

The evenings and a great part of nights were spent in conversations by the singing gas-light – the village had no electricity – and Brendan told us about his life or commented on topical subjects. He grew up as one of ten children in a working-class home in Dublin. When he was only eight years of age he became a member of the IRA (Irish Republican Army), the illegal organisation – using terrorist methods – that fights for the union of Northern Ireland with the Republic. At the age of sixteen he was sentenced to three years at a Borstal in England in connection with an attempted Irish bomb outrage. This was the first of his prison spells, which were to comprise eight years in all.

I shall never forget the week that followed. It was one of the richest in my life.

On the face of it, it was ordinary enough. We drove around the Dingle Peninsula in a small car together with Brendan and his wife, made short trips of twenty-five to thirty miles and stopped at small pubs or inns (groceries-cum-pubs) to have a beer and chat with the locals. But we had the opportunity of seeing a great Irish artist among his own people; we saw how well liked he was, and how he was one with the surroundings, how humble and sensitive he was in the midst of all his pranks and whims.

As soon as we stopped Brendan entered the pub and we followed in his wake. In five minutes he was the centre of attention by virtue of his witty, loud and extremely unlicensed conversation. His English, spoken with a strong Dublin accent, is sparkling, highly poetic and extremely witty. He talks like one of his own fictional characters and his facial expressions keep shifting.

A born dramatist, he thinks in parts and illustrates his conversation by mimicking different imaginary characters. Yet, one never tires of him, and one soon discovers that this is a very wise man and an acute observer.

He also tried to make people use Gaelic, which he himself speaks fluently. In these parts there are still many villages where Gaelic is the everyday language among the locals. To me, having mostly heard Gaelic used in monosyllabic comments on the weather or in solemn poems, it was an experience to hear Irish speakers rattle away with explosive force in heated debates on religion and politics. Even if Brendan was the life and soul all the time, he had a marvellous talent for engaging all those present in the conversation and having a personal word for everyone. An old man who stood away from the crowd was asked by Brendan why he looked so sad. 'My wife died last Thursday.' In a similar situation I would have withdrawn with some words of condolence, but Brendan did not. 'Then you have lost the one person in the world who really cared for you', he said immediately. 'I understand how you feel – for children never really care for their parents and *vice versa* – but the person with whom you have lived your adult life, that's the person who matters to you.'

During these days and nights my picture of Brendan Behan was formed, a man whose appearance may be bizarre, but whose inner self is shy and sensitive, and whose inmost core is indestructible goodness. His shyness makes him overact at large parties, especially with journalists present, when he feels he has to live up to the expected part as Brendan Behan, the bizarre boozer and jailbird. I think this explains the occasional scandals that occurred when he attended performances of his own plays.

One day we were to visit a churchyard where one of my best friends in Ireland, an old priest, is now at rest. First we went into the church, where Brendan prayed devoutly, but on coming out he could not refrain from sprinkling holy water on a sign for a Catholic temperance society. Later, in the churchyard, which was littered and cluttered up with big unwieldy memorial stones, he found a broken-off chrysanthemum, stuck it in his buttonhole and assumed the face of an undertaker.

Immediately afterwards we all knelt in the high grass praying for the soul of Father Hurley while summer winds murmured under the clear blue sky.

Later still we passed some boys who were playing ball. Brendan at once ordered us to stop, jumped out of the car and joined in the game. In a street in Limerick there were two street musicians with a cap in front of them. 'Can you play "The Blackbird"?' 'Of course.' And while they were playing Brendan performed a solo jig to an ever-growing audience. Then he took the cap, made a collection, which he offered to the little band. Outside the house in Dublin where Brendan lives there is a little park where some circus horses graze. One of them was trained to drink beer out of a bottle, and it was a priceless sight to see Brendan drinking to the horse, which was swigging away at a bottle standing on its hind legs.

Our friends in Dublin were a bit worried about Brendan's impending visit to Sweden and somewhat maliciously emphasised our friend's propensity to get into scrapes with the police.

We need not have worried. From the very start Brendan and Beatrice took to our way of life. Brendan enjoyed the Swedish summer in the archipelago to the full; he angled for perch in the early morning, he imitated Tommy Steele[2] to the older kids, played football and acted the changing of the guard with the younger ones, and it was hard to say who enjoyed it most.

Beatrice Behan is the daughter of the well-known Irish artist Cecil Salkeld, and is a painter in her own right. She forms a contrast to her husband with her fine, thin face, dark hair and big blue eyes. She is quiet, and one tends to regard her as harmless, until she reveals a gift of repartee with a sting to it, which will often give the conversation a new turn.

Brendan had brought the manuscript of his play *An Giall – The Hostage –* which had been such a success in the Irish version at the Abbey Theatre, and which was now to be recast into English. He got up at sunrise and began his day at about four o'clock by making tea – he had brought ten pounds of tea from Ireland as he requires a special blend which he thought was unavailable in Sweden. Then he attacked the typewriter, and about nine o' clock he put away a substantial breakfast of ham and eggs, porridge and loads of tea!

In the evening he read out what he had written during the day and commented on the best places: this is fun – this will go home – this verges on libel, and so on. There were no songs put in as yet, but every night he sang Irish ballads to us in his warm tenor. One night Jussi Björling – who lives on a neighbouring island, Siarö – gave a concert at the rural community centre. Brendan enjoyed it immensely, listened with rapt attention and was silent for a long while afterwards. To him it was one of the highlights of his visit to Sweden.

One night we went to town to go to the Gyldene Freden, the famous restaurant he had heard so much about. Brendan looked forward to this visit with childlike delight, and his turnout was unrecognisably bourgeois, sleek-haired with a red Irish tweed tie and a dazzlingly white nylon shirt.

The cloakroom attendant gave our friend the once-over, turned to me and said, 'This gentleman has been drinking!' I expected an explosion as I translated, but Brendan smiled blandly, 'Tell him it is a magnificent understatement.' Eventually, we got in and I gave him a survey of Swedish attitudes to drinking. To my surprise he was positive to the Swedish temperance policy and said among other things that the Swedish standard of living is a very strong argument for a sober way of life, and that it is significant for a sober nation that PUB[3] should mean a place where you buy clothes and not spirits. The next morning Brendan went to Mass in the little Dominican church at Linnégatan. He appeared in slippers, without a coat, wearing braces and an open shirt. 'God is not the Gyldene Freden.'

In the country, meanwhile, *The Hostage* was taking shape. As time went on it grew into a new play, songs were inserted, the plot was somewhat changed.[4]

One day there was a large parcel from Dublin. It contained the final proofs of *Borstal Boy*, which has now been published in Swedish. All the dirty words had been carefully replaced by dashes, and the names had been changed to fictitious ones. In the original Brendan had used the real names, which had had to be changed now. I read the book in the night; in the morning it had to be posted as soon as possible. In the little post-office at Linanäs Brendan copied the first page in longhand, writing with a Swedish steel-nib. It is the facsimile page serving as cover of the English version. As the book was sent off to the publisher he turned to me: 'Do you regard this as a religious book?' I answered yes; in my opinion it is marked by a deep religious feeling. 'But nobody in Ireland will understand that. It will be banned immediately.' It was.

The impression he made on our children will be best illustrated by Patrick's reaction. Last winter Patrick found some Irish coins given him by his friend Brendan, and he at once began packing his toys in a small bag. 'I've got to pack. I'm going to Dublin to see Brendan.' My objection that Brendan would not have time to play with him was countered with 'But I'm not going to play with him, I'm going to live with him.'

To my mind the unlimited confidence that he inspired in a small Swedish boy, who did not even understand a word of his language, illustrates beautifully the personal charm that Brendan develops in happy moments.

Recently I had the opportunity of seeing *The Hostage* at Göteborgs Stadsteater,[5] and, when Karin Kavli[6] asked what Brendan was like, I could only say, 'He's just like his play. You couldn't find a truer self-portrait.'

His father once said something to me that might sum up Brendan's life: 'Some people are born to greatness, others achieve it, but some are hit by it.'

Brendan Behan has been, as it were, hit by genius and talent, so much so that, at times, it has been a burden to him.

But the whimsical element in his character is just the superficial 'image', and anyone who has become his friend will disregard it in favour of the great artist and writer and the profoundly good man.

NOTES

Dr Olof Lagerlöf, Swedish ophthalmic surgeon who is interested in Irish culture.
1. 1957.
2. A well-known British rock-and-roll singer.
3. Short for Paul U. Bergström, a large department store in Stockholm.
4. Beatrice Behan, in her memoir of her husband, *My Life with Brendan* (London: Leslie Frewin, 1973), pp. 134–9, indicates that the translation of *An Giall* into English had not started in Sweden. Dr Lagerlöf, on the other hand, assures me in a letter dated 18 October 1976 that Behan 'actually got started when with us and had the first act finished going back – how could he otherwise have had the play ready in mid-October 1958?'
5. The municipal theatre in Gothenburg.
6. A well-known Swedish actress.

My First Visit to Dublin*

RAE JEFFS

Back in the office, I tried to readjust myself to a certain degree of normality but the prospect of publishing a book of *Borstal Boy*'s literary merit was hardly an everyday occurrence, and as the day of publication[1] came nearer a feeling of excitement swept through the office. There were so many requests for personal interviews with Brendan both from the press and television companies that it became impossible to deal with them with the Irish Sea separating us. I was detailed to go across to Dublin to straighten out a few of the entanglements that must surely follow without Brendan's full co-operation. I was to stay in the house of a senior counsel at the Irish bar, a man who knew Brendan from his earlier days and whose wife was also an acquaintance. They would be prepared for emergencies. As the aircraft touched down at Dublin airport on the first of my many visits to Ireland, I could not help wondering whether the return flight would find me in a comparable state of health.

With my hostess, I went to see Brendan and we carefully selected the hour between 2.30 and 3.30 to do so as the pubs would be closed during that time. (The Holy Hour, Brendan called it, adding that the politician who introduced it in the Dáil[2] was shot dead an hour afterwards.) I was several minutes knocking on the door of their ground-floor flat in Herbert Street before Beatrice half opened it. Her assertion and regret that Brendan was out, followed by Brendan's booming affirmation from the adjoining room that he was in, were somewhat bewildering. As we hovered on the doorstep, there was no time to decide on our next move for a hand pulled Beatrice to one side swinging the door wide open, and Brendan stood in front of us, barefooted, the bottom of him just covered from the point of indecency by pyjamas, while the top half sported a white shirt, the collar of which was stretched tightly around his neck as he manfully struggled to do up the button.

The extent of his welcome for me was totally in opposition to the look of distaste he gave to my companion and I was confused and embarrassed, both on her account and my own. Beatrice, who had still not recovered from being made to look a barefaced liar in front of comparative strangers, was unable to help. He ushered me in, and the sight of the room which we

* *Brendan Behan: Man and Showman* (London: Hutchinson, 1966) pp. 51–2.

entered did little to alter my confusion for it looked as if it had been ransacked by a burglar. Brendan beckoned me to sit down while seating himself in the only other available chair and, while I trod gingerly across the floor, Beatrice apologised for the mess and explained that the builders were trying to combat the dry rot with which the house was plagued. All at once I felt stupid and rude for not having warned her of our visit. Of course she would object to our seeing her home for the first time in this condition.

Slowly Brendan began putting socks on his feet, but with a lack of concentration revealing that his mind was not on his work. Deliberately and with a dignity completely out of character, he turned towards my hostess.

'Would you ever tell me what you had to do to get those briefs for your husband?'

NOTES

Rae Jeffs first met Brendan Behan when she was publicity manager for his publisher, Hutchinson. She later resigned to help Behan tape record *Brendan Behan's Island* (1962), *Brendan Behan's New York* (1964), and *Confessions of an Irish Rebel* (1965). Now Mrs Peter Sebley, she lives in Sussex.

1. *Borstal Boy* was published in London by Hutchinson in October 1958.
2. The Irish Parliament.

Book and Author*

MICHAEL CAMPBELL

At the last London publishing party of importance, in an imposing panelled room at Hutchinson's, a romantic head with brows knit and a proud mien, multiplied many times across the whole of one wall, gazed out and away towards some distant and disturbing prospect of the mind. 'Borstal Boy' was written under the dimpled but strong chin. It was a display of highly effective jackets containing many books of that name.

At the centre of the room stood the more human reality, large, flushed and tousled, with an old coat spread wide to reveal scarlet braces, and an unequivocal voice that warmly welcomed arriving guests and invited them to find a blankin' drink.

The worst-dressed person in the room was on this occasion the most

* *Irish Times* (Dublin), 25 Oct 1958, p. 6.

important. Mr Brendan Behan has hit London rather like Mr Somerset Maugham, in his youth; it is surely beyond all imagination to think of two people more dissimilar hitting anywhere. Mr Behan's new play, *The Hostage*[1] has left the London theatre critics breathless and invigorated. His first play, *The Quare Fellow*, a former success, is shortly to be televised. (This winter it will be running in Paris and New York, and the film rights are sold.)

His *Borstal Boy*, officially published this week, was preceded by continual fanfares and has already received critical acclaim.

At the pre-publication party, therefore, Mr Behan already had reasons for celebrating, while his publishers made nervous conversation and wore brave faces. Not many moments had passed when the hubbub created by the distinguished guests was rent by a raucous and familiar voice declaring that Mr Patrick Campbell, the well-known humorous writer, formerly of the *Irish Times*, would now give a rendering of 'The Old Musheroon'.

In the sudden hush this suggestion was gracefully rejected, whereupon the guest of honour himself broke forth into 'Oh the praties over there, they were small, they were small'.

No one has ever sung at a publishing party before, but it was accepted without undue surprise and slowly overborne by the conversation.

Mrs Behan, quietly removed from the central din, was telling me that her husband is writing a novel set in Dublin during the last war which is 'very funny'. Also present was Dr Brian Inglis, formerly of the *Irish Times*, who was also about to have a book published by Hutchinson's, called *Revolution in Medicine*, though one could have been forgiven for not knowing it.

There was also Mr Gerard Fay, whose history of the Abbey Theatre[2] had just been published, though by another firm, Hollis and Carter; and Mr Valentin Iremonger,[3] the Irish poet of the Irish Embassy, who once made part of that history with a declaration from somewhere in the stalls.

At about this time Mrs Iremonger, with great calm, sang a solo in the Irish language to the 80 per cent alien assembly who heard it in reverent silence. The scattered applause was broken almost at once by a duet of tremendous volume between Mr Behan and Mr Hugh Delargy, the Labour MP, who were standing at opposite sides of the room: 'Glory-o, Glory-o, to the bold Fenian men'.

The staff of Hutchinson's was faintly smiling again and the distinguished London men of letters were regaining their sense of importance, when two young guests of schoolboy age[4] made a late but breezy arrival. A number of people looked as if they could not believe it. This was particularly so when Mr Behan treated the newcomers with more solicitude than the men of letters, personally serving them with two blankin' drinks that caused a moment's hush, in their vicinity. They came of a well-known Irish family, were old friends of Mr Behan's and were totally at home amidst their eminent elders.

But one could understand the passing astonishment.

It was lost again, however, in a spate of songs that made no bones about the treacherous tyranny of the English. In short, hilarity was general. Mr Shinwell, beaming, said that when he spent five months in prison as a striker in 1919 the warders never spoke like that to him. Mr Behan took time off to report that in prison Neville Heath, the murderer, had complained to the governor about *his* blankin' language.

It was growing late. The two younger guests I observed at work on the end wall, tucking samples of that noble head underneath their arms and making a gleeful departure. Having delivered a somewhat schoolboyish protest, I was given permission to do the same. There was little cause to stay longer and wish Mr Behan success. Books, in the main, succeed or fail before publication, when the booksellers order them. *Borstal Boy* was a success too. No publisher is ever likely to give such another.

NOTES

Michael Campbell (1924–), Irish novelist and journalist living in London.

1. *The Hostage* had its first production in London at the Theatre Royal, Stratford East, on 14 October 1958.
2. Gerard Fay, *The Abbey Theatre: A Cradle of Genius* (Dublin: Clonmore and Reynolds; London: Hollis and Carter, 1958).
3. For a note on Valentin Iremonger see p. 90.
4. Garech and Tara Browne, of the Guinness family.

Behan: the Last Laugh*

ALAN SIMPSON

I founded the Pike Theatre in 1953. We had been in existence for almost a year when we presented Brendan Behan's first play, *The Quare Fellow*, in the autumn of 1954. I had known Brendan since 1945. He had been released from an internment camp and I had come out of the Army. I had been a military engineer at the Curragh when Brendan was on the other side of the barbed wire. I did not know him then, nor was I guarding him; it

---

* Des Hickey and Gus Smith, *A Paler Shade of Green* (London: Leslie Frewin, 1972) pp. 210–19.

was simply that we had our training-ground alongside the internment camp. But in 1945 I was out of the Army and working with Edwards and MacLiammóir at the Gaiety. Some friends of mine had a studio over the Monument Creamery which had been leased to them by John Ryan, who was to be the editor of *Envoy* magazine, and it was here that I first met Brendan Behan. We became friends and by the time I founded the Pike he was writing for the *Irish Press*. He didn't actually tell me he was writing a play, but Sally Travers, Micheál MacLiammóir's niece, told me that Brendan had sent a play to Hilton Edwards.

It was not Hilton's sort of play and obviously they were not going to do it, so I asked Brendan to let me have a look at it. As soon as I read *The Quare Fellow* I wanted to stage it. I liked the play and was excited by it. I suppose this was some time in the summer of 1954, but it was autumn before I was able to get it on. It was a frightfully difficult play for our tiny theatre. There was a cast of twenty-one and the play created all kinds of technical problems for us, apart from the problems of finding actors. But we produced it and ran it for as long as we could afford. After a month it became too costly to keep going. Brendan came to the rehearsals. He was easy and uncritical, not in the silly sense; he was not one of those playwrights who see everything differently to the director or try to mess him around. We rearranged rather than rewrote some of the play. I still have a copy of the original script, which is very rambling. A character would change subjects as though in a genuine conversation. We made Brendan sort it out so that one subject was dealt with at a time. We probably made cuts; in fact, I am sure we did, and we tied up loose ends such as curtain lines.

We never discussed his theme of capital punishment. That was a delightful aspect of his play: it was not propagandist in the ordinary sense of the word. Brendan wrote *The Quare Fellow* out of his experiences of English and Irish prisons as an almost documentary record. I would not say that he set out to write a deliberately anti-capital-punishment play.

Dermot Kelly played Neighbour, Derry Power the young Gaelic-speaking prisoner and David Kelly the part which Brendan called Fatser, but which we renamed Mickser because David wasn't by any means fat. I would not say that Brendan was conscious of having written anything theatrically important. He was delighted and enthusiastic simply because I was putting on his play. He loved coming to rehearsals; in fact, he turned to somebody during rehearsals, nudged him and said, 'I wrote that!' He had been to the dress rehearsal, but it would have been dangerous to bring him to the first night; in such a small theatre he would have made too much noise. We kept him in the office across the laneway and the manager, Tim Willoughby, gave him a drink every fifteen minutes. If we hadn't given him a drink he would have gone off to a pub to buy one. On the other hand, if we had given him as much drink as he wanted he would have been incapable of walking into the theatre to take a curtain call. During the last ten minutes of the play we steered him into the auditorium. He refused to make a speech; instead he sang 'Red Roses for Me'.

The play was hailed by various Dublin critics as the best since O'Casey. Its potential was obvious to me. It was rather a shocking play for a Dublin which wasn't very sophisticated at the time, and I had been slightly afraid when I put it on that it might be libellous; indeed, somebody might have seen fit to take an action if it had received its first production in a large theatre. But obviously there was no point in taking an action against either Brendan or the Pike because neither had any money. People from Mountjoy Prison had even come down to see the play and once it was hailed as an important work they could not very well have taken any action. The nuclear-disarmament movement meant that a lot of middle-class people who had never been inside a prison or approached a policeman except to ask the time now knew what went on behind prison walls. But at the time of *The Quare Fellow* prison life was still a mystery to the man in the street. Brendan's play was shocking in the sense that it revealed things which had not been revealed before. I wanted to establish the play in Dublin by putting it on after its Pike production in a large theatre. I lined up a cast which included Denis O'Dea and Noel Purcell. I approached the Gaiety Theatre first, but they had no available dates at the time. I then approached the Olympia, but the management was suspicious of Brendan because his brother had once worked there and sold the *Daily Worker* in the gallery when he should have been operating the spotlight. It was a pity, because Joan Littlewood was able to steal our thunder by presenting the play in Stratford East. At the time we were very cross about this, but I suppose it is hard to blame the Dublin managements.

The Pike seated only fifty-six persons and with a full house, which included persons standing, we took about a hundred pounds a week. We played to packed houses, so if Brendan was working on a 10 per cent basis, which I think was our agreement, and the play ran for four or five weeks, he got forty or fifty pounds. I later staged three short plays of Brendan's: *The Big House*, which he wrote on commission for the BBC'S Third Programme and which I adapted for the stage with his blessing; and two other short plays, *Moving Out* and *The Garden Party*. *The Hostage* was commissioned as *An Giall* for Gael Linn.[1] They gave him seventy-five pounds to write a play in Gaelic and promised him a further seventy-five pounds when it was written. He spent the first advance and wrote nothing until about three weeks before the deadline. Frank Dermody directed *An Giall* at the Damer Hall and it was the first, if not the only, controversial play written in the Gaelic language for many a long year.

Meanwhile Joan Littlewood presented *The Quare Fellow* at the Theatre Royal in Stratford East and it transferred to the Comedy Theatre in the West End. It established Brendan as an important playwright. During the run of the play at the Comedy, Brendan made his famous television appearance with Malcolm Muggeridge. He was stoned. This turned him, so far as the English were concerned, into a celebrity overnight. Joan Littlewood commissioned him to translate *An Giall* into English and gave him her flat in Blackheath in which to work whilst she went off on a holiday. Needless to say, when she returned she found that Brendan had hardly put pen to paper. She forced him to translate the play and when it went into rehearsal at the Theatre Royal she and her partner, Gerry Raffles, kept him in the pub opposite the theatre in Angel Lane, so that whenever they wanted a change made or needed a new song, they could go across to the pub and say, 'How about it, Brendan?' That is how *The Hostage* got its embellishments. Half the characters in the English version were not in the Irish version.

Joan Littlewood produced *The Hostage* for a London audience and coloured it in a London way. When I came to direct the play in Gaelic for the Taibhdhearc in Galway I worked from the English version and had the embellishments translated into Gaelic. But I related the play to Galway, which is exactly what Joan did for London. Obviously an Irish audience could not be expected to accept *The Hostage* as directed by Joan Littlewood because it did not seem true to the Irish character. When you come to work on the play, however, you realise that this difference is superficial.

If I liked *The Quare Fellow* because it was documentary, I liked *The Hostage* because it was the reverse of documentary. Both plays reflect the period of their first performance, and in this *The Quare Fellow* has suffered more than *The Hostage*. I directed *The Quare Fellow* at the Abbey Theatre in 1969 at the invitation of the directors and because of my associations with the play. I think this may have been a mistake. I found that Irish audiences had lost their relationship with the work. So many of the situations had become common-place and much of the material had been used again in *The Hostage* and in the adaptation of *Borstal Boy*.

Somebody told me that Brendan wrote a short play when he was in jail which was never published; I don't think it can have been of great importance. The short story which John Ryan published in *Envoy* was, I suppose, his first significant piece of writing. He might well have lived longer had the lionising he received by the press in England not gone to his head and made him drink heavily. One must remember that Brendan was in no sense arty. He was an artist in spite of himself. His way of life was that of an artisan, a house-painter like his father, who regarded work simply as a way of earning money. Whether you worked with a typewriter or a paintbrush was immaterial to him. Brendan changed from the brush to the typewriter when he found that the typewriter could earn him more money. Then he discovered he could make money just by talking to people in pubs, so he didn't bother to type any more. His later works were tape-recorded. Brendan made more money than he probably intended to, and this helped to destroy him. He was not a compulsive writer; he was a compulsive thinker and talker. He had wonderful ideas, and if he dispensed these ideas to some drunken fellow in a pub who went away and forgot them, Brendan was as satisfied as if he had dispensed them at a pound a line. I lost touch with him after I moved to London and he was spending long periods in America. Shortly before I left Dublin I staged a revival of *The Big House* at the Gate Theatre and Brendan gave me the royalties from the play for my *Rose Tattoo* Fund.[2] That was 1959, the year in which I directed his brother Dominic's play *Posterity Be Damned*, first in Dublin and then in London. Brendan came to the rehearsals at Stratford East and after that period I never saw him again.

Brendan had the philosophy of a working house-painter. Out of the money you earned every week you spent so much on the basic necessities of rent and food and clothing and the remainder you spent on drink. This is a straightforward philosophy when the money involved is reasonable, but when you earn large sums of money you must adjust to a new situation. When you have a few pounds you can get stoned twice a week, but you can't get any more drunk than that. When you have as much money to spend on drink as you like, something must give. This, rather than anything else, was Brendan's big problem. He did not know when to stop drinking, and his physique just didn't stand up to it.

The plots of Brendan's plays are nothing very much. *The Quare Fellow* is a documentary and the plot of *The Hostage* is unbelievably simple. What makes these works so lively is the characters and their talk. We can meet a person in a pub and laugh our heads off at his remarks, yet how many of us can write them down afterwards? Brendan had this ability. He was a raconteur and as entertaining on the page as when he reached the right stage in drink. Even at the time of *The Quare Fellow* he was using his earnings from the *Irish Press* to keep him in drink. He was basically a shy person and quiet when sober. When he took a few drinks to break the ice he was the most wonderful company in the world. When he took one over the eight he became violent and unpleasant. He was frightfully generous, yet hardheaded about money and he would not write for nothing. He drove a hard bargain, yet would press a hundred pounds into the hand of somebody he thought needed it. He was not unlike Bernard Shaw in this respect, but when drunk he had been known to sell the rights of a work to four or five competing parties.

I always found Brendan good company, although other people considered him noisy and tiresome and something of a menace to polite society. When I first met him he wasn't a writer, so far as I knew, except for his newspaper work. When we talked it was about politics or horse-racing or other people's writings. John Ryan was simply a friend to whom he gave that first short story and said, 'Would you like that for *Envoy*?' Presumably I must have seen him when he was interned at the Curragh. He would have been one of a number of men walking around in the mornings between the huts and the barbed wire.

The English, on the whole a staid people, had this love affair with Brendan who overpowered them with his flow of poetic prose. His bad language on television at a time when television was still rather pompous had almost as much to do with his popularity as his actual writing. By degrees Brendan came to realise that he was expected to behave outrageously. His personality, combined with the quality of his work, made an enormous impact. I think that a share of the success of the stage adaptation of *Borstal Boy*[3] can be attributed to the fact that Niall Toibin was able to impersonate Brendan so cleverly. The similarity was so alarming that it upset some members of the Behan family.

Dominic is not so good a playwright as Brendan. His sense of humour is not so ebullient as Brendan's and he has the natural exaggeration of a lyrical writer. *Posterity Be Damned* was too Irish for the English to understand it thoroughly. It was concerned with the relationship between Fianna Fail[4] and the IRA and had an appeal in Ireland as a controversial play, but it lacked that innate warmth and humanity which is to be found in all Brendan's work.

The year after I had staged *The Quare Fellow* at the Pike I wrote to Samuel Beckett for the rights of *Waiting for Godot*. The Pike production in 1955 was the first production of *Godot* in the English language, although there was one beginning about the same time in England. Dermot Kelly played Vladimir, Donal Donnelly Lucky, Austin Byrne Estragon and Nigel Fitzgerald Pozzo. I met Beckett before and after that production and found him a kindly and delightful person, reserved but in no sense standoffish. He was cagy about publicity and has spent considerable effort in dodging newspapermen. He attracts culture vultures as a jampot attracts wasps.

He was fond of Brendan, and Brendan once borrowed money from him in Paris when he was broke. Both writers have a compassion for humanity. On the whole I would say that audiences in Dublin were less puzzled by *Waiting for Godot* than audiences in other countries. Without distorting the play I exploited its Irish aspect, which brought it near to an Irish audience. Beckett did not altogether approve of what I had done and subsequently told me so. He saw *Godot* as a universal play, but I must say that I think a theatre should relate a play to its audience. I believe I was right at the time, although if I directed *Godot* again I would not necessarily direct it in the same way.

Dubliners appreciated the Pike Theatre, but after the *Rose Tattoo* case we lost custom. Although they might not have seen *The Rose Tattoo* and knew the case had been thrown out of court, people decided that there was no smoke without fire. Since those days the law has been brought into disrepute, but at the time of the *Rose Tattoo* case ordinary people believed that nobody went to jail unless he had done something rather wicked. I believe my indictment was the first of its kind in the world. It did us harm at the Pike. Until then we had been well thought of, but now people withdrew their support because they were frightened. We had been thinking of building or converting a larger theatre, and this would have needed capital and assistance. We had received a grant from the Dublin Theatre Festival Committee to stage *The Rose Tattoo*, but we never fully recovered from the setback of the court case which dragged on for a year. During that year our lawyers would have been distressed if we had staged anything that might have been considered controversial in the mildest sense of the word; so the plays we staged were particularly innocuous.

An organisation must grow; it cannot stand still; but there was no hope of our raising additional capital. It would have been an admission of defeat if we had closed the Pike after the court case. Except for a number of friends, however, people did not want to be too closely associated with us. Our loss was not just financial; there was an incalculable loss of goodwill which slowed down our operation until it came to a halt. Perhaps it was for the best. For me, at any rate, the day of the small theatre as we knew it is gone. The Pike was exactly right for that particular decade. I am not saying that we shouldn't have small theatres today, but they should work on totally different lines.

Curiously, it was in a small Dublin Theatre, the Peacock, that I directed the first production of Brendan's last play, *Richard's Cork Leg*, in the spring of 1972. Although the play was written by Brendan in 1960, most of us believed that it was unfinished and contained only one act. Early in 1972 I asked Beatrice to search her home for any manuscripts of Brendan's. It was then that she found the draft of a second act of the play. I myself completed the play.

Although most of Brendan's later work was dictated into a tape recorder, this play was written in longhand. It is set in an Irish cemetery and highlighted by the same ribaldry and wit that made *The Hostage* so entertaining. Here is an extract which Beatrice considers typical of Brendan's sense of song and insight into the Irish character:

THE HERO (*Sings*) (*rise*):

> The child that I carry will have to be
> laid on the steps of a nunnery.
> The man I call my own,
> Has turned funny and screams like
> a queen for cologne.
>
> His nails are all polished and in his hair,
> He wears a gardenia when I'm not there,
> Instead of flittin' he sits knittin'
> for a sailor he met in Thames Ditton.
> I must find another, for he loves me
> brother, not me. (*Exit off left.*)

CRONIN (*addressing the audience*). My wife tries to cheer me up by saying that girls like me – that she loves me. But then she is my wife. I mean, I don't mean that she just loves me because a wife is supposed to love her husband. But she is a very, very, exceptional person, and she is very kind to everyone, and particularly to me.

But I'll tell you something for nothing. There's a lot of nonsense given out by the English and Americans about our attitude to women. They say it just to flatter themselves. Some old Jesuit in America attacks the Irish for not screwing early and often enough. A hundred years ago screwing and having kids was out of fashion and Paddy was being lambasted because he got married too soon, and had too many kids. It's like saying all Jews are capitalists because Rothschild is a capitalist, and all Jews are Reds because Karl Marx was a Jew – if they don't get you one way they get you another. If they don't get you by the beard they get you by the balls.

The English and Americans dislike only some Irish – the same Irish that the Irish themselves detest – the ones that think. But then they hate their own people who think. I just like to think, and in this city I'm hated and despised. They give me beer, because I can say things that I remember from my thoughts – not everything, because by Jesus, they'd crucify you, and you have to remember that when you're drunk, but some things, enough to flatter them.

The great majority of Irish people believe that if you become a priest or a nun, you've a better chance of going to heaven. If it's a virtue to meditate in a monastery and get food and shelter for doing it – why then isn't it a virtue outside? I'm a lay contemplative – that's what I am.

NOTES

Alan Simpson, Irish theatrical director and co-founder, with his former wife, Carolyn Swift, of the Pike Theatre, Dublin. He directed the world premiere of Behan's *The Quare Fellow* and the English-speaking premiere of Samuel Beckett's *Waiting for Godot*. See his *Beckett and Behan and a Theatre in Dublin* (London: Routledge and Kegan Paul, 1962).

1. The Irish-language organisation which produced the periodical *Comhar*.
2. *The Rose Tattoo*, by Tennessee Williams, was produced by Alan Simpson at the Pike Theatre in 1957. Simpson, however, was arrested and charged in the Dublin Court District with 'producing and showing for gain a performance which was indecent and profane'. See Des Hickey and Gus Smith, '*The Rose Tattoo*: Arrest and Trial', *A Paler Shade of Green* (London: Leslie Frewin, 1972) pp. 128–33.
3. Frank McMahon's adaptation of *Borstal Boy* was first produced at the Abbey Theatre on 10 October 1967, during the Dublin Theatre Festival.
4. A middle party formed in Ireland by de Valera (1923) when he turned from armed to political opposition to the Free Staters. It first formed a government in 1932.

Talk with the Author*

FRANK MELVILLE

Burly Brendan Behan, thirty-five, now living with his painter wife, Beatrice, in a ten-room house near Dublin, agreed to talk to an interviewer, provided the process did not upset his daily rhythm of pub-crawling. Accordingly, *Newsweek*'s Frank Melville donned his drinking cap and set out with the roistering author.

First stop was a public house on a blind alley of Dublin slum dwellings where Behan, in open-necked shirt and trench coat, joined his friends and a former IRA colleague in singing, dancing, and – of course – drinking. They greeted him with the warmest affection. A former IRA man shuffled up with his leathery face beaming: 'How's your big self today, Brendan? Sing us a song about the old days.' A withered hag sipping her gin and stout by the door marked 'Latrines' pulled herself to her feet and started to dance a jig, in which Behan joined. 'I write in order to keep myself in liquor', he presently explained, lacing five pints of Guinness stout with double jogs of Irish whiskey. 'I have nothing against the Church as long as they leave the drink alone.' Pope John's recent call for the unity of all Christian churches had Behan's suspicions thoroughly aroused: 'The day the Catholic and Protestant churches combine, it's the end of all drinking. I'll have to go to Rome to sabotage the affair.'

Moving on to another staging post – which he entered with the IRA battle cry of 'Up the Republic' – Behan turned his talk to politics: 'I was brought up in one of the worst slum areas in the world, very near this pub. The kids literally begged to keep alive. Sure, I hate capitalists. That's why I want to be a rich Red. Don't think I'm a rich fellow, though. I like some capitalists like the Guinnesses [who brew the stout]. They're a fine lot and Irish patriots.'

Mention of one Irish institution, the Censorship Board, which banned publication of *Borstal Boy*,[1] stirred Behan to a genuine fury: 'The trouble with that lot of bastards is that they're illiterate. They've never blue-pencilled anything I've done in Gaelic because they couldn't read it.' He is especially mad because he considers *Borstal Boy* his finest work.

Behan, immensely proud of his serving with the IRA, declared, however, that his days of illegal soldiering are over: 'I'm too scared of big

* *Newsweek*, LIII (23 Feb 1959) 106.

bombs to care any longer about small ones.' Another reason for his caution is almost certainly that Behan is greatly enjoying the financial security (£200 to £300 per week) which his writing career is bringing him. Hanging proudly in the Behan bedroom is one distinctly capitalistic artifact, an expensive Savile Row tuxedo. To keep it there and himself in the chips, its portly wearer has loaded his schedule with new work, including a TV play, a movie, a column in *The People*, a leading London Sunday newspaper, and a new book. His recipe for success in literary and all other matters: 'Be courageous.'

NOTES

This interview was given on the occasion of the publication of the American edition of *Borstal Boy* in 1959.
1. See 'News in Brief: Eire Book Ban', *The Times*, 12 Nov 1958, p. 6.

My Husband Brendan Behan*

BEATRICE BEHAN

I suppose my husband must be one of the most widely-discussed men in these islands. Discussed not only for his brilliance as a playwright and an author, but also for his drinking habits.

The notable time when he was drunk while being interviewed on TV is only one such occasion. There have been many others. For example, he danced a jig on the stage of the Theatre Royal, Stratford, in London's East End – interrupting his own play, *The Hostage*.

Maybe you have wondered what it is like to be married to a turbulent genius like my husband.

He is a man who never combs his hair, but who will spend thirty guineas to buy me a dress. He will spend ten pounds a day on drink – yet would give his last penny to a 'down and out'. He will bring home for lunch a gang of tramps he has met in a pub.

I knew what I was taking on when I married Brendan. Although we were married only four years ago, we knew each other for fifteen years before that.

I first met Brendan when I was seventeen. He was nineteen. My father, Cecil ffrench-Salkeld, a well-known portrait painter in Dublin, brought

---

* *Irish Digest* (Dublin), LXIV, no. 4 (Feb 1959) 12–14.

him home one day. They had met in a pub, which Brendan, who worked then as a house-painter, was redecorating.

We met on and off at parties after that. Once he suddenly turned up at a party on Inishmore, one of the Aran islands.

Brendan has been banned from Inishmore because he had locked the local police up in their barracks and thrown the key away. He'd had a row with them over pub-opening times. But he managed to sneak over to the party without being caught.

Trying though it is sometimes to be married to a genius, I have never regretted it. One of the most attractive things about Brendan is his kindness. His brother Brian, a building labourer, was recently one of the strikers at a skyscraper office site near Waterloo Station, London.

When Brendan heard about the strike he took the first hundred pounds he had earned in royalties from his new play, *The Hostage*, went down to the site, gave every one of the thirty or forty men on strike one pound each and bought them all drinks.

I agree with Brendan that it is better to spend money like this helping people than leaving it lying in the bank. He believes that money is to be spent, not saved.

And he never forgets that he has been poor. When people tell him that he allows himself to be 'sponged' on too readily, he replies, 'Well, I was a sponger, too, once.'

Brendan always likes to have about twenty pounds in his pocket when he goes out. Then he is well-equipped if he meets friends.

When he is out I get on with doing the housework, or I paint. My pictures have been exhibited in Dublin from time to time.

Sometimes I wish Brendan would drink less for his health's sake. He often puts away more than fifteen pints of stout a day – and some Irish whiskey besides. This may seem a lot, but you must remember that Brendan comes from a very hardy family who are used to drinking after a heavy day's manual work.

Mind you, Brendan hates it if I ever get merry. Once, we went to a dinner where we had a different wine with every course. I am not used to mixing my drinks, and afterwards I began hopping and skipping about a bit.

Brendan said nothing at the time, but a day or two later he said. 'I was furious with you. You had too much to drink.'

Some people say they are frightened of Brendan when they first meet him because he looks aggressive and has rather an abrupt way of speaking.

It's true that he wants to fight when he has had a few. Once he knocked a man off a bar stool because he didn't agree with his views. If he feels he is in a 'shockable' atmosphere, he sometimes tells a shocking story to break the ice.

But Brendan is a very gentle, affectionate person. He cares about and is interested in people more than anything else in the world – including drink, money or his success as a writer. He adores children, and I hope we shall have some one day.

Luckily I am a very easy-going kind of person, else marriage to him would be difficult. I would far rather be married to him than to some stuffy and strait-laced person who never gets any fun out of life.

Recently we went into a big store to buy me a new coat. Brendan took hold of one of the wax models and started waltzing it round the shop. The shop assistants were in stitches of laughter – and I found it difficult to keep a straight face myself.

One just can't be angry with him for very long.

NOTE

For a note on Beatrice Behan see p. 68.

Brendan Behan Insists on Use of Irish in Bray Court*

Mr Brendan Behan, playwright and author, aged thirty-six, Anglesea Road, Dublin, was yesterday fined forty shillings at Bray District Court by District Justice Manus Nunan, for being drunk and disorderly at 1 a.m. at Greystones, Co. Wicklow, on the morning of 4 March last.

Mr Behan insisted that the case should be heard in Irish. He admitted that he was drunk and apologised for his language. Witnesses said that he called policemen murderers, scruffhounds and dirt birds.

When the case was called, Mr Behan said (in Irish), I want this case to be heard in Irish, please. According to the Constitution of this country, I have a right to be heard in Irish.

District Justice (in Irish): Sit down.

Inspector James Kelly (in Irish): Be quiet.

Mr Behan (in Irish): I have a right that only the Irish language is used in this case.

Guard J. A. Molloy, who began his evidence in Irish, said that on the morning of 4 march, he got a call from a civilian named Terence O'Reilly that a man was lying in Church Road, Greystones. At 12.45 a.m. he went to Church Road where he saw the defendant, Behan.

* *Irish Times* (Dublin), 7 Mar 1959, p. 9.

BRENDAN BEHAN INSISTS ON USE OF IRISH IN BRAY COURT

Mr Behan (in Irish): Justice, can I speak to you for a moment?
District Justice (in English): No.
Mr Behan (in Irish): According to the Constitution of this State, I can speak in Irish, and have the right to be heard in the language of the State.
District Justice (in Irish): Sit down.
Guard Molloy then began his evidence in English. He said that he went to Church Road. 'I saw the defendant . . .'
Mr Behan (in Irish): That man is not talking in Irish. I want the case to be heard in the first official language of the country.
Guard Molloy, continuing his evidence in English, said that he asked the defendant what he was looking for. He was lying down. A local doctor, who was also on the scene, told him that Mr Behan was not ill and that it appeared to be a case for the police. He said that he was 'looking for his wife', the witness said, and added that 'she was in one of the local houses'. He was dishevelled and appeared to have been in a struggle. He said, 'Here are the —— bloodhounds,' and 'You —— murderers.'
Mr Behan: Correct.
Witness: He then left the scene, and went towards another hotel, where he hammered on the door to gain admittance. I remonstrated with him, and he used vile language. Then I telephoned for a patrol car, and two *gardai* came along in it.
Mr Behan (in Irish): Well, at least you know one word in Irish – *gardai*.
Guard Molloy: He said that we were '—— bloodhounds.' He resisted violently when we tried to arrest him, and used foul language. You could hear him all over the place.
Defendant (in Irish): No doubt it was not in the Irish language.
Guard Molloy said that the defendant had to be forced into the patrol car, and had to be forced out of it again at the police station. He was forcibly searched, and then forcibly put into a cell. He added: He kicked at the cell door from 1.30 a.m. to 4.30 a.m. He said that the police were '—— murderers', and said 'You are no —— good.' He was discharged at 8 a.m. when he was still in the same tone of voice.
Defendant: As I always am.
Guard Molloy said that when he attempted to take the defendant into custody he had no idea who he was.
Mr Behan, cross-examining the guard in Irish: When I asked you for a drop of water during the night, did you give it to me?
Witness: Yes.
Mr Behan: You gave it to me five minutes before I left in the morning. Now you know I have no great love for you, don't you? You are a perjurer.
Addressing the district justice, still in Irish, he said: He said to some of the others, 'We have the quare fellow now.'
Inspector Kelly: I must ask you, Justice, to treat this behaviour as gross contempt of court. He has abused this guard, and has called him a perjurer. This should not be allowed.

The next witness, Guard Denis O'Leary, said that he was called to Church Road in a patrol car on the morning of 4 March. When he attempted to arrest the defendant he called him a bloodhound and said that he would get him in the morning. He had to be forced into the patrol car and out of it at the station.

Defendant: You recognised me as Brendan Behan?

Witness: Yes, I had seen your photograph in *The People*.

Defendant: Not in *Forga Tora*?[1]

Guard L. C. McEntaggart said that he was in the patrol car which came to arrest the defendant. When he tried to get him into the car, he called me a '—— guttersnipe', said witness.

District Justice: It would be hard to translate that one.

Mr Behan (in Irish): I'll do it for you.

Witness added: His language was vile, and he could be heard all over Greystones.

Mr Behan: Did you recognise me?

Witness: I did not know him, and I do not know him. I have never heard of him and never read him.

Mr Behan (in Irish): Can he read at all?

Asked to make his defence, Mr Behan, speaking in Irish, said: I went to the Grand Hotel, Greystones, on the evening of 3 March because I wanted to do some writing for a film. I was in the bar, and was having a few drinks. I had booked into the hotel for a couple of days. While I was in the bar, a man, who said his name was Charlie Reynolds, came up to me. He wanted to drink with me. He told me that he was an old policeman. I told him that I would not give a drink to any policeman, old or new. Then I went out into the open and the police came. They put me in the car. They would not even give me a drink of water in the cell. I have been in jail in Belfast and in Britain and have never been refused a drink. I am on my oath now, so I must admit that I was drunk on this occasion.

District Justice Nunan called Mrs Beatrice Behan to give evidence. She said that when her husband left Dublin for Greystones he was sober, and that he had gone there to finish some work so that he would not be interrupted.

District Justice: Isn't it obvious that he went there on a skite?

Mrs Behan: I did not think so. He just wanted to be somewhere quiet.

District Justice: I am trying to keep him out of jail. I don't seem able to do that. You don't seem able to control him.

Mrs Behan: I would have if I had been there.

Inspector Kelly said that if the case had been carried on in the proper manner, he would not press it. It was a shame that an otherwise very talented man should behave like a blackguard. He was drunk and he was violent, and he had behaved very badly.

District Justice: Will you make an apology for your behaviour?

Defendant (in English): How can I make a sincere apology? I regard you as representative of the Irish people. But I will apologise for my language.

District Justice: Is that an apology?

Defendant: Which would be the greater insult – to apologise if I was not sincere or not to apologise?

District Justice: That is a matter for your own conscience.

Defendant: All right, I will apologise.

District Justice: Fined forty shillings.

NOTE

1. *Hue and Cry*, the Irish equivalent of the *Police Gazette*.

'The Only Thing I Blame Paris For'*

BRENDAN BEHAN

I was born on Holles Street, Dublin, on 9 February 1923. During that year my father was in an English camp with 10,000 other prisoners, including the present President of Ireland, Sean T. O'Kelly.[1]

My family has always been Republican. We are socialistic and trade-unionist. My father, Stephen Behan, is the President of the Irish National Painters' and Decorators' Trade Union and the Ship Painters Union.

The Behans have always been Catholics and anticlerical. None of us became a priest, but everyone is dying for clerical help. I wish God were for hire!

My father was excommunicated in 1922 because he was a member of a Republican party. I made it in 1939. . . .

Furthermore, it consists of a simple formality. In Ireland, a Catholic country, no one worries, the priests least of all. One can always get married and be buried in the Church.

I was brought up in the poor district of North Dublin – a district with huge Georgian houses, where each family crowds together in one room. We, however, had two rooms, one of them being the kitchen. A huge stove sat enthroned in the kitchen, which also served as a living room. My father and mother as well as the baby of the moment – we were eight, seven boys

---

* *L'Express* (Paris), 9 Apr 1959, p. 36. This is the first appearance in English.

and a girl – slept in the kitchen. The rest spent the night in a room which adjoined one of the rooms of a brothel situated in the street.

In 1936 I joined the technical school as a house-painter apprentice. The following year, the Dublin Corporation relocated us in a housing estate in Crumlin, south of the Liffey, near the countryside. We had electricity, a bathroom, a toilet, and air...I detested all that. Not that I don't like being clean; but I missed the old street. I love the sea, not the countryside. The days there are endless. The only thing I blame Paris for is the absence of the sea.

It was in 1947 that I came to France for the first time. Everyone admires the Paris of the artists. I love the Paris of the barricades. I love Delacroix,[2] who, I think, represents perfectly these two Parises. In France, I worked as a house-painter on the buildings of the Aeronautical Exhibition, the Invalides station, and at St Gratien.

When I visited France last time, I was involved in an incident at Orly Airport. Since the Press distorted my statements, I seize this opportunity to make a clarification. I was quoted as saying that I did not want to 'die for France'. I am known for having no desire to die for France or Ireland, or to die at all if I can help it. Consequently, the newspapers wrote that I had shown violent anti-French feelings. What I actually said was: 'I have no wish to die for Air France.'

I love France: the Republican France. I love Ireland: the Republican Ireland. I did not appreciate being put in a cell at the Choisy-le-Roi police station.[3]

All policemen are peasants, who are delighted to be in town, in uniform, and armed with revolvers. They crawl through the cities with a strange fear, as if they are disembarking from the countryside. It is not their fault. Lenin said that the aim of all politics was the abolition of the village idiot.

The police is a necessity...for those who have money.

When I say that I love France I am not thinking of those who are peasants and feeble-minded, as elsewhere. The world being a madhouse, is it right to let prisons be supervised by armed lunatics?

I cannot say anything about what I am writing as this might spoil the comedy. As far as drinking is concerned, I can only say that in Dublin, during the Troubles, drunkenness was not considered a social disgrace.

I have recently established that drunkards are ill-omened...as far as the following day is concerned. Furthermore, I suffer from dreadful pain which sometimes prevents me from walking. Proust[4] said, 'We do not obey any doctor as we do our pain.' Perhaps I shall reform. Perhaps.

NOTES

Behan was in Paris to attend *The Hostage*, which was selected to represent Great Britain in the Théâtre des Nations Festival in 1959. It was presented on 3 April.

1. Sean T. O'Kelly (1882–1966), Irish journalist and political leader; one of founders of Sinn Fein; Speaker of the first Dáil Éireann (1919–21); Irish envoy to USA (1924–6); Vice President of Executive Council and Minister for Local Government and Public Health (1932–9); Minister of Finance (1939–45); President of Irish Free State (1945–59).
2. Ferdinand Victor Eugène Delacroix (1798–1863), French painter; leader of the romantic school in painting.
3. The word *roi* in French means king.
4. Marcel Proust (1871–1922), French novelist.

A Cry*

GEORGES WILSON

I knew Behan's work before I knew the man. An American, Jacqueline Sandstrom, brought me a play which she had had translated by Boris Vian, and we worked together.

The play pleased me. It was the work of an Irishman then thirty-eight years old – my own age. I have Irish ancestors myself, and I felt for this story of prisoners. Finally, I put it on at L'Oeuvre, having helped Boris Vian a little with the translation, for the author's language was certainly not easy. It was called *The Quare Fellow*, which Boris Vian rendered as *Le Client du Matin*.[1] I asked his American friend if Brendan Behan would come to Paris, we invited him, and at last I was able to meet him.

I had not in the least expected his physical appearance. He was a man who appeared unhinged; during my two months of work on his play, I had constructed for myself a quite different image of him, but that was a matter of no importance. We went out together. He seemed to me rather sad, and very reticent. He saw a rehearsal of his piece and said to me, 'It's very good, better than what I wrote' – but that was a sally.

I saw later that he only ever talked in riddles.[2] It was a defence. Oversensitivity? I do not know. He would always help his partners, but never expose himself; in spite of my Irish origins, my knowledge of English humour was insufficient. Then I saw that I could not interest Behan. In spite of everything, I had interpreted his sense of humour on the stage. I realised that this man loved the game of conversation. If one did not come up to his expectations, he would abandon one.

* *Les Lettres françaises*, no. 1022 (26 Mar–1 Apr 1964) p. 8. This is the first appearance in English.

I know the Irish well, their way of hiding themselves, of baffling one, of protecting themselves. But I quickly saw Brendan Behan was a man perpetually playing a part, and I must admit that I did not find him *sympathique*. Let me explain.

We actors, we know all the machinery of illusion and dissembling. But, on the other hand, in ordinary life we do not like to act, we're natural, we rest. We do not lie among ourselves. We are sincere in our relations with others. I do not like someone to have so little trust in me that he must act a part for me in ordinary life; I am not a dupe, I see through it straightaway, for it is my own *métier*. Behan, however, had invented a style which was peculiar to him, and he would not allow anyone else to share it. If he was sad, he would start to drink. His eyes began to trouble him, he would break something, he would begin to sing. Everyone was astonished to see this man who passed so brusquely from sadness to mad gaiety. Everybody looked at him. Myself, I was irked, for I dislike noise. I know how to make it in the theatre, but that's different. He was actually himself the characters in his plays, throughout the day, that is to say, these characters playing their roles. *It is very Irish, to play oneself as a part, and not to believe in it.* But not in the theatre. Thus he was astonished to see his plays put on – for one was, if I may put it like that, reconstructing his life, which he himself did throughout the entire day.

He came to the dress rehearsal, applauded inappropriately loudly, shouted and created a disturbance, and I believe he was like that to show himself off and get back into the swing of things. He no longer knew if it was against himself or against the rest of the world. He lost himself in this continual performance, he perplexed himself. But his work, that was well organised. He had an extraordinary sense of theatre – and there lies the value of his work really, this kind of popular genius. He had, and I repeat the word, a genius for dialogue, which is why he carried on a dialogue throughout the day, and was even reduced to soliloquy, when he could not find a partner. When he could write down his soliloquy, it was brilliant. He was a marvellous playwright, which is not to say a man of letters. He also had a genius for playing with words, for fracturing them, for the unexpected, which is very Irish.

I lost track of him. Then he sent me his second play, which we have called *Un Otage*,[3] and which I put on because he insisted that it should be I who staged it.

We worked with Jacqueline Sandstrom and also with Jean Paris. It was extremely difficult to translate – at first reading, it seemed impossible. We put it on at Barrault's; we telephoned Behan, but he was ill, in hospital. He was drying out. He got better. Three days before the dress rehearsal, he came out of hospital, and do you know what he did? He sent a telegram – to the Comédie Française!

There. I did not see him again. I retain the memory of a kind of typhoon, a terrifying force, a man who consumed himself, in every sense. I believe he was not aware of his self-destruction. For one thing, there is no pessimism in any of his plays. On the contrary, he is an optimist, a great poet of life; but as a result of alcohol, he was bound to confuse everything a little. One might also say that his death – his alcoholic death, one hears – was to some extent caused by the fact that the fight against England was over. The fact that its finish was to fizzle out must have thrown him into great bitterness. This is not official, certainly, but I believe it was so. He carried rebellion within him. He was a rebel against the police, a rebel against religion, a permanent rebel.

In the street when he went out he was terrible, he could not bear to see a policeman. It was a physical thing. He was an anarchist, let's say in the nineteenth-century sense. It worked out well because Ireland was in a state of rebellion, so he became a hero. He was a rebel to his finger-tips. But when there was no more force in the rebellion, he became disenchanted, and in the end he talked of the 'flabbiness' of the Irish, of their surrender of principle. Without a struggle, he lost his aim.

He wrote his first play like a jet of water; he had spent several years in prison as a political prisoner. He threw out his first piece like a cry, during the first week after his release. The second was slower, but it was so anarchic in its form, that one could well imagine the author writing a couple of scenes in a café, forgetting them on the table, then remembering vaguely that he had written it when reuniting the bits. . . . And his disorderliness was the charm of his work. It had no logic (except the first play) but I, who put on *The Hostage*, I used to push the emphasis towards anarchy because I was thus moving towards the author, I was supplying the 'ruptures'; and at one point Behan wrote in parenthesis on his copy 'There, I don't know how to finish, so you can do as you wish.' That was not cunning, it showed his sense.

His theatre, I believe, will influence the modern theatre, because in his genre he is one of the most pure popular authors. It is a CRY, by which I mean a Gorki had had the same force – but not the same eccentricity. He was of the people, and genuinely poor. Through his plays, I felt his poverty, and it was lacerating. He knew all the social difficulties resulting from poverty – prostitution, for instance. The taste he had for prostitutes was nothing more than a fraternal meeting. His mother and father were workers, and he saw his mother die a domestic servant.[4] He had a hatred of poverty, yet at the same time could not do without it: it was the climate in which he lived: truly, anarchy. And with it, an enormous sensitivity.

He could have written many more fine things. He had a third play on the stocks. I never saw him again, I can tell you no more. But truly, this popular poet, with his songs, his marvellous dialogues, has touched and marked the theatre of today.

NOTES

1. 'The Morning Customer.'
2. Literally 'sallies'.
3. *The Hostage*; literally 'A Hostage'.
4. Brendan's mother is still (1981) alive; she is ninety-two.

'Success Is Damn Near Killing Me'*

RAE JEFFS

Once settled in the cab, Brendan's tension burst out of him in volleys of abuse at Beatrice. He was over-wrought, desperately unhappy and mentally and physically sick, and had to release his pent-up emotions in this way or be devoured by them. Beatrice sat impassively without saying one word. She understood completely. The lull would come when the storm was over. But I was confounded and dismayed by his unhappiness and, pleading a headache, I asked to be excused from travelling further with them.

Brendan was in the office early next morning, and while I was getting used to his mercurial changes of mood, I was once more astounded to find him in good humour, calm and completely at ease. He had signed a contract with Hutchinson to write a comprehensive book on Ireland,[1] he said, and had agreed to return to Ireland because Paul Hogarth, who was illustrating it, would shortly be coming over to work on the project with him.

We had a farewell drink at the Mason's Arms, and when I waved him off from Great Portland Street I did not expect to see him again for a while. A few days later, however, Beatrice telephoned me from Dublin to say that while Paul Hogarth had arrived as arranged, Brendan's contribution was to take off immediately for London. 'He's on his way to you at this very minute', she said. 'I thought I had better prepare you for the event.'

Indeed, within a few hours Brendan was in the office and asking for money. He gave no reason for the purpose of his return, nor did he mention that Paul Hogarth was in Dublin. He merely indicated that he would be staying with Joe and Kathleen McGill, friends of his from earlier days. As I

* *Brendan Behan: Man and Showman* (London: Hutchinson, 1966) pp. 88–90. Editor's title.

knew that both Joe and Kathleen would be largely tied to their flat by domestic duties, I became aware that Brendan had not called on me simply to collect money. He was expecting me in some way to be responsible for him and to be part of his erratic and abnormal behaviour so that he could gallop around London on a free rein and be sure of a friend to pick him up when he fell. For a moment I wavered. I resolved to get rid of him and spare myself the appalling state of anxiety which accompanying him necessitated. But then I reflected that the demands he made on me, consciously or unconsciously, were part of a real need for self-protection and were well worth the indignities which I might have to endure. It became plain that he had come back to London to drink, and I was not prepared to watch him drain his talent into the sewers of the Thames without some effort to stop him.

In the next few weeks I was turned out of more pubs with Brendan than I care to remember. People who had previously sought his company now avoided him, and I was left standing on the corner of the street, one arm propping up Brendan while the other waved in anguish at the taxi-drivers who passed without caring to notice us.

His health deteriorated rapidly. The strain of the continental tour, coupled with his junketing around London, had left him in considerable need of medical help. But to get him into hospital willingly was an impossible task for he was without a vestige of common sense in his loathing for the place, and looked upon his admittance as a form of drastic punishment. I waited for the inevitable collapse, but while he still had the determination to stand on his feet, he announced he wanted to go home and asked me to make the necessary arrangements. His gratitude was both touching and pathetic.

'If the Lord God Almighty were to tell me that your friendship was not genuine,' he said, 'I would not believe him. You're a gentle and understanding person, and I would rather cut off my right arm than hurt you. When I've had a few, I may say a lot of nonsensical things, but I don't mean them. You know that.'

'Brendan,' I answered. 'I wish I could help you more. I believe so much in your work and I hate to watch you throw away your talent.'

A shy smile broke across his lips and his tired eyes reflected momentarily the humour as he replied. 'Ah, that's the rub. Success is damn near killing me. If I had my way, I should prescribe that success should go to every man for a month; then he should be given a pension and forgotten.'

He did not laugh, but sat gloomily looking at the floor in front of him; I wondered now if there ever could be a cure for Brendan Behan.

NOTES

For a note on Rae Jeffs see p. 109.
 1. *Brendan Behan's Island: An Irish Sketch-book* (London: Hutchinson, 1962).

The Doctors Warn Behan*

Carraroe, Connemara

Rumpled, rumbustious Brendan Behan was downing whiskey and stout chasers here tonight, despite the fact that he should have been in London for the West End opening of his play *The Hostage*[1] – and despite doctors' warnings that if he keeps on drinking it will kill him.

Officially he is here to 'rest and recover' from the mysterious ailment which, in three months, has robbed him of three of his sixteen stones and some of his roaring zest for life.

But give up the drink? Not he. Today he was knocking it back in half a dozen pubs in Connemara and neighbouring Galway, singing Irish songs, telling stories of IRA battles during the Troubles, holding animated conversations in Gaelic.

Between the drinking and singing and laughing he told me, 'You are right. I am not well. I sometimes feel terrible. But I don't know what the trouble is. So have another drink.'

But wife Beatrice told me 'I am worried to death, but no one can control a man like Brendan. It is too much for anyone. He drinks too much and won't eat at all.

'In the last couple of months he has been seeing his doctor in Dublin at least once a week. He has been told to stop drinking completely. But what can I do with him?

'I have dragged him down here for some rest. He has done too much travelling lately and he is tired. He wouldn't go to London. His trouble began just before our tour of the Continent.

'While we were away Brendan drank everything from every country and ate practically nothing. It's his own fault. He is ruining his health. I wish he would stop for a little while.'

Said Brendan in Flaherty's pub, 'A man's got to have a drink.' In the Swinging Bridge he downed some more, sang Irish songs, and roared, 'I don't drink stout any more, so I have to drink whiskey.'

And in the Malthouse in Galway he flung his arms round my neck, ignored the serious matter of his health, and with a thumping fist announced loudly, 'Kingdoms fall, empires crash – but we shall rise again. I will go on...'

* *Daily Mail* (London), 12 June 1959, p. 3.

In London, Joan Littlewood, who is directing *The Hostage*, said, 'Believe me, Brendan is really ill. We are very worried about him.

'He was in poor shape nearly all through his recent Continental tour, and he looked dreadful.

'Then the French raved over *The Hostage*, and it bucked him up so much that he got into a few fights and came home last week with a couple of black eyes. But he still wasn't his old self at all.'

NOTES

Behan did not go over for the first night of the West End production of *The Hostage*. A *Daily Mail* reporter interviewing him in Connemara recorded Brendan's reaction to the premiere.

1. The play was produced at Wyndham's Theatre, London, on 11 June 1959.

I Swear I'll Beat It Yet*

BRENDAN BEHAN

It has never been a habit of mine to say anything bad against myself and as far as possible I've always tried to stop anyone else from doing likewise.

But this morning I'm going to take off my shirt, part my hair, expose my soul and answer some of the questions about me which have caused so much gossip, argument and malicious rumours – and wasted so much valuable printer's ink – during the last fortnight.

I am going to lie back in this hospital bed in Dublin, take a good look at myself, and tell you how and why I am where I am.

I am going to tell you how I booze, why I booze, when I booze and what the booze does to me.

I am going to tell you exactly why I went on that riotous jag in London. But let's not delay the confession.

I hear the man over in the corner of the ward asking for the first page already and the nurse has warned me that if I let this typewriter fall off my knees and frighten the patient beside me she'll break the water jug on my head.

God forgive her! I've a baby bottle of whiskey hidden in that.

For a start let me tell you that I'm neither dead, dying, drunk nor dotty. I'm just damn sick, but getting better all the time.

* *The People* (London), 19 July 1959, p. 6.

My liver, I'm told, is like the sole of a hobnailed boot: my inside feels as if it's been scoured out with sulphuric acid and my head occasionally thumps like a pneumatic drill.

But sure I could be worse and indeed I often was.

Nevertheless it's true that at the moment my health isn't the best.

But there is nothing disastrously wrong with me and I am not going to kick the bucket just yet.

It is true, however, that I am an alcoholic and that excessive gargle is responsible for my present condition.

But I am not without hope.

I have been in this hospital now since last Wednesday night and I've been gradually getting off the drink all the time.

As a matter of fact I had nothing to drink yesterday and I will be back to work and dry as a sponge next Wednesday.

Why do I drink so much? That's easy answered.

First because I like the stuff, secondly because I like company, and thirdly because a pint of orange or lemon juice is twice the price of a pint of stout.

Furthermore, it would be very hard for me to miss the beer bug seeing as I was at the stuff with me grandmother since I was six. By the time I was ten I knew the taste of it better than tea.

Anyway, I'm a lonely so-and-so and I must have people around me to talk with.

Bars are usually the best places because most of them are full of poor people, hard-chaws, ex-convicts, chancers, and tramps who'd lift the froth off your pint if you didn't keep your nose well in over the edge of the glass.

So long as I am working I am OK. I'd never ask to stop writing. It's only when I've nothing to do that I hit the bottle.

Lately, it has been with more serious impact than in former years, but that's simply because of my different financial position.

My pockets kept a strict rein on my drinking then, but nowadays I can afford a little more.

Many wild theories were put forward as to why I went on that terrible batter to London last week. But the truth is simpler than any of them.

I went to London because I was getting fed up in Dublin, because I wanted to collect a few Nelson Eddies, readies, or pound notes, and because I wanted to see my show in Wyndham's Theatre in the heart of the West End.

I managed to achieve all objects – though at great cost to life and limb and a night in Bow Street cop shop.[1]

I got drunk, I sang, I jigged and generally kicked up hell over there. But sure you know that part of the story better than me.

The press certainly kept the world well informed of my activities.

I have only one apology to make about the London skite and that is to my wife, Beatrice.

She hadn't a moment's rest with phone callers and interviewers and I am deeply sorry that I caused her so much trouble.

Otherwise, I have no apologies to make to anybody. I enjoyed myself in my own way.

I'm not proud of being an alcoholic, but neither am I going to apologise to anybody for being one.

I might also mention here the people who abuse me for giving a 'wrong' impression of the Irish abroad.

Frankly, I don't care two hoots what impression I give. Nobody ever paid me anything for being Irish.

I know I can cure myself from drink and that's what I am doing here in hospital.

Remember that during that skite last week my average consumption was between two and three bottles of whiskey a day, washed down with, maybe, a dozen or two of stout or beer.

Since I came into hospital on Wednesday I cut that down to a dribble and I took nothing yesterday or today.

And – with the possible exception of the little bottle hidden in the water jug – I will take nothing until I come out a new man this week.

I'll go back to work then and take an occasional drink just like I used to before all this rumpus started a few months ago.

I'll go out for walks with Beatrice then and we'll go to the sea and we'll talk just like we used to.

I know people are always gossiping about how we get on, why we got married, and 'I don't know how his poor wife puts up with it all, and her such a sweet, quiet creature, too!'

Well. I'll tell you.

It happens that Beatrice and I like each other very much and when I'm on the wagon we go out and talk and laugh like so many other couples.

Beatrice is a wonderful girl. By nature she is a much happier person than me, and when I get out of sorts she always cheers me up.

And no matter what I do she won't lecture or nag about it. Without her I don't know where I would have got myself over the last few years.

Incidentally, before I leave you, let me get a free lost-and-found ad. into *The People*.

Does anybody know where the blazes I left my dinner-jacket, pants, shoe, shirt and dickey-bow?

They are somewhere between here and Bow Street and would ye mind keeping an eye out for them.

I fear my cousin, Jim Bourke, the theatrical costumier in Dublin will be asking me about them.

Well, I think I've pretty well washed my soul in public now, so if you don't mind I'll turn over and call for a glass of milk.

Long live the cow!

NOTE

1. Behan appeared at Bow Street Magistrates Court, London, on 11 July 1959 on charges of being drunk. See 'Playwright Fined 5s.', *The Times*, 13 July 1959, p. 4.

His London Appearances*

DONAL FOLEY

The prostitutes outside Bow Street Police Court called out warmly; 'Come back soon Brendan – Good old Brendan.'

Looking tousled and dishevelled and with a grin as wide as O'Connell Street Brendan bellowed back at the girls, 'I'll be back – don't worry.'

It was one of the promises that he did not keep. But his appearance on 11 July 1959 at Bow Street will be remembered by those of us who were present. The previous night Brendan Behan, who was then at the height of his popularity in London, was found in a state of coma in Mayfair. As a result the next morning he was charged with being drunk. He arrived from the prison cells looking a little shy and subdued. The London constable read out the charge and the magistrate asked the routine question: 'Anything known?'

There was a quiet titter in court at the absurdity of the question; but the constable was not at all flurried: 'Not in this court', he replied.

Brendan, a stickler for accuracy in these matters, reminded the magistrate of his sojourns in various prison establishments and then went on to pay his own special tribute to the London police: 'I was given fourteen years for shooting at two coppers but this black eye didn't come from the cops. They were very kind and very civil.'

The magistrate – Clive Burt – ordered him to pay a fine of five shillings and fifteen shillings expenses. Immediately afterwards Brendan left for London Airport. No less than thirty cars manned by Fleet Street reporters joined in the calvacade to the airport. The inevitable stop for refreshment came at a pub on the Great West Road. The landlord seemed a little apprehensive at the strange invasion in the normally quiet period of a

* *The World of Brendan Behan*, ed. Sean McCann (London: New English Library, 1965), pp. 151–7.

Saturday morning. Reporters were falling over themselves to buy the great man a drink. It was not surprising because at this stage Brendan was worth his weight in gold to the Fleet Street newspapers. His play *The Hostage* was still packing Wyndham's Theatre and every word he uttered, drunk or sober, was faithfully recorded for posterity. But today Brendan was having some fun at the newspapermen's expense. He spoke entirely in Irish and advised me to cash in on the situation: 'Charge them translation fees', he chuckled in Irish.

Nobody enjoyed the joke more when he heard me making a bargain for the golden words. It was the only time in my life that Irish proved of any practical value; unfortunately there are only a few Brendan Behans around. Brendan drank three whiskies and two bottles of stout and left London, his four-day spree having cost him £150.

Incidentally, when another Irish playwright, Oscar Wilde, appeared in a London court he was not accorded the affectionate farewells by the prostitutes that were given to Brendan. The prostitutes jeered and cat-called at Wilde in furious fashion, fearful perhaps that Mrs Warren's profession was in some little danger from the new cults. There could be the explanation that the street girls instinctively sensed Brendan's infinite compassion and anarchic frame of mind.

Brendan was always at home with the down and outs, the wayward and the men of no property. (Although he could quaff champagne with the best of us.) One night in a pub in Victoria in London two young Teddy Boys were told to leave the pub by the landlord who objected to their offensive behaviour. Brendan, who had taken more than one drink himself, followed the boys out and talked to them for about ten minutes on the pavement. At first they told him to 'Eff off Paddy', but by cajolery and sheer charm Brendan succeeded in establishing rapport with them. Eventually Brendan had the pair of Teds back in the pub with the permission of the landlord. Between them they had a bottle of red wine and spent the night roaring with laughter listening to Brendan's stories.

Not all our experience together in pubs were so happy. I remember the evening we were barred in a well-known Irish house in London for talking Irish. Brendan loved the language but he never paraded his knowledge of it with other Irish people. On this occasion his only reason for the use of it was that he wanted to borrow some money from me unknown to the other two Irishmen present who had no knowledge of Irish. We began to talk Irish because I had to explain that although I had not got any money there was a possibility of getting a cheque cashed in a nearby tavern. We had to raise our voices a little above the normal din to get our nuances of meaning across to each other. The head barman looked at us suspiciously: 'Enough of that now', he warned.

Neither Brendan nor I took any notice.

'That settles it – ye've 'ad enough t' drink', he said with tremendous finality at the same time removing our two pints from the counter.

We protested, Brendan more vehemently than I. But it was to no avail. We were asked to leave the pub and not to come back. Brendan had the last word: 'I've been barred from pubs for many things but I've never had the distinction before of being barred for talking Irish.'

We both laughed and went across the road to the Cheshire Cheese where Brendan regaled visiting Americans about the literary Doctor Johnson whose house is not far away. He told the story of the Cockney who collapsed in the street and his friend rushed up to Doctor Johnson's believing that the great doctor was a GP for that area.

Brendan's impact on London was in many respects greater than in his native city. The occasion when he appeared drunk on BBC television with Malcolm Muggeridge made him into a national hero with the British working class. He became the toast of every Cockney pub overnight. They identified themselves with this rumbustious Irishman who refused to conform to any pattern. To flout BBC conventions in these new far-off conventional days was of course something. The morning after the broadcast Brendan was walking up Victoria Street when a Cockney newspaper-seller approached him and grabbed his hand enthusiastically: 'You were great, Mr Behan – I didn't understand a word you said but I didn't know what Mr Muggeridge said either.'

It was the latter part that tickled Brendan. He was aware of his own lack of articulation that evening but pleased that Mr Muggeridge's well-phrased and well-moderated accents meant as little to the Cockney ear.

During the run of *The Hostage* and *The Quare Fellow* in London Brendan had a rare time. Some said that his arrivals in London from Dublin were carefully timed with falling attendances at the shows. True or false his visits certainly stepped up interest in the Behan plays. One never knew what to expect from him. One night, sitting with him watching *The Hostage*, I remember his great big body would shake with laughter and he would turn to me, give me a dig in the side and roar, 'Wasn't that great.' Then at last completely overcome he roared out, 'Up the rebels.' He began to call out to the players on the stage.

'Are you a member of Equity?' Howard Goorney who played Pat in *The Hostage* called out.

'No', says Brendan. 'The NUJ.'

Brendan was by now completely convulsed with laughter and he kept up a running commentary with the players. The actors improvised their lines and one quipped, 'Brendan didn't write that.'

At this point the play stopped completely, the actors unable to continue because of their own laughter. It was audience participation at its highest level. After the play Brendan took his curtain call with the rest and danced a hornpipe to the great delight of the audience. Need one add that it was impossible to get a seat at *The Hostage* for many weeks. Brendan remained around and held court nightly at the Salisbury Tavern in St Martin's Lane.

His audiences were mostly journalists but Brendan was happy in their company. He was always conscious of the value of publicity and only on rare occasions have I seen him angry at something written about him. One piece which suggested the possiblity of his early death angered him particularly. Brendan did not like what he called 'this death lark' at all. This is why perhaps he called himself 'a Catholic after dark'.

Brendan Behan's language could at times be foul, the four-letter words of the Dublin streets, of *Borstal Boy* and the Army. Women present did not matter to him. But if there were children present Brendan was most careful about the words he used. At a *Yorkshire Post* luncheon where there were many children present Brendan, forewarned by his friend Val Iremonger, spoke for nearly an hour without once using any words to which anyone could object. But later when he had finished his speech he could not contain himself any longer: 'Look at that professional Jesus!' he whispered to his companion when a well-known editor of a literary magazine passed across the room.

There is a parrot in a garden in Chiswick, the London suburb, which owes something of his vocabulary to Brendan Behan. Brendan when he stayed with the Iremongers in this most respectable of suburbs used to pass the parrot every morning on his way to the station and in his friendly manner he would bid the parrot the time of day. A friendship developed. The parrot now has a vocabulary which would shock any Dublin docker and much to his owners' embarrassment he exercises it freely.

When Brendan lived permanently in London for a short period during the early 'fifties his only income came from articles in newspapers and magazines. His main source was the *Irish Press* to which he contributed a weekly column. The column was in my opinion the best of its kind to appear anywhere at that time. It was racy, anecdotal, uproariously funny and full of acute observation. Brendan wrote it at an amazing speed. One day at three in the afternoon he came into the *Irish Press* office in London where I worked and asked for an advance of twenty guineas on four articles. I consulted the Editor who authorised me to give him the money, provided I got the four articles in advance.

Brendan looked at me as if horror-stricken when I told him the situation. I explained firmly that I could not hand over the money without first getting the articles. Brendan did not say much but warned me to have the twenty pounds [*sic*] at seven o'clock that evening. Meanwhile he retired to the sedate quiet of Lincoln's Inn Fields with a pencil and a sheaf of paper. He was back promptly at seven with 7000 words written. He demanded that I should read the articles before I passed him the money.

'If you're going to be so bloody stern you'll do your own job too', he shouted at me in mock anger. He was in great form as a result of his achievement: 'A good journalist should work against the clock', he said proudly.

The articles have since appeared in book form[1] and it is incredible to recall that they were written in such a short time. I believe Brendan enjoyed writing more than anything else and it was this infectious quality which gave his column its character. His robust love of life shone through every line he wrote.

The following day Brendan arrived in Fleet Street in the company of an ex-professional boxer – an obvious victim of the free-for-all boxing booths at the old Blackfriars ring. They had spent the morning together in Billingsgate Fish Market where you can get a drink at the crack of dawn if you are on market business. This was easy for Brendan Behan who was an old hand at the Dublin markets. The Billingsgate and Covent Garden porters knew him as well as the Moore Street shawlies.

Brendan had brought his boxer friend along to meet a mutual friend, a pious Irish newspaper executive for whom he had a great affection but whom he also liked to shock. (He rang him on his honeymoon in London to confide that he was in bed with a woman, omitting to mention that he had been married the previous day, and that the lady was his wife Beatrice.) But the shocks that day were to come from Brendan's boxer friend. Brendan introduced him as of good Irish Catholic stock. Whereupon the boxer began to talk about the good old days in the most colourfully phrased foul language I have ever heard. The newspaper executive finally remonstrated with him.

'That's strange language for a Catholic.'

The boxer looked at him puzzled and replied:

'I said I was a Catholic not a fanatic.'

Brendan sat there drinking his pint and enjoying every moment of the unusual encounter. His impish sense of fun was satisfied.

Brendan Behan had many good friends in London but he was happiest in the East End, particularly in Stratford East near the Theatre Royal where he saw his first big stage success under the hand of Joan Littlewood. Here in the cafés and taverns in the little mean streets Brendan would sit for hours with obscure unlettered Cockneys giving them his wit and listening to their lore. He became an expert at Cockney rhyming slang and dialects. His Cockney imitations were pure music hall. Many Londoners have pleasant memories of his ballad-singing for he was liable at any moment to burst into song. He did so one particular evening in the Coal Hole public house on the Strand. The house was cleared instantly. A bewildered Brendan found himself unceremoniously bundled onto the pavement.

The Behan first nights at Stratford East were something to remember. The playwright in evening dress which never seemed to fit him properly would greet almost every person present. The party in the long bar at the Theatre Royal would be well under way before the rise of the curtain and the result usually was that a certain anarchic atmosphere prevailed even before the anarchy began on the stage.

The first night of *The Hostage* attracted the oddest collection of people; there were so many people with beards and unusual dress that one playgoer was heard to remark, 'What's this – the annual meeting of the Explorers' Club?' Ultimately the play began with members of the *avant-garde* standing all round the walls. It seemed rather appropriate that the first scene should take place in a Dublin brothel. But the play had a lyrical gusto that carried it along and the players helped by their tremendous enthusiasm.

The author came on stage immediately the curtain came down. There was tremendous applause and irreverent shouting before Brendan, his head inclined to one side made himself heard: 'If you want to know what it was all about, you'll have to read my colleagues in the morning. I, myself, am a fully paid up member of the National Union of Journalists.' The play was well received by the critics and, as I have said, went on to the West End.

It received the final accolade of approval when Princess Margaret attended a performance. Brendan's reaction to the Royal visit was: 'I knew her husband – a decent youngster. I spent a night with him in Dublin when he came over to take some photographs.'

The Irish middle-class in London did not take kindly to Brendan. They felt that he was reviving the image of the stage Irishman and that he was a disgrace to Ireland. He was often refused entry to the more respectable Irish clubs. Not that he cared much.

Those who knew him well will remember him for what he was. A man of genius and compassion. As he would say himself, 'an 'oul softie'. His governor in Borstal, where he spent formative years of his youth, wrote of him some time ago, 'You may think of him as the genius and the drunkard, but I remember him as a boy of nineteen who wanted to serve God and who loved his mother and his country.'

It is no bad epitaph and it is one that Brendan would have liked. One thing is sure. It will be some time before an Irishman of such colour and wild genius will strike London town. He gave his friends eight years of joy and despair. God rest him.

NOTES

Donal Foley, London Editor of the *Irish Press*: now Editor of the *Irish Times*. See also his references to Behan in his recently published book *Three Villages: An Autobiography* (Dublin: Egotist Press, 1977) pp. 79–80.

1. *Hold Your Hour and Have Another* (London: Hutchinson, 1963; Boston: Little, Brown, 1964).

His Tremendous Humanity*

DAVID ASTOR

I admired him because of his tremendous humanity, his detachment. He seemed to me like George Orwell, incapable of prejudice against any class because it was a class. He was just in favour of people. He disliked injustice, no matter where it came from. In *Borstal Boy* the Governor is as much a hero as the Warder in *The Quare Fellow*. There are no conventional good chaps and bad chaps – just human beings. I wrote to him simply because I heard he was in a mess and I thought it was terrible to think of this marvellous man destroying himself.

* Ulick O'Connor, *Brendan Behan* (London: Hamish Hamilton, 1970) p. 234. Editor's title.

NOTE

David Astor, English journalist who admired Behan and who offered to help him give up alcohol when Behan was in London. On 2 April 1960 Behan signed a note authorising Astor, then Editor of *The Observer*, to supervise his treatment: 'I agree that David Astor should supervise medical treatment for me, and I authorise him to prepare such measures as he sees fit.'

Meet the Quare Fella†

EAMONN ANDREWS. Well, now, the purpose of this is to try and find out what makes Brendan Behan tick. We may be no wiser at the end of it, but at least we're going to try.
BRENDAN BEHAN. I don't imagine that you will be any the wiser at the end of it, but, however, we can try.
EAMONN. Well, how would you describe yourself?
BRENDAN. Well, I would describe myself, Eamonn, in the following way.

† BBC television interview shown on 29 Nov 1960.

Whistler, the English painter, remarked that the world is divided into two classes: invalids and nurses. I'm a nurse.

EAMONN. How do you make out that you're a nurse and not an invalid?

BRENDAN. I'm a nurse in the sense that in my plays and in my books I try to show the world to a certain extent what's the matter with it, why everybody is not happy. The fact, of course, that in my private life I'm rather a gloomy sort of person has nothing at all to do with my public ministry – if I may so describe it. But what makes me tick? I don't know. Sometimes I wonder how long effectively I'm going to tick. I'm a person put into a position that in some ways suits me, but in other ways doesn't.

I'm a very ordinary person. A great number of people say that with their tongue in their cheek, but I say it with my tongue in my gums. I've a great deal of fame, a certain amount of glory, a certain amount of infamy. And I can only repeat, with John Keats's saying, 'God help the poor little famous.'

EAMONN. Now I wonder why you've become famous. Is it because you're a brilliant writer or because, apart from that and for some extraordinary things, you've hit the headlines?

BRENDAN. Well, I don't know why my books sell. And if people are willing to pay nearly a pound for a book of mine – thousands of people are willing to do so – well, it shows that they're not merely buying it because they heard I was drunk on television, for instance. Or that I sang a song for the buskers[1] outside the Wyndham's Theatre in the West End of London while my own show was going on. I thought it a perfectly natural thing to do. I've been a busker myself...not a very successful one.

EAMONN. Do you consider it a perfectly natural thing for an author to go into the West End to attend his own play and instead to take over from the buskers outside this theatre?

BRENDAN. Yes, in my case, yes. Why not? I mean you might say...it says the Sabbath was made for man, not man for the Sabbath. In the same way, the West End was made for me, not me for the West End.

EAMONN. Yes, but did you sing there because you wanted to sing or just because you're an exhibitionist?

BRENDAN. I'm not by any means an exhibitionist. I wish I was...or I wish I were, shall I say.

EAMONN. Well, I was coming back on the contradictions because somebody said, restated a Cyril Connolly saying, and said that perhaps there is inside the coarse exterior a sensitive man trying to conceal the fact he would like to get out.

BRENDAN. Oh, yes. Wasn't it that he said that inside every fat man there's a thin man trying to get out? It's probably true. There was a great French painter who was asked what he did during the siege of Paris in 1870. 'Oh,' he said, 'I stopped in the cellars.' He said, 'Moi, Je suis poltron.' 'Me, I'm a coward.' Well, I'm all for cowards. I know that there is a tendency among some very great writers such as Hemingway and Liam O'Flaherty, who is a countryman of our own, to extol violence. Hemingway goes in for bullfighting and fishing, and Liam O'Flaherty for football, hurling, horse-racing and bullfighting and boxing. Hope I'm not treading on your toes there when I attack the noble art! But I think it was done for the reason that they had the opinion that writers were supposed to be aesthetes – if that's the right way you pronounce it – and supposed to be kind of precious.

EAMONN. But you, of all people, criticising those writers for introducing violence into their books!

BRENDAN. I don't criticise them for introducing violence into their books. There's plenty of violence in my work. But I criticise them for being so childish as to make it into a praiseworthy...it's not comfortable. The principal aim in this world after the age of sixteen should be comfort. And when I say comfort, I don't mean people getting fat like myself.

EAMONN. But you, now, do you think you've made yourself comfortable in your definition?

BRENDAN. Oh, I'll never be comfortable. I'm lost years ago. The only thing that enables me to survive...I'm essentially a gloomy man and a shy man. Now there's a school of opinion that holds I'm a sort of a natural playwright in the sense that I simply write by inspiration or something. But in actual fact I'm a very highly trained one for the reason that I went to the hardest school of all. I used to go to the music hall and see plays at my uncle's[2] theatre, the Queen's Theatre, Dublin, from the age of four to the age of fourteen. My father and mother used to go on Monday – allegedly to censor the jokes – and we used to go on Tuesday.

EAMONN. I wonder if that's why a number of people say there's a quality of music hall about *The Hostage*?

BRENDAN. If there is a quality of music hall...I hope there is. You won't get away with much on music hall. I mean on other stages...I mean in the Abbey Theatre, for instance, you can go and say, 'Musha, will you put down a pot of rashers and eggs for the decent man.' I sometimes think that the Abbey company must be the best-fed company in the whole of Europe, because every time the action slacks they eat something. You can't get away with that on revue. Anytime you're not cheering the people up, well you get some fellow to sing a song or do a dance. People don't go into a theatre to cry their eyes out.

EAMONN. Well, sometimes they do. But let's come back to you for a moment. What sort of person, thing or institution commands your respect?

BRENDAN. Well, I'm a bad Catholic, like many another great artist, like Rabelais, Michaelangelo.

EAMONN. So now you're telling me what you haven't got respect for, but have you respect for anything? Do you believe in God?

BRENDAN. I do, of course. I said I'm a bad Catholic; it's the religion of great artists.
EAMONN. What about the background to this book and the background of your plays – a background of violence and prisons? Do you feel you're going to get away from this theme for the future?
BRENDAN. Yes, I hope so. The thing that I'm going to write next is a book called *the catacombs*.[3] I might make it into a play, too. It's about Dublin, naturally – I don't write about anywhere else. The Irish are not my audience. Somebody asked me...someone said to me about my books...I had a book banned here, *Borstal Boy*, and they said what do you think of it? The Irish are not my audience; they are my raw material.
EAMONN. Would you like the Irish to be your audience?
BRENDANN. No, I don't care.
EAMONN. You don't care what opinions the Irish have of you as an Irishman?
BRENDAN. Well, I think that the Irish that I know and the Irish who I like, who are ordinary blokes, taxi-drivers, house-painters, bookies' runners – I don't say honest workers...some of them are extremely dishonest workers – but they're the people I care about. And in any country they don't buy books very much and they don't live by books or by literature, except newspapers with the racing results.
EAMONN. I think somehow that perhaps you're a bit of a snob.
BRENDAN. Me? I am, I suppose, but I'm a snob in various directions. I mean to say that the only people that I don't like here are the theatre-going public; what passes for society here, I don't like. They don't like me, so there's no love lost. But the ordinary people I like.
EAMONN. But when you keep saying ordinary people and saying that your friends are house-painters or bookies' runners or whatever it is, this implies a form of snobbery, doesn't it?
BRENDAN. I don't think so. Unless you're going to be very clever and talk about inverted snobbery or something. I'm a house-painter myself. I don't see why I shouldn't like the company of house-painters.
EAMONN. Neither do I, but if you don't care about Irish readers, what about Irish writers – the Shaws, O'Caseys?
BRENDAN. O'Casey's a great man. I mean for me to praise any of these people would be a piece of impertinence. It would be like praising the lakes of Killarney...saying they were rather nice looking. O'Casey's a marvellous man, a great man.
EAMONN. Has he influenced your own writing?
BRENDAN. Oh, I should think so. I think any playwright, certainly any Irishman writing plays in the past forty years that denies that O'Casey influenced him is a fool – a liar. Yes, of course he influenced us all...a marvellous man.

EAMONN. How do you feel, for instance, about the comparison they so often make between you and Dylan Thomas?
    And let me remind you of a quotation of a journalist called Leslie Mallory, who speaking of you said, 'If you've met one Dylan Thomas, you've met them all.'
BRENDAN. Well, I since met Leslie Mallory in Paris during the festival...during the International Theatre Festival this year...and I discovered that he was a Dublin man. And naturally, as Dr Johnson said, the Irish are very honest people – they seldom speak well of each other!
EAMONN. But, Brendan, back to the late Dylan Thomas. What about him?
BRENDAN. I think, of course, that he was a great fellow, but I think in some ways he was very different to me. I mean his talent was a different one. He wrote a poem, called 'To a Child Killed in an Air-Raid Fire in London',[4] that I most certainly could not have written, not in a thousand years, not if I was to sit up like the famous monkey in the British Museum. They were supposed to give it a typewriter and it was said that, by the law of averages, in 50 million years it would write the complete works of Shakespeare. Well, if I were the monkey and you gave me the typewriter, I would not have written the poem of Dylan Thomas about the child killed in the London air-raid. The poem to his father... 'Do not go gentle into that good night . . . .' I think it was a different person. Well, none of us is very different from the other.
EAMONN. But one of the elements of comparison, of course, has been that, like so many great talents, Thomas was one of these fellows who turned to strong drink.
BRENDAN. Oh, yeah. Well, that's only incidental – it's not very important.
EAMONN. Do you not think it's of importance in your life?
BRENDAN. Well, no, I drink too much, but it hasn't anything to do with my work. I mean, when I'm working I don't drink, and I'm sure when Thomas was working he didn't drink.
EAMONN. But why have so many great writers and painters turned in this way to drink to excess?
BRENDAN. I never turned to it; it seemed to turn to me. I don't ever remember not drinking, but I think in the case of Thomas too much has been made of it. I think he was a great artist and I don't think he would have given a damn one way or the other what they said about him after he was dead. But people like to fix on something they can understand. Well, they can't understand his poetry, but they can understand his boozing. I think that is the top and bottom of it.
EAMONN. But is it the top and bottom of it, Brendan? As far as you're concerned. You've appeared on television, quote 'drunk', unquote – and it's your own quote at that. Did this please you?
BRENDAN. I didn't care very much, actually. I shouldn't use that word, actually. It shows that I'm extremely sober. Anyone that says 'actually',

'the lot' or 'I couldn't care less' should be shot, or beaten over the head with even a beer bottle, if you can't get anything else.

EAMONN. It seems to me that you've gone down to the corner once too often. To put it mildly, Brendan, you don't appear at your best on television when you've got one over the eight. Does this not make you feel embarrassed, being a shy person, that people should see you like that?

BRENDAN. I'm embarrassed being there at all. I'm embarrassed now, and I haven't one over the eight – I haven't even one over the seven.

EAMONN. All right. No you don't have much respect, it would seem, for your fellow Irish.

BRENDAN. I do. I've plenty of respect for my fellow Irish. Don't I write about them? I immortalise them.

EAMONN. Fair enough. What would you like to have said of you in fifty years' time?

BRENDAN. That I've celebrated my eighty-sixth, my eighty-seventh, birthday!

EAMONN. In addition to that, what would you like to have said about your work, your writing?

BRENDAN. Well now, again I have to quote somebody else. I was one time arguing with a person who writes plays and has another occupation...he's an officer of the law, he's a legal person in Ireland. And he said to me, 'My plays will be remembered when you're dead and rotten.' Well, I said, I want to tell you something and that is this. Number one, I'm not interested in having my plays remembered when I'm dead and rotten. And, number two, I'm not particularly attracted by the idea of being dead or rotten, anyway.

EAMONN. I bet you're not. Now, you did say to a journalist at one time two things at the one occasion. You said everyone should be successful for one month, but that's all.

BRENDAN. That's all. I believe that, Eamonn.

EAMONN. Why?

BRENDAN. Ah, because after that it gets a bit of a nonsense. You can't go out for a drink or you can't walk up the street without some person, usually, that hasn't bought a book you've written or that hasn't paid into a play you've written. The cash customers, of course...they're quite welcome. They can shake my foot as well as my hand!

EAMONN. Now, in July 1959, you said that your doctor said if you didn't stop drinking you wouldn't last eighteen months. That gives you till about January 1961.

BRENDAN. You mean you saw that in the paper.

EAMONN. Attributed to you.

BRENDAN. Yeah, well a lot of things are attributed to me. He didn't exactly say that, but he chastised me very severely.

EAMONN. Do you intend doing anything about it?

BRENDAN. Of course, I've done plenty about it.
EAMONN. You said a moment ago that what you'd like to have said about you in fifty years' time was that you'd celebrated your eighty-seventh birthday.
BRENDAN. Yes, indeed.
EAMONN. Well, if you don't take the doctor's advice, you might never celebrate it. Do you fear death, or don't you care?
BRENDAN. I do care. I don't like it. I don't like the dying lark at all. I don't think anyone does. I can give you instances of very eminent men surrounding themselves with all kinds of quacks, all sorts of doctors and surgeons and scientists, in an attempt to stop in this world just a little while longer. A fellow said we know where we are; we're not quite sure where we're going.
EAMONN. Well, none of us is quite sure where we're going, but wherever...
BRENDAN. You are. You're quite sure you're not going to die. Anyone that appears on television so often as you do is under the opinion that they're going to live to be about 130. And then you'll have one of these things[5] over you to get your last minutes.
EAMONN. All right, Brendan. Wherever you're going, success on your journey.
BRENDAN. Thank you very much.

NOTES

This film was directed by Fred O'Donovan and produced by Louis Elliman. The conversation was edited by Ken Stewart.

1. Itinerant musicians or actors.

2. Patrick J. Bourke (1883–1932), Irish impresario, actor and playwright in the Boucicault tradition; father of playwright Seamus De Burca. He was married to Behan's maternal aunt, Margaret, and he made the Behans welcome at his shows at the Queen's Theatre.

3. Behan began work on this novel early in 1958 when he was in Ibiza, Spain. Before he returned to Ireland in March he had completed at least thirty pages of it. When *The Quare Fellow* opened in New York in November 1958, Behan did not attend the opening night, for he felt that he must get on with the writing of this novel. *the catacombs*, however, was never finished. In a letter to Iain Hamilton dated 26 Sep 1957 Brendan said, 'I'm starting a book called *the catacombs* (the lower case is intentional) which I will submit to you.' See also Colbert Kearney, *The Writings of Brendan Behan* (Dublin: Gill and Macmillan, 1977) pp. 137–40.

4. The correct title of this poem is 'A Refusal to Mourn the Death, by Fire, of a Child in London'.

5. A camera.

But Not in the Pejorative Sense*

W. J. WEATHERBY

The idea had been to interview Brendan Behan, to report a conversation with one of our leading dramatists, but at the first literary question Mr Behan spat eloquently into the fire and said, 'Let's go to the pub.'

He had been working on his new play adapted from *Borstal Boy*, his autobiographical book, and standing at his ancient typewriter – 'the oldest machine in the world' – he looked like a bull at a gate anxious to escape. 'Oh, damn it', he said at last (though he didn't say 'damn'), 'I've had enough of going over the same bloody Borstal ground for one day.'

Thus began a whirlwind tour of Brendan Behan's Dublin, so different from the guide-book version that had earlier refused to come alive for us. He had already brought himself up to date on the Manchester he remembered – Strangeway's Jail, Platt Lane police station, and the street where he was arrested – and so he was able to inform the first barman we called on that a hangman of his acquaintance in Manchester now kept a pub. This seemed to impress the barman and led to a talk about the famous Judge Lynch, of Galway, who hanged his son because nobody else would do it. Mr Behan's comment about him was to the point and unprintable.

'I saw you on television the other night', a new customer confided. 'What was my mug like?' asked Mr Behan, and he seemed dispirited by the non-committal reply he got. And so, like a character with drooping spirits in a Behan play, he began to sing a musical medley, a mixture of rock 'n' roll, Irish ballads, and the kind of ditties popular with the infantry. He had a boisterous, not very musical voice, but we all felt better after the song. Dublin was beginning to come alive.

We tried a literary question – something about the writers who had influenced him – but without any more success. 'Let's go and call on my half-brother', Mr Behan suggested, already on his way to the door and exchanging jovial farewells with everyone he passed. His half-brother was at one of those large Georgian houses that Dublin is famous for. The front door was open and decorators in paint-splashed white overalls were busy transforming the ground floor. Mr Behan tracked down his relative, who

---

* *Guardian* (London), 4 Mar 1960, p. 9.

was working in the hallway, and then enthusiastically picked up a paintbrush and a tin of paint and went up a ladder. He had once been a housepainter and obviously hadn't lost his touch. The other painters showed us their work, and one of them shook our hands to mark the birth of the Queen's baby. This brought Mr Behan down from the ladder to join in and soon there was general hand-shaking.

He wanted to buy a copy of the *New Statesman*, so the next stop was at a bookshop where every book seemed to have been autographed by its author and which had the kind of pleasant literary atmosphere every bookshop should have. It was the ideal place for Mr Behan to break down in and be literary. But it was not to be. Among the customers was a poet, John Montague, and so Mr Behan led us all over to another pub, where he said over his fourth soda-water that his country's representatives abroad seldom went to see his plays, that Princess Margaret had been to see *The Hostage* – 'She's all right' – and that an author's first duty was 'to let down his country'.

That needed some explanation, and Mr Montague suggested an author should let down his country when he was supposed to hold it up. Presumably he meant 'hold it up' in the sense of writing propaganda, but it was too late to inquire, for the conversation was off in another direction. Mr Behan said gloomily he might go to live in Paris. But weren't his roots in Dublin? 'A man's got his damned roots by the time he's thirty', he replied (though he didn't say 'damned'). He was thirty-seven – and the fact seemed to weigh heavily that day.

Mr Behan had recently acquired the phrase 'in the pejorative sense' from some criticism he had read, and he dropped it into the conversation as if it were a great joke. Asked if So-and-so was a journalist, he replied, 'Yes, but not in the pejorative sense.' A reference to the IRA reminded him of how he had once taken a French journalist to the IRA headquarters. 'I thought the French might give it some objective publicity. After all, they've no bloody axe to grind. But they told us, "Come back in the afternoon when our PRO will be here." We went back and the PRO was there but he couldn't hear our questions. He was stone deaf. So we went away.' Mr Behan shook his head sadly. 'They were always doing things like that. And today they just seem little beside the H-bombs.' Then he added, 'But not in the pejorative sense!'

After an interval at home Mr Behan headed for the hills. At first all of his directions led into cul-de-sacs, but gradually we found the route which he and his wife used to take out of the city on long walks years ago. And on passing a prison-like building he recalled that a man, who was said to be mad, was once imprisoned there. 'The IRA decided he wasn't mad so they rescued him. But when they put a tommy-gun in his hands they found out soon enough that he really was mad.' This inspired Mr Behan to bellow a jolly song, which unhappily is unprintable.

At a pub – with a distant view of the battleground used in the film of

Henry V – he won two out of three games of darts and learned enough about some of the customers standing at the bar to fill another book. He must be one of the most industrious questioners in Dublin. Everything interested him from a man's views on education to the number of working-men's clubs in Westmorland. And his blunt, teasing manner established good relations at once.

Someone told a story about a royal personage who was warned not to visit a certain club because the police were going to raid it. When the police arrived he was sitting in the club and they had to call off the raid. The teller interpreted it as a story against the royal personage, but Mr Behan said that it proved he was a jolly good sort. He automatically took the side of the underdogs even if they were in the wrong. As a former 'Borstal Boy' he seemed to have a natural dislike of the police and almost all authority. One day he may accept them into the human family, but not yet.

This was probably why he made such a grand but slightly rebellious entrance into the grill-room of the hotel where we had lunch. This was where Authority might dine. A waiter began by taxing his patience with lofty talk about the wine list, and eventually Mr Behan, no mean wine man himself after working in France, said flatly, 'Is it red or white? He seemed surprised at the lack of interest in his devotion to soda-water throughout the day. 'I've been on it for a week. I can't work if I'm drinking.' Mrs Behan mentioned admiringly Peter Sellers's imitation of her husband, and said the line about having 'the thirst' was most accurate. 'I've heard you use it, Brendan', she said.

Mr Behan couldn't remember, but beamed, and was unexpectedly at last in the mood to answer literary questions. He thought Dublin was still the city Joyce described so accurately...Critics seemed to think he was new to the theatre but he had been going since he was four...He had traced the Behans back in Leinster history and they were said to be an ancient literary family.... He liked Joan Littlewood's conception of the theatre in the Theatre Workshop: a mixture of moods, music, dialogue, songs, and dancing....

Then – with the suddenness of a princess changing back into Cinderella – Mr Behan slipped back into his non-literary manner as if he feared he was being disloyal to the people he grew up with 'I know somebody who works in your kitchen', he told the waiter who appeared majestically at the table.

And so to coffee in the lounge with Mr Behan sitting grimly in an armchair glowering round at the other guests. A man who looked like a visiting South American millionaire came over and asked for his autograph for three relatives. Mr Behan graciously signed his name three times. 'They're the same everywhere, these places', he said when the man had gone. 'They don't do any good, but they're harmless.'

It was a definite concession, for Mr Behan has mellowed a little since his early days; he must now know as well as his critics that he will have to embrace the hotel lounges as well as the underdogs if he is to develop as a writer. But he is tremendously loyal to the past. As if dreading that he might be weakening again, that he might be playing the literary figure, he scowled round the lounge with his bull-look and ordered a whisky. 'But not in the pejorative sense!' he added – an essentially warm-hearted, sensitive man putting his armour on again.

NOTE

W. J. Weatherby, English author, journalist, and novelist.

Meet the New Brendan Behan*

ALAN BESTIC

In a large, comfortable house in Ballsbridge, one of Dublin's most fashionable suburbs, Beatrice Behan is brewing tea by the gallon these days.

Her husband Brendan, the boisterous, bewildering 'Quare Fella', is pushing it down by the potful, as he pounds at a typewriter with stubby fingers. For perhaps the first time in his life, he is writing a play without the aid of porter, whiskey, brandy, Châteauneuf-du-Pape, or any similar lubricant.

The play is called *the catacombs*.[1] He told me that it was going to be 'a sort of stew, set in Dublin to a Spanish Civil War background, garnished with boy and girl trouble'.

But even if it falls flat in the searing oven of his mind, it is almost certain to succeed; for Brendan has managed to make himself a legend at the age of thirty-seven, which is rather like running a four-minute mile in army boots.

I have known him for years now; yet I can never remember where we first met – which is rather like saying that I cannot remember the first time I was run over by a jet-propelled steamroller.

My wife, however, does remember her first meeting with Brendan. She recalls how we gave him a lift one day from Baggot Street to Duke Street in

* *Irish Digest* (Dublin), LXIX, no. 4 (Oct 1960) 13–16.

Dublin. His shoes were too big for him, she says, and there were huge holes in his socks.

She also remembers that before he left the car he had managed to slip half a crown into the ready hand of our small daughter, Penny. It was almost certainly his last piece of silver for that was long before he wrote *The Quare Fellow*, *The Hostage*, or his best-selling autobiography, *Borstal Boy*.

In those days, Brendan was usually broke. And, like most people who are usually broke, he was generous. Occasionally he had money, but never for long.

Around that time, for instance, he was paid seventy-five pounds by the Irish News Agency for his life story, which was only really beginning. Next morning he had six and eight pence left.

Some of it had gone to pay his bar debts. But most of it had strayed into other pockets. Spongers have long ears and Brendan can never carry money quietly.

The next time we met I was working for a Sunday newspaper in London. A note in a strange mixture of English, Irish and French was sent up to me from the front office.

It was from Brendan and, freely translated, it read, 'Have you any —— money?' It was Friday and I had.

I arranged to meet Brendan at Paddington in time to catch the last train to Maidenhead, where I was living. I arrived to find him reasonably plastered, but it was a pleasant journey. Brendan sang, and so did the rest of the carriage, it being pay night. The morning seemed very far away.

But it arrived eventually and inevitably. I had to go to work and bring a sadly hungover Brendan with me. We staggered into a carriage that was infested with bowler hats, brief cases, and copies of the *Financial Times*.

Brendan flopped down beside a pair of striped trousers, and the city gents jerked up their newspapers, like guardsmen presenting arms. But as the train pulled out, Brendan leant forward, tapped a striped trouser leg in front of him, and said, 'Mister, do you mind if I sing a song?'

The *Financial Times* was lowered three inches. A pale, calm, directorial face gazed over it, and a clipped voice snapped, 'Not-at-all.'

To a backcloth of pink newspapers he began. For the first time in the history of British Railways the 9 a.m. from Maidenhead trundled along to the strains of:

> The old tri-angle goes jingle-jangle
> Down the banks of the Roy-al
> Canal!

I would say they are still talking on the Stock Exchange about the day Brendan tangled with the bulls and the bears.

Yet in spite of his jingle-jangle, I know Brendan Behan as a sensitive person. I have seen him hurt bitterly by a jeer from one of my more Borstalian children. And I have seen his sensitivity work positively, too.

That was when I went back to Dublin after an absence of three years and arrived broke, owing to a formidable farewell party. I called on Brendan, feeling as if I had been pummelled with broken bottles.

Without a word he led me gently over to Tommy Devine's pub, ordered a large Irish and stood over me, like a vet over a sick pup, while I edged it down. Then he ordered a pint of draught stout and I managed to sink it, inch by inch.

After that we went home and Brendan roared, 'Alan's here, Beatrice, and he's sick. Cook him some liver.'

The antennae were still waggling. The postman brought a registered envelope and Brendan came in with it, dancing a jig. It was loot from his publishers.

He pushed a handful of notes across to Beatrice and said, 'That's for scoff.' He shoved another handful in his pocket and said, 'That's for booze.' And then he pitched a fiver over to me and said, 'You'd better have some, too.'

I had not said a word. He had simply sensed I was broke!

He is sensitive – and he is shy, particularly of showing his emotions. And he reveals that shyness in *The Hostage*.

Most critics hailed it as a comedy. In fact it was a tragedy in which Behan lashed out at the futility of narrow nationalism, whether British, Irish, or any other breed.

He jibes mercilessly at the remnants of British imperialism. He is no less harsh with the new IRA. And this, remember, from a man who was an extreme nationalist himself and has the jail scars to prove it!

At the age of sixteen he was sent to Borstal for illegal possession of explosives in Liverpool. His Counsel – Eoin 'the Pope' O'Mahony, [2] from Crok – told the bemused jury that he was 'but a love child of the revolution', a description which Brendan has been trying to live down ever since.

Then came deportation to Ireland and a fourteen-year sentence for shooting at de Valera's police. This was commuted and he went back to Britain, where he was jailed again for defying an exclusion order.

That was by no means his last appearance in a British jail. Yet, in spite of it all, Brendan shows little bitterness.

In fact, I have sat up until dawn, listening to him talking about his jail experiences and watching him heave with laughter as he described his rebel days.

'You should have met my granny', he said one night. 'A marvellous woman. She lived on tinned salmon, snuff, and porter, and never got out of bed except for funerals.

'I'll never forget the day the rozzers searched the house and found arms in her bed and she got a suspensory sentence of six months!'

It was his granny who gave him his first drink of porter at the age of eight when she took him to his first funeral.

Brendan has subsidised Messrs Arthur Guinness, Son and Company Ltd handsomely since then – and a few distillers, too, as the BBC know to their cost.

In Broadcasting House, indeed, they still talk in whispers of the night he rolled in front of the TV cameras, paralytic, to be interviewed by Malcolm Muggeridge.

As he says himself, 'After the show they all looked at me as if I had a bomb in my pocket. All, that is, except Muggeridge, who behaved like an English gentleman. Instead of blowing me out, as he had a right to, he just said, "Brendan, you could use a drink." And then he brought me off to his club!'

Muggeridge would hardly recognise Brendan today, as he sits at home, gulping Beatrice's tea and pounding out his play.

NOTES

Alan Bestic, Irish journalist.
1. For a note on *the catacombs* see p. 148.
2. See The Bellman, 'Meet "The Pope" ', *The Bell*, XVI, no. 4 (Jan 1951) 15–20.

OHIO UNIVERSITY LIBRARY

Please return this book as soon
have finished with it. In ord
fine it must be returned by